Viking Nations

To Dave and Billy for reminding me to drop my science with defiance

And

To Jerry who has been there from the beginning

Viking Nations

The Development of Medieval North Atlantic Identities

Dr Dayanna Knight

PEN & SWORD
ARCHAEOLOGY

First published in Great Britain in 2016 by
Pen & Sword Archaeology
an imprint of
Pen & Sword Books Ltd
47 Church Street
Barnsley
South Yorkshire
S70 2AS

ISBN 978 1 47383 393 7

A CIP catalogue record for this book is available from the British
Library

Typeset in Ehrhardt by
Mac Style Ltd, Bridlington, East Yorkshire
Printed and bound in the UK by CPI Group (UK) Ltd,
Croydon, CRO 4YY

Pen & Sword Books Ltd incorporates the imprints of Pen & Sword
Archaeology, Atlas, Aviation, Battleground, Discovery, Family
History, History, Maritime, Military, Naval, Politics, Railways, Select,
Transport, True Crime, and Fiction, Frontline Books, Leo Cooper,
Praetorian Press, Seaforth Publishing and Wharncliffe.

For a complete list of Pen & Sword titles please contact
PEN & SWORD BOOKS LIMITED
47 Church Street, Barnsley, South Yorkshire, S70 2AS, England
E-mail: enquiries@pen-and-sword.co.uk
Website: www.pen-and-sword.co.uk

Contents

List of Illustrations   vi
Preface   x

Chapter 1   General Aims and Research Context   1

Chapter 2   Theory and Methodology   22

Chapter 3   Settlement, Economy and Lifestyles in Zone 1
                  c. AD 800–1250   44

Chapter 4   Settlement, Economy and Lifestyles in Zone 2
                  c. AD 870–1250   83

Chapter 5   Settlement, Economy and Lifestyles in Zone 3
                  c. AD 1000–1250   111

Chapter 6   Trade and Economics   137

Chapter 7   Religion   157

Chapter 8   Building and Maintaining Identities in the North
                  Atlantic – A Material Perspective   177

Appendix A: Grœnlendinga Saga   200
Appendix B: Norse Place Name Elements   218
Appendix C: Glossary   221
Appendix D: Sampling and Analysis   226
Notes   230
Bibliography   250
Index   262

List of Illustrations

Unless otherwise stated all drawings and photographs included in this work are © the author.

Fig 1.	Beach near Bornais, west coast South Uist. Photo taken by Dr R Lenfert.	2
Fig 2.	Norse expansion across the north Atlantic.	4
Fig 3.	Major North Atlantic oceanic currents.	6
Fig 4.	Koppen designations for the north Atlantic region explained in brief.	7
Fig 5.	Island geographic data from Koppen designations.	8
Fig 6.	Land areas of the north Atlantic region.	9
Fig 7.	*Knórr*, after Crumlin-Pedersen.	12
Fig 8.	Aspects of *landnám* associated with each Zone.	13
Fig 9.	The Lewis Chessmen on display at the National Museum of Scotland. Photo taken by Dr R. Lenfert.	17
Fig 10.	Schematic of individual interaction.	24
Fig 11.	Key terms associated with the Annales School.	32
Fig 12.	Practice Theory as utilized in this work.	33
Fig 13.	Generalization of Traditional Core and Periphery.	36
Fig 14.	Diagram of Alternative Core and Periphery interactions. Roles are more flexible in this view as a mode and a medium for change is expressed.	37
Fig 15.	Shetlandic archaeological sites from the Norse period of occupation.	43
Fig 16.	Comparison of Gardie 1 and Hamar.	44
Fig 17.	Generalized longhouse plan for Shetland.	46
Fig 18.	Shetlandic steatite forms.	48
Fig 19.	Major sites in the Faroe Islands.	49
Fig 20.	Medieval church and landing area at Kirkjubøur.	50
Fig 21.	Niðri í Toft at Kvívík.	51
Fig 22.	A collection of Faroese spindle whorls and wooden distaffs.	52
Fig 23.	Generalized artefact placement for the Faroe Islands.	53

Fig 24.   Shieling sites in the Faroe Islands.   54
Fig 25.   Choices involved in the exploitation of the wild.   55
Fig 26.   Iron fishing hooks from I Uppistovibeinum and Argisbrekka on
          display at Forøya Fornminnisavn.   55
Fig 27.   Steatite vessel forms and wooden implements.   56
Fig 28.   Faroese sheep shot on the island of Litla Dimun during the
          nineteenth century.   57
Fig 29.   Shared characteristics of Shetland and the Faroe Islands.   59
Fig 30.   Changes to the Zone microscale identity over time.   60
Fig 31.   Influences upon choices of marine and terrestrial cultural
          practices.   61
Fig 32.   Division of Labor.   63
Fig 33.   Zone 1 farm progression.   64
Fig 34.   Byre at Niðri í Toft.   67
Fig 35.   Need for human work diagram.   68
Fig 36.   General life of turf built longhouses in the North Atlantic.   69
Fig 37.   Farm productivity cycles presented chronologically.   71
Fig 38.   Vectors on choice in the context of local exchange.   73
Fig 39.   Gender based consideration of identity orientation on Zone 1
          Norse farm sites, including data from Gulatingslog.   75
Fig 40.   The amount of specialty equipment required for exploitation in
          relation to productivity of marine, littoral and terrestrial areas.   77
Fig 41.   Division of Labor.   78
Fig 42.   Division of labor on North Atlantic settlement farms.   79
Fig 43.   Zone 2: warm water and colder water currents.   82
Fig 44.   Zone 2 saga sites.   83
Fig 45.   Zone 2 Textual sources by type.   85
Fig 46.   Hólmur sunken feature building.   90
Fig 47.   Skallakot.   92
Fig 48.   Aslakstunga fremri.   93
Fig 49.   Stöng.   94
Fig 50.   Major Characteristics of Zone 2.   101
Fig 51.   Seals described in Konungsskuggsjá.   102
Fig 52.   Format of the Althing.   104
Fig 53.   Zone 2 artefact choices.   105
Fig 54.   Reconstruction of vertical loom utilized in the weaving of
          vaðmal from Þjóðminjasafn Íslands. Reconstruction made
          utilizing ethnographic and archaeological evidence from
          throughout Zone 2.   107

Fig 55.   Whale bone weaving sword utilized in the weaving of vaðmal
           from Þjóðminjasafn Íslands.   108
Fig 56.   Map of Norse Greenland.   112
Fig 57.   Glacial runoff leading to the Eirikssfjord, as seen from Signal
           Hill, Narsarsuaq.   113
Fig 58.   The Inland Ice of Greenland, as viewed from an airplane.   113
Fig 59.   Zone 3 textual sources by type.   114
Fig 60.   Narsarsuaq house site overgrown with dwarf Arctic willow.   115
Fig 61.   Igaliku tithe barn front, after Roussell.   116
Fig 62.   The Farm Under the Sand longhouse.   118
Fig 63.   L'Anse aux Meadows site map.   120
Fig 64.   House styles and characteristics in Zone 3.   127
Fig 65.   Zone 3 artefact decision diagram.   132
Fig 66.   Trade and exchange via merchant intermediaries.   136
Fig 67.   Diagram relating transportation to equipment, speed and
           cargo capacity.   137
Fig 68.   Transport descriptions relevant to this period.   138
Fig 69.   Norse vessel types. All of these vessels would have been
           constructed using the clinker-building techniques.   139
Fig 70.   Norse landing area and medieval pier, Isle of Lewis. Photo taken
           by Dr R Lenfert.   140
Fig 71.   Modern rowing vessels from Torshavn, Faroe Islands.   142
Fig 72.   Efficiency in long distance travel.   143
Fig 73.   Traditional portrayal of the World Tree remembered in Norse
           pagan mythology.   156
Fig 74.   Generalized Social Space conceptions of Norse farms in the
           North Atlantic. Table explaining is on the following page. Also
           includes following page.   157
Fig 75.   Social space terms with relation to Norse North Atlantic sites. 158
Fig 76.   Bishop from the Lewis Chessmen on display at the National
           Museum of Scotland. Photo by Dr R. Lenfert.   160
Fig 77.   Papar place name locations and movement map.   163
Fig 78.   Bónhústoftin chapel site, taken within the site enclosure.   164
Fig 79.   Hog back from St Boniface chapel, Papa Westray, Orkney.   165
Fig 80.   Chapel dedicated to St Boniface on Papa Westray, Orkney.   166
Fig 81.   Qassiarsuk, Greenland.   169
Fig 82.   Igaliku, Greenland.   170
Fig 83.   Kirkjubøur, Faroe Islands.   171
Fig 84.   St Magnus's Cathedral, Kirkwall, Orkney.   172

Fig 85.   Designation of internal and external group elements.   176
Fig 86.   Hierarchal interaction applicable to both microscale and
           macroscale levels of identity.   177
Fig 87.   Identity expression vectors in the ninth and tenth centuries.   178
Fig 88.   Identity expression vectors during the eleventh century.   181
Fig 89.   Identity expression vectors in the twelfth and thirteenth
           centuries.   182
Fig 90.   The Lewis Chessmen King on display at the National Museum
           of Scotland. Photo by Dr R. Lenfert.   183
Fig 91.   Hierarchal interaction applicable to both microscale and
           macroscale levels of identity.   186
Fig 92.   Initial construction of history.   187
Fig 93.   Maintenance of history.   188
Fig 94.   North Atlantic identity orientations in context.   190
Fig 95.   The Atlantic Zone and its Changes over time.   192
Fig 96.   Leif Eriksson statue at Qassiarsuk, Greenland.   194
Fig 97.   The reconstructed Viking Age longhouse located at Qassiarsuk,
           Greenland.   198
Fig 98.   Modern Igaliku, Garðr that was, as seen from the peaks above
           the settlement.   199
Fig 99.   Location map for the site of L'Anse aux Meadows.   202
Fig 100.   Excavated Norse Church foundations at Qassiarsuk.   208
Fig 101.   The Eiriksfjord.   210
Fig 102.   Criteria used in data creation.   224
Fig 103.   Table detailing the relative ranking system applied to site
           evidence.   226

Preface

This book is an adaptation of my doctoral thesis undertaken at the University of Nottingham entitled *Identity Construction and Maintenance in the North Atlantic c. AD 800–1250* – the product of both research and a huge amount of effort. I'm indebted to everyone at Pen and Sword Books for the opportunity to discuss medieval identity. There is a list of people and organizations who assisted the production of this work. I'll go over the research related aspects first.

Many thanks go out to Fróðskaparsetur Forøya who funded a portion of my research in the Faroe Islands. Other thanks go out to those who I met across the North Atlantic, particularly Drs Steffen Stummann Hansen and Ole Guldager who very kindly took time to talk to me. Thank you to Drs John Lindow and Carol Clover, both of the University of California at Berkeley, for teaching me the basics of Old Norse. Much appreciation also goes out to Drs Judith Jesch and Christina Lee, both of the University of Nottingham, who supported a fellow Viking enthusiast in her attempts to translate Old Norse sources. Thanks also goes to James Rackham and Dr Doug Gray, DVM, for discussing livestock shipping with me so I could explain the terrestrial aspects of this system more completely. Several of the photographs illustrating this work were shot by my friend Dr Robert Lenfert, owner of Lenfert Film and Digital Photography. One of the most difficult to quantify must go to my academic advisor Dr Christopher Loveluck of the University of Nottingham. He went above and beyond assisting with both pastoral care and all the while trying (and succeeding) to advise an obstinate American historical anthropologist on how to write a British archaeological thesis. Thank you for not giving up on my situation when so many others did.

All people know we're kept sane and grounded by our friends. Thank you to Dr Peggy Scully-Linder who led by example being first an inspirational anthropology professor then an amazing mentor for this early career researcher. Another thank you must go out to my parents who provided support and didn't freak out when I said I was going to graduate school abroad. Every computer that has ever touched this book or the thesis that it's derived from has been kept going far beyond warranty by Mike 'Badger' Bristow. Mead, amusement, bemusement and commiseration has been provided by my local Isle of Misfit

Toys – you all know who you are. Finally, the biggest thank you of all must go to my husband who made the trip across half the planet because his wife wanted to study Vikings.

Unless otherwise stated, all drawings and photographs included in this work are my own. All mistakes and omissions are purely my own.

Dr Dayanna Knight

December, 2014

Chapter 1

General Aims and Research Context

Introduction

The western expansion of Viking Age and Medieval Norse into the north Atlantic has long been subject to debate fuelled by a substantial corpus of both archaeological and written sources. Each of the North Atlantic islands and archipelagos would come to feel the impact of the Norse migrations in their own way as the Norse moved beyond the Scandinavian homelands to the Northern and Western Isles of Scotland, the Faroe Islands, then, Iceland, Greenland, and, North America. These islands and island groups each have their own unique natural and historical contexts that made unique impacts upon the incoming Norse populations and have helped the subsequent local identities to evolve into modern nationally recognized identities. This work is an investigation of Scandinavian identity formation and cultural structures within the north Atlantic that looks specifically at the construction and maintenance of the island identities within this region, circa AD 800–1250. It not only includes consideration of the incoming Norse settlers in rural areas but also the effects of contact between the emerging island cultural identities and continental Europe. This period corresponds with the so-called Viking Age, AD 800–1050, and the Medieval, AD 1050–1250, and at times is referred to as such within this book.

Humans identify themselves and others through a series of negotiations of similarity and difference that is an important part of identity and how humans interact with the world.[1] They produce their existence in a wide variety of ways. Indeed this is composed of complex topics such as ethnicity.[2]

Ethnicity is important because it is socially constructed and thus believed to be important to those who exercise it and so has weight and meaning in the social world. This is similar to concepts of religion, history and nationalism. This process leaves varying degrees of physical evidence of its presence from nothing to magnificent examples of landscape utilization. Identity is determined partially by the context of an individual actor's situation, including whether or not there are other individuals with whom to interact.[3] This book focuses upon the aspects of group identity created and maintained in the Norse north Atlantic settlements. This work follows a trend of thought that has its basis in the French Annales School.[4] It also follows with some concepts of multivocality.

For ease in consideration and presentation within this work, the physical region has been broken into three zones of settlement that all experience a form of Scandinavian *landnám*, 'land taking'. Land naming is a broader reaching concept – it is the initial step of establishing a geographically based identity in a new region, in a similar fashion to the process of how a baby becomes socially human to adults. This process adapts previously utilized naming conventions with new geographic forms in unsettled areas. When the process of *landnám* occurs on previously inhabited areas there can be connotations of a cultural takeover with only occasional survivals in the maintenance of established names such as Mousa in Shetland. The term *landnám* is widely used in Icelandic archaeological publications to discuss the period from AD 870–1000. In English translations of these sources it is referred to as the Settlement Period. This conveniently covers the pagan period of Iceland as well as the time when both Iceland and later Greenland were settled. *Landnám* is also a term utilized by Scandinavian literary specialists in relation to two works associated with the medieval author Ari Þorgilsson. In relation to textual sources, *landnám* conveys a set of information primarily of the period covered by the texts, but also to the direction of movement west from a coastal western Norwegian origin.

Fig 1. Beach near Bornais, west coast South Uist. Photo taken by Dr R Lenfert.

Within this work, *landnám* is used to designate the initial Norse settlement period in all zones – it is a temporal and culturally biased concept. This is done for consistency and to prevent confusion when discussing physical aspects of archaeological sites. It is also to clarify the complex set of information conveyed by the term *landnám* about the migrating Norse population. In the instances when a settlement event has occurred in a zone, i.e. in Iceland, it is referred to as a *landnám* event to prevent confusion. This is a feature of Norse medieval settlement particular to areas that are rural in nature.

Geographic Organization Of Analysis

In order to compare the changes that occurred in each of the island groups settled by north Atlantic travelling Scandinavians it was necessary to designate zones across the entire region, please refer to Fig 2. These zones were designated on physical location and historical precedence. Zone 1 is composed of the Northern and Western Isles of Scotland and the Faroe Islands – the nearest island groups to the Scandinavian homelands within direct sail during the Viking Age. This is the North Sea and Irish Sea region that has been an interconnected web of exchange and power networks since the Neolithic and early Scandinavian interest in the area is unsurprising. As there are several island groups in Zone 1 the case study for this zone utilizes evidence from Shetland and the Faroe Islands. Shetland and the Faroe Islands have been chosen for the Zone 1 case study to gain clarification on the reality of identity construction and maintenance in the island groups. Due to historical precedence during the Middle Ages, Orkney and the Hebrides are more widely studied by modern researchers and will be referred to within discussion chapters. This is due to the more numerous publications related to this period. Excavation plans and environmental studies in particular are more plentiful concerning Orkney and the Hebrides due to British archaeological efforts. There are also direct reliable textual sources simply not available for Shetland and the Faroe Islands that highlight identities as opposed to Icelandic textual sources only. Shetland and the Faroe Islands, on the other hand, both remained under the control of Scandinavia for a longer time as well as having received less widespread publication and archaeological survey in the modern era. They will form the bulk of evidence presented within the case study for Zone 1. Each of these archipelagos is within a direct sailing voyage from the Scandinavian homelands, in particular western Norway. Examination of Shetlandic and Faroese evidence will show a different social, economic and political situation to the more southern affluent and agriculturally viable islands of Orkney and the Hebrides. The islands of Zone 1 also all exhibit evidence of highly restricted wood resources at the time of Norse *Landnám* whether due to heavy previous human exploitation or a total lack of presence in general due to remote island location from European arboreal populations.

Zone 2 is primarily composed of Iceland. Iceland has an incredibly large body of evidence in publication including archaeological reports, but also sagas, their related critiques, formalized trade agreements and medieval law codes. This has required sampling of the available material and as a result the Southern Quarter of Iceland, which historically received the heaviest *landnám* population, and the Eastern Quarter of Iceland, which is the closest geographically to Zone 1, has been focused upon within the case study for Zone 2. In addition, this area is best warmed by north Atlantic currents. As the majority of modern excavations

Fig 2. Norse expansion across the north Atlantic. Zone demarcation utilized throughout the work is also shown.

have been conducted in the Northern and Western Quarters of Iceland, however certain full farm complexes such those found in Mývatnssveit have been included as well to help provide the more complete data sets provided by modern excavations. Palaeobotanical data and toponymic evidence point to the fact that Iceland was wooded at the time of the initial Norse *landnám,* however both physical evidence and textual evidence support the fact that subsequent populations caused the forest resources to be exhausted. The entirety of Iceland shall be considered within Chapters 6, 7 and 8 of this work.

Zone 3 is composed of the Eastern settlement of Greenland as well as the New World Norse site at L'Anse aux Meadows, Newfoundland. This designation is primarily due to differences in available locations for settlement and the effects that this has on the available resources as well as the presence of non-European indigenous inhabitants. The Western Settlement of Greenland is much farther north than the rest of the study area and so is more difficult to include in this sample. Greenlandic Norse farms are known from the areas designated as the Eastern and Western Settlements and so the entirety of Norse Greenland shall be considered in Chapters 6, 7 and 8. The singular New World site has been included as Greenlanders and Icelanders, via Greenland, attempt to settle and conducted any subsequent trading in the region that implies the presence of a Greenlandic *habitus*, rather than a separate New World based Norse identity.

Ecological Environments of the North Atlantic

Norse settlement of the north Atlantic was successful in no small part because of the variety of environments which corresponded to those experienced in the coastal fjords and islands of Scandinavia as well as the early movements into Zone 1, for instance a Shetlandic *voe* is merely a fjord with a land aspect which is much less dramatic. However, island archipelagos create the very real concern of limited future resources for growing medieval populations. Initial *landnám* populations took the best lands available that were primarily located on the coast or had a coastal element to them.[5] Lands that are more marginal became places of subsequent secondary and tertiary settlement as the *landnám* population expanded over generations. With such a large area to consider, certain aspects of location become more influential than others. Ocean currents such as the Irminger Current and the Norwegian Atlantic Current provide warming and cooling effects on land and water masses ranging from continents to small island archipelagos. The movements of currents provide catalysts for fish migrations, driftwood systems and greater water transport mobility. Some of the most influential ocean currents that influence the north Atlantic zones are shown in Fig 3.

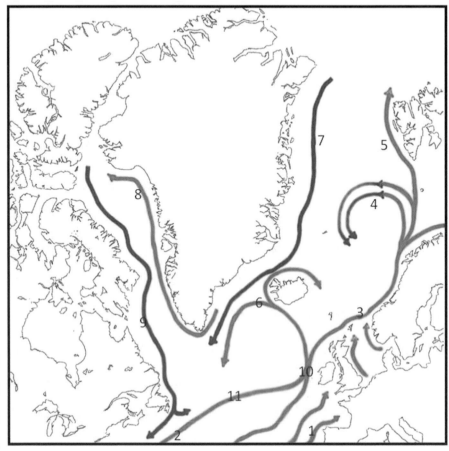

1. Portugal Current
2. North Atlantic Current
3. Norwegian Current
4. North Cape Current
5. Spitsbergen Current
6. Irminger Current
7. East Greenland Current
8. West Greenland Current
9. Labrador Current
10. Shelf Edge Current
11. North Atlantic Drift
Current

Fig 3. Major North Atlantic oceanic currents.[7]

Linked to currents is the global climate, which has been associated with significant impact in north Atlantic settlement. The entirety of the region under consideration is classified as either **Cfb** or **Cfc** according to the Koppen-Geiger climatic designation system that would not have changed overall during the period under consideration. This classification system has been utilized to provide several consistencies within the ecological and climatic data presented in Fig 5. These are well-established designations that are based upon vegetation types and geologic weathering present within geographic environments.[6] Land areas are included in Fig 6.

Koppen designation	Common name	Precipitation	Month of warmest average	Number of colder months
Cfb	Maritime Temperate Climate	All months	Warmest average month will be below 22°C	At least 4 months will be above 10°C
Cfc	Maritime subarctic climate	All months	Warmest average month will be below 22°C	Less than 3 months will be above 10°C

Fig 4. Koppen designations for the north Atlantic region explained in brief.[8]

There were some quite influential global climatic trends at work during the period under consideration. The period, which resulted in overall warming of the Northern Hemisphere from circa AD 600–1200, is known as the Medieval Warm Period or Optimal.[9] The terrestrial impact of this can easily been seen in Europe and North America in particular through greater agricultural production, greater areas of associated political and social power consolidation as increased amounts of human migration.

The maritime impact of the Medieval Optimal is much more ephemeral in terms of direct evidence Due to the fluid nature of the medium although comparative modern examples exist. The increased temperature conditions resulted in calmer waters for longer periods during the Optimal period.[10] Sea ice, which had developed during the colder winter months, did not form as far south, which resulted in the possibility of more direct and hence shorter voyages to the various north Atlantic islands.[11] This easier period would end earlier in regions above 60°N especially in Arctic polar climates with the onset of the Little Ice Age, which would truly affect Europe and North America during the fifteenth century.[12] In the higher northern latitudes, glacial ice-core samples show that these regions began to experience harsher longer winters centuries earlier than locations to the south.[13]

Marine regions contain a variety of ecological environments available for exploitation. Of all of these, open water is one of the most difficult to prove due to the nature of the material. The best evidence this environment's exploitation is marine artefacts found on land as well as the physical remains of exploited open water material.[14] This can range from the exploitation of marine fish and mammals to seaweed and littoral zone shellfish. Live marine mammal exploitation in this pre-Modern period, and which continues in areas like the Faroe Islands, consisted of tiring animals to bring them into coastal waters.[15] Deep sea fishing on greater than subsistence levels would require cooling global temperatures and the proper economic climate on the European national market to grow in importance.[16]

Island groups	Koppen Symbol	Modern Annual Rainfall	Basement Rock	Arability
Orkney	Cfb	948mm	Old Devonian Red Sandstone	80%
Shetland	Cfb	1003mm	Complex: Old Devonian red Sandstone but also Lewisian, Dalradian and Moine metamorphic outcrops in a confluence of several fold and fault axes in accordance to the various plates.	35%
Hebrides	Cfb	1297mm	Primarily Lewisian gneiss.	47%
Faroe Islands	Cfc	1433mm	Basalt – the remnants of an ancient continent.	2.14%
Iceland	Cfc	779mm	Primarily basalts and other minerals of volcanic origin which are subject to active glaciers in some areas.	0.07%
Greenland	Cfc, Ef	526mm	Crystalline granites of the Laurentian Shield which are in close proximity to active glaciers.	0%
L'Anse aux Meadows	Cfb/c	1514mm	Primarily granites and marine sedimentary rocks to the south	0%

Fig 5. Island geographic data from Koppen designations.[17]

Coastal waters include the water aspects of fjords and any areas where shallower relatively open waters occur. Artefacts found on land evidence this. Evidence includes net weights used to hold down nets used in coastal fishing as well as hooks and line weights. Species exploited here include Gadids and shoaling flatfish as well as available marine mammals such as seals, walrus and porpoise.[18] The littoral margins including beaches, the terrestrial aspects of fjords and other immediate coastal areas such as *geos* provide such material as ecofacts, pollen and other palaeoecological evidence. This is where landing sites and boat nausts were located.[19] Shore fishing, shellfish and seaweed collection all occur in this environment. Some marine bird exploitation also would have occurred in these regions.[20]

Meadows naturally either occur in the flattish areas near littoral margins or are within terrain that is more mountainous. These are the regions preferred for building construction. The arable lands provided the locations necessary for the infield and outfields.[22] Drainage is a major concern across much of this region, particularly for the areas nearest to glaciers, and occurs in the rarer sandy soils of the north Atlantic. Grasslands also provided immediate and future fodder as well.[23] Pastures utilized for animal husbandry will tend to have an available source of fresh water and outbuildings for areas of larger size, and possibly pens

Fig 6. Land areas of the north Atlantic region.[21]

for holding animals as well.[24] Haymaking fields on the other hand, will be much more remote and may or may not have outbuildings. Haying was a manual task, as it is in parts of the Faroe Islands to this day.[25]

Marginal areas were those regions that were less directly involved in the production and collection of food and raw resources. These were the locations of secondary and tertiary settlement. This is where wild species exploitation would have occurred. In the areas furthest west, Zone 3, where species such as fox, arctic hare, caribou and musk oxen were exploited to fill the need of protein and raw materials.[26] Marginal areas also include those haymaking pastures which are too small to support a population of medium to large herbivores yet are still productive enough to contribute to the over-wintering strategy.[27]

Although one is hesitant to ascribe cultural identity development merely to the contextual environment, a trend in theory known as environmental determinism, it is incredibly hard to deny the impact of the environment in this consideration of north Atlantic settlement. This may have something to do with the fact that islands and coastal environments themselves are often quite marginal in nature themselves, with limited carrying capacity in terms of human and domesticated animal populations. The subsistence strategy of any culture prior to the modern period is quite closely tied into the local environments those cultures inhabit and the north Atlantic region during this period is no exception to this.

The available resources show broad similarities amongst certain species and share some of these similarities with the rugged Scandinavian coastlines. The early-medieval Norse subsistence strategy was based upon the farm unit outside of trading centers. The farm unit has a series of basic needs only satisfied by certain locations in the north Atlantic. They include a place to keep stock as well as a place for the people required for their care.[28] A place to gather or grow fodder, especially for the winter, was vital in the higher latitudes.[29] A means of communication and exchange with other farms was necessary as well as this could be used to obtain materials unable to be locally produced. Due to this early exposure to similar conditions as would be found in the north Atlantic islands the *habitus* of the *landnám* era settlers developed in such a manner as to become specialized generalists as well. Specialized generalists are those groups that specialize in the exploitation of a wide variety of local resources. In the case of the north Atlantic archipelagos, this included the exploitation of marine birds, fish, mollusks, seaweed and marine mammals amongst other species as well as inanimate goods such as driftwood.[30] This exploitation was integrated into the local trade and exchange network with interior sites on the islands. The diverse resources would have required somewhat specialized knowledge in certain cases such as knowing when to exploit migrating birds and fish as well as the much larger community task of whale exploitation.[31]

The overall marginal nature of the archipelagos found within the north Atlantic required the exploitation of every available resource by farm groups just in order to survive the harsh winters. This fact does become part of the laws codes of several of the island archipelagos as time passes and the world climate moved from the Medieval Warm Period onto the cooler Little Ice Age.[32] This is reflected in the medieval laws which dictate not only collection rights with regards to coastal resources but also, in the case of Iceland in particular, dictate unaffiliated people to become part of a farm for the year or else to risk being *útlaga*.[33] Following the adoption of *oðal* system during the late Medieval period an effort was made to provide a balanced collection of available island resources so that a greater variety of resources were available to the public farms.

Research Context of the North Atlantic

The Norse settlement of the north Atlantic occurred at a convergence of major events any of one of which could have potentially resulted in significant changes to society. As northwestern European peoples began their settlement into sometimes quite marginal quality lands which were increasingly farther from the long-established networks of trade and community in the North and Irish Sea area we also began to see global climatic conditions warm and mellow in general.[34] Maritime technologies advanced to the point that long-distance travel over open water became much less of an obstacle than it had in the past – this included masts and the flexible yet strong clinker construction which the ships of Scandinavia became famous for.[35] Evidence for such vessels has been found in a variety of locations ranging from defensive scuttles found within Scandinavian harbors, to ship burials to even the boat nausts that once held vessels over winter.[36]

Concurrent to this the Scandinavian homelands began to consolidate into medieval nationalities, the beginnings of modern nations. This consolidation is highlighted in several Icelandic sagas as the primary reason for the Scandinavian Diaspora across the Atlantic. Some relate this to growing interaction and emulation of kingdoms of the Continent while others cite it in relation to a particularly strong period of economics.[37] This process began first in the most southern of the early-medieval kingdoms, Denmark, but spread north along with the conversion to Christianity until Sweden was converted by the early twelfth century, much later than the north Atlantic settlements to the west.[38] Due to the spread of Christianity Latin text was acquired and resulted in a wide variety of textual resources being produced by a people with a previously strong and complex oral tradition.[39] Increasingly researchers are faced with some form of the text in question related to the actual and perceived liminality of the expanding Scandinavian populations and any impact this may have had in the subsequent descendents.

The expansion of peoples into the North Atlantic has been a topic of much academic consideration and publication over the years, fuelled by a substantial corpus of both archaeological and written sources that are primarily associated with Early-medieval Norse. There have been fewer considerations regarding the peoples aside from this Scandinavian tradition, such as the *Papar* who preceded the Norse in the movements west and the Thule who shared the Greenlandic waves.

Knorr

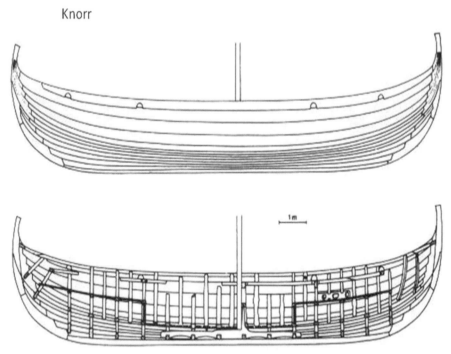

Fig 7. *Knórr*, after Crumlin-Pedersen.[40]

Norse

Although there have been several considerations of the entire North Atlantic they have been primarily associated with the Norse movements and resultant human impacted landscapes alone as opposed to a wider variety of cultural vectors.[41] North Atlantic settlements have long been a subject of archaeological research as well as more textual based considerations. This interest is linked to the early efforts of antiquarians who had been inspired by saga material and folk legends. In this view, the evidence provided by Icelandic sagas in particular was seen as being a true representation of the past able to be easily corroborated via archaeological excavation.[42] The impact of this cannot be underestimated, particularly in Iceland but also in the Faroe Islands as well. By the beginning of the twentieth century, this individual interest was being funded by nationally interested museums and universities, involving the local infrastructure to a lesser degree.[43] One of the most influential of these during this period and even to this day is the Department of Antiquities and the National Museum of Denmark, which funded much of the earliest excavations in the Faroe Islands and Greenland.[44]

Archaeological surveys and excavations which were conducted during the inter-War period and immediately following World War II also exhibited the nationalistic influences of the previous decades although not necessarily always from museums and universities.[45] Due to this, some of the more remote sites of the North Atlantic were found. On the other hand, excavations were conducted under rescue conditions, often due to the effects of coastal erosion that are almost unavoidable when working with maritime and littoral populations. A striking example of this can be seen in Kvívík in the Faroe Islands, where the Viking Age longhouse and stable had partially eroded into the North Atlantic by the time of excavation.[46]

Zone	Time frame	Names	Geographic area	Cultural assumptions via texts
Zone 1	Pre-AD 800 [varies] to 1000	Some assimilation of old names and descriptive	Previous settlement, coastal areas	Networks previously established; pagan population converted fairly quickly
Zone 2	AD 870–1000	Initially descriptive	Coastal areas and nearby valleys to the interior	Primarily pagan with some Christians mostly coming via previous settlements in Zone 1
Zone 3	c. AD 950–1050	Difficult to comment upon as many Norse place names have been lost – personal name elements is what survives	Coastal portions of the interior fjords	Pagans and Christians with Christian population growth as time passed

Fig 8. Aspects of *landnám* associated with each Zone.

Localized considerations became much the standard practice during the mid-twentieth century, with little in the way of cross-regional integration. Each island group were considered to be metaphorical and physical stepping-stones for Norse culture to move *en masse* west across the Atlantic. By the 1970s and early 1980s sites in the Northern and Western Isles of Scotland as well as Caithness began to be excavated which intensively began to change this point of view, however.[47] These excavations were the result of rescue work and previous survey and highlighted the fact that this was a region of great importance in its own right prior to modern times. Contemporaneous to these events, archaeological excavations began to be conducted in a much more standardized fashion – a prerequisite for interregional comparisons and considerations. This included systematic and widespread use of fine mesh sieves, sampling, and floatation techniques amongst other things. That has resulted in the standardization of archaeological data in accordance to quantifiable scientific evidence. Theories and ideas based on not only the individual but also societal impacts on site and text construction began to find their way into archaeological thought. These theories began to provide an ideological framework more suited to the multi-contextual situations found in the north Atlantic and are discussed in detail in Chapter 2 of this book.

As time passed, more and more researchers interested in north Atlantic topics began to realize and recognize the high degree of integration found within the region within publication. By the late 1980s the first major conferences, regional considerations and edited volumes began to appear in publication.[48] The idea that the islands were not just peripheries to a continental European power, but also held other functions within this system, spread during this time, in turn influencing up-coming graduate students. This concept became central to subsequent works of the region and recognition of the culture contact that occurred during the Viking Age became more widespread in published considerations.

The peopling of the Atlantic archipelagos is not considered in a similar manner to Pacific archipelagos primarily due to historical precedence with heavy nationalistic overtones indicative of the early modern period. Comments such as these began to help change this view. International research groups such as the North Atlantic Biocultural Organization (NABO) spread these ideas and concepts further while providing an ever-increasing research network. The early 1990s saw not only the first cross-regional considerations but also wider growing interest in culture contact studies within archaeology and anthropology in general. This was especially evident within former colonial areas of the world. Whether this is a reflection of the wider multicultural movement found within the social sciences and humanities during this period or a wider need on the part of former occupied lands to determine where the history books told the truth and where they lied is somewhat dependent on the personal context of the researchers at the time. This is important in relation to the north Atlantic as every settlement became colonial in relation to the medieval Scandinavian kingdoms over time.

Alongside this intensification were published works on Greenland and Newfoundland that were more associated with the millennial celebration of

Leif Eriksson's landing on the North American continent. In the light of the anniversary the materials which have resulted have focused not only on the context of north-western European movements, such as the Fourteenth Viking Congress held in Torshavn in 2001 which was directly themed 'Viking and Norse in the North Atlantic,'[49] but also indirect considerations of Vínland and Leif Eriksson.

An example of the latter is the 1999 international colloquium organized by the Sigurður Nordal Institute at the University of Iceland which was themed *Vester um haf*, the repeated term found within saga evidence which refers to the travel of ships westwards beyond Iceland.[50] Directly translated this term is 'west over sea' and has subsequently become a favoured title reference to pertinent publications.[51] The *Vester um haf* colloquium proceeding's preface in particular, as well as other volume introductions from this period, also highlights the heavy involvement of nationally politically-minded institutions. Myth maintenance being integral to the maintenance of modern ethnic groups has become a particular problem in relation to Scandinavian archaeological and historical research over the centuries.[52] Certain regions in particular are strongly associated with certain saga episodes and sagas while artefacts and sites that do not necessarily promote this view as strongly are given less weight than they would in a more ethnically and/or politically neutral situation. This interest exists in more than just the international researchers based outside of the north Atlantic region. However, as major museum exhibitions and publications have shown, the Smithsonian's 'Viking: The North Atlantic Saga' exhibit and publication not only held a successful place within Washington DC but a smaller travelling exhibition also travelled throughout major American museums for several years. Much of this past decade has been spent continuing the trends towards interdisciplinary international considerations. The publications of the conference proceedings from the late 1990s and early 2000s have largely been completed and published.

International conferences and colloquiums held in recent years seem to have focused upon the contextualization of the new material into the existing Viking Age and medieval North Atlantic corpus as well as more global events. In 2008, the *Maritime Societies of the Viking and Medieval World* conference was held in Kirkwall, Orkney. The aim of this endeavour was specifically detailed within the title.[53] The NABO conference for the same year was associated with the International Polar Year efforts of the global research community. However, as in previous conferences this was also a time to update the NABO international research community and audience on current work in the field. This trend was also expressed in the *New Directions in Medieval Scandinavian Studies*

Conference held at Fordham University's Center for Medieval Studies in 2010. This particular conference advocated intense discussion of all aspects and regions of Scandinavian influence.[54]

Thanks in no small part to the efforts and funds of institutions such as NABO and the variety of National Museums, libraries and archives data related to the North Atlantic region there is a wealth of reliable evidence available for modern researchers. The recognition of the necessity of interdisciplinary work within the north Atlantic dominated the 2011 *Viking Society for Northern Research Student Symposium* where each of the speakers advocated greater interdisciplinary communication between archaeologists and literary specialists.[55] This work attempts to fit within this scheme of multivocality.

Pre-Norse North Atlantic Populations

Although this study is primarily focused upon the Scandinavian related settlements of the north Atlantic it is very important to remember that this is not the only population for which there is evidence for, it just happens to be the population which has the majority of the evidence attributed to it. There is a long history of folklore and interest in the peoples who came before, up to and including the incoming Norse populations of the seventh and eighth centuries. Icelanders in particular appear to have held a strong interest in the history of the land and its people and as a result, such topics are the focus of several sagas and informative Scandinavian texts such as the *Historia Norwegiae*.[56]

This is a topic with little in the way of solid evidence due to the maritime environment and the organic nature of the material evidence. In fact the earliest voyages would have been undertaken in wooden or hide covered boats that could have easily been drawn up onto shore rather than requiring a proper harbor.[57] Vessels of similar types and their predecessors would have been involved in the early settlement of Orkney, Shetland, the Hebrides and the islands of the Irish Sea. They may originally been following currents, winds or even migrating birds and animals. They would not have left much evidence of this movement visible in the land or seascape. Networks of trade and exchange maintained through hierarchies of social obligation, similar to elsewhere in Western Europe, would have extended from the Continent to at least the North Sea and Irish Sea regions extending networks to early urban centers in north-western Europe. How far these early voyages actually went is lost to time unfortunately, however, because of their occurrence a particular type of folktale developed: the *immrama* tale. This type of tale also in turn was partially absorbed by Christian tradition. In fact, the Christian element of this earlier maritime population is that which subsequent populations have best remembered. Amongst the contemporary non-Norse sources, particularly Adomnán and Dicuil, are descriptions of hermetic priests who lived on the most remote of those islands and sea-stacks at sites such as the sixth century monastery at Skellig Michael.[58] The other body of evidence, which may or may not be directly linked to these ascetic priests described above, is related to the *Papar* described within Icelandic and Norwegian sources and remembered within the toponymic geography of the north Atlantic.

The *Papar* present a unique situation in terms of this consideration, as they are not equally represented across the various types of evidence available. Migratory populations more often than not leave little in the way of physical evidence must be considered. With relation to considerations of *Papar* the lack of physical evidence has caused a dominance of written and toponymic studies of the topic-, it is easier to find evidence for the *Papar* in these sources than anywhere else is. The Papar, as ecclesiastics and not a biological population, are discussed in detail in relation to the Church in Chapters 6, 7 and 8.

Geographic Organization of Analysis

In order to compare the changes that occurred in each of the island groups settled by north Atlantic travelling Scandinavians it was necessary to designate zones across the entire region, please refer to Fig 2. These zones were designated on physical location and historical precedence. Zone 1 is composed of the Northern and Western Isles of Scotland and the Faroe Islands – the nearest island groups to the Scandinavian homelands within direct sail during the Viking Age. This is the North Sea and Irish Sea region that has been an

Fig 9. The Lewis Chessmen on display at the National Museum of Scotland. Photo taken by Dr R. Lenfert.

interconnected web of exchange and power networks since the Neolithic and early Scandinavian interest in the area is unsurprising. As there are several island groups in Zone 1 the case study for this zone utilizes evidence from Shetland and the Faroe Islands. Shetland and the Faroe Islands have been chosen for the Zone 1 case study to gain clarification on the reality of identity construction and maintenance in the island groups.

Due to historical precedence during the Middle Ages Orkney and the Hebrides are more widely studied by modern researchers. They will be referred to within discussion chapters in Chapters 6, 7 and 8 comparatively due to the more numerous amounts of publications related to this time period. Excavation plans and environmental studies in particular are more plentiful concerning Orkney and the Hebrides due to British archaeological efforts. There are also direct reliable textual sources simply not available for Shetland and the Faroe Islands that highlights identities as opposed to Icelandic textual sources only. Shetland and the Faroe Islands on the other hand both remained under the control of Scandinavia for a longer time as well as having received less widespread publication and archaeological survey in the modern era. They shall form the bulk of evidence presented within the case study for Zone 1. Each of these archipelagos is within a direct sailing voyage from the Scandinavian homelands, in particular western Norway. Examination of Shetlandic and Faroese evidence will show a different social, economic and political situation to the more southern affluent and agriculturally viable islands of Orkney and the Hebrides. The islands of Zone 1 also all exhibit evidence of highly restricted wood resources at the time of Norse *landnám* whether due to heavy previous human exploitation or a total lack of presence in general due to remote island location from European arboreal populations.

Zone 2 is composed of Iceland. Iceland has an incredibly large body of evidence in publication including archaeological reports but also sagas, their related critiques, formalized trade agreements and medieval law codes. This has required sampling of the available material and as a result the Southern Quarter of Iceland, which historically received the heaviest *landnám* population, and the Eastern Quarter of Iceland, which is the closest geographically to Zone 1, has been focused upon within the case study for Zone 2. This is also the area which is best warmed by north Atlantic Currents. As the majority of modern excavations have been conducted in the Northern and Western Quarters of Iceland, however, certain full farm complexes such those found in Mývatnssveit have been included as well to help provide the more complete data sets provided by modern excavations. Palaeobotanical data and toponymic evidence point to the fact that Iceland was wooded at the time of the initial Norse *landnám* however both physical evidence and textual evidence support the fact that subsequent populations caused the forest resources to be exhausted. The entirety of Iceland shall be considered within Chapters 6, 7 and 8 of this book.

Zone 3 is composed of the Eastern settlement of Greenland as well as the New World Norse site at L'Anse aux Meadows, Newfoundland. This designation is primarily due to differences in available locations for settlement and the effects that this has on the available resources as well as the presence of non-European indigenous inhabitants. The Western Settlement of Greenland is much farther north than the rest of the study area and so is more difficult to include in this sample. Greenlandic Norse farms are known from the areas designated as the Eastern and Western Settlements and so the entirety of Norse Greenland shall be considered in Chapters 6, 7 and 8. The single New World site has been included as Greenlanders and Icelanders, via Greenland, attempt to settle and conduct trading in the region implies the presence of a Greenlandic *habitus*, rather than a separate New World-based Norse identity.

Specific Aims of this Work

The primary aim of this book is to examine the construction and maintenance of Scandinavian-based identities involved in settlements found within the north Atlantic from AD 800–1250 via the utilization of multiple data sets. This has the benefit of not only providing an internal means of crosschecking findings but also highlights the multilayered complexity of the human condition.[59] This is an area known to have a high degree of inter-regional homogeneity concerning material culture. As a result, this has necessitated a more interdisciplinary approach that encompasses a wider variety of evidence including archaeological evidence as well as medieval written material. This allows for the utilization of multiple data sets that have the benefit of not only providing an internal means of crosschecking findings but also highlights the multi-layered complexity of the human condition.

In order to study the multi-layered complexity of the north Atlantic situation some breakdown is necessary for analytical reasons.[60] This includes analysis of the cultural structures of society, which affected not only the community and society but also family units.[61] This practice is evidenced by a variety of human impacts and products, some of which are physical in nature and some of which are more ephemeral, and so as a result this investigation must too be multivalent. Although this is not necessarily a new idea in terms of social theory, its application to the North Atlantic as a unit as opposed to a portion of the area is new to research in this Scandinavian settled region. It is important to highlight the strategies that became part of being an inhabitant of any of these island archipelagos including the generalized Norse responses as well as the more localized pragmatic strategies that dictated by the environment. In order to better examine and compare this region has been broken into three zones for consideration.

Another specific aim is to examine what happens when nationalistic elements imposed by colonizers of the north Atlantic impacted cultural identities following the initial settlement period rather than prior and during settlement as experienced in more modern efforts of colonization. This occurred when Norway and the Hansea controlled the north Atlantic trade thus encompassing the informally settled archipelagos in medieval political and economic networks.[62]

Unlike the more widely studied post-AD 1492 movements of Europeans west, the nationalistic elements which are found within the vast majority of the written sources from the medieval period through to well into the twentieth century are largely anachronistic to the onset of the Norse north Atlantic settlement. The impact of modern European nationalism is something that cannot be downplayed when it comes to research in the North Atlantic. There are beneficial aspects to this such as funding for major archaeological excavations, for example the Danish *Gård under Sandet*, GUS, site excavations conducted in northwestern Greenland as well as the means necessary to conserve medieval manuscripts and as such, much acknowledgement must be made. On the other hand, however, the negative impact of nationalism is also felt in the North Atlantic, particularly in publication and has been for quite a long time. Saga research and archaeology in particular have become linked over time through the utilization of pseudo-history as fact. Another specific aim of this work is to examine what happens when those nationalistic elements imposed by other colonizers of the New World impacts cultural identities following the initial settlement period as occurred when Norway and the Hansea controlled the north Atlantic trade networks.[63]

Lastly, the final aim of this work is to utilize written texts for their anthropological insight into Norse north Atlantic identity construction and maintenance. In order to do this personal translation of Old Norse texts and passages has been undertaken. This is not a common technique for modern archaeological considerations outside of Scandinavia.[64] There is a distinct difference in how the study of Norse culture is conducted modernly in comparison to the major late nineteenth century Scandinavian excavators as those modern researchers who study the archaeology of the region and those who study the substantial amount of literary material have imposed a definite distance between themselves. This was not always the case with the earlier studies conducted and to a certain extent some of the sense of an entire culture has been lost as a result. The utilization of such material in this work is to correlate data concerning societal and class structures as opposed to utilization of such material as an infallible written history of events – one of the critiques often imposed on those earlier studies.[65] Internal and external views of identity construction, history and daily domestic life are provided by contemporary written sources. This provides a view not only from within the culture under consideration but also a view of how people not within the group considered the group in question – the emic and the etic views.

Study Format

Evidence for this consideration of medieval Norse identity construction and maintenance is presented in a manner that highlights both the microscale and macroscale aspects of identity. As the concept of Norse identity, of what it means to be a part of the Norse culture and what other people considered that identity to consist of, changes through time and across the space of the region a method of simplification and categorization has been utilized in the format of this work. Evidence data is presented in table form within the text of these chapters as well as more completely by site presence and absence tables found within the Appendices. The criteria utilized in the creation of these tables is derived from artefact lists of well excavated and dated maritime Scandinavian farms and settlements and is presented in a manner similar to skeletal presence and absence charts for ease in consideration. In some cases they have also incorporated textual evidence related to certain regions and farms as well to more directly compare aspects of identity practiced in a variety of media.

Chapter 2

Theory and Methodology

Introduction

This chapter explores the theoretical concepts behind this consideration of the Viking Age and early-medieval north Atlantic. The Norse settlement of the north Atlantic occurred at a convergence of major events. Any one of these on its own would have formed a major driver and/or vector for change within identity construction and maintenance of the region's populations. This topic requires the consideration of a wide variety of evidence. The utilization of a multivalent and fluid concept of identity and ethnicity allows this material to be more efficiently used and considered in light of the development of actor-networks described by Latour and Sindbæk. By doing this the relationships and social obligations of these Atlantic populations, the very drivers and vectors of social change, are highlighted to a greater degree. At the basis of this is an essential perspective that at its most basic culture has been created by groups of people initially to provide humans with a 'blueprint' of how to relate and inter-relate within their environments. Society is not only embedded in the individual actor but is also produced by the actor. In order to do this an explanation of what identity and ethnicity means in relation to this work is necessary.

Identity and Ethnicity

This work relates to the multivariate nature of identity and ethnicity as conceived of by Jenkins[1] and its application to the discipline of archaeology.[2] As such, definitions for identity and ethnicity need disclosure. These are concepts that have become increasingly more focused upon as the fluid nature of identity and ethnicity is more widely accepted. They recursively compose and direct the concepts of habitus and doxic practice. Identity is the name for the collection of personal assumptions, beliefs and knowledge utilized in the internal and external identification process that occurs during all individual and group interactions.[3] It has a wide variety of expressions both conscious and unconscious produced – some of these are tangible while others are not. Identity is important because it provides a means of exploring the human experience in the span necessary for study of cultural structures only visible in considerations of the longue durée, which in turn are a portion of the complete culture and group identity.[4] Identity presents most consistently through the examination of choices made.[5] Thus, choice becomes a common denominator of study. In studies of living populations, examination of choice occurs through fieldwork and interview as well as the examination of the intangible and physical residue of such choices.[6] Hence, in fieldwork the choice of who to talk to is considered alongside the physical aspect of what was brought home for dinner. This process is possible archaeologically, particularly when studying archipelagos.

The environment including the social context of social hierarchy and power networks influence identity.[7] Social theorists including Jenkins and Jones have taken efforts to acknowledge the contextual choices made during the construction and maintenance of identities, both individual identities as well as group. In terms of evidence, this will be reflected in varying degrees to object choice that ultimately results in archaeological assemblages on sites. It is in a similar manner to the authorial and editing choices made during the construction of written material. Ethnicity is another important factor to consider in frontier situations. For instance, in New Spain ethnicity was the most important factor in finding a position within the peripheral area's economic and social hierarchies.[8]

Meskell cites there being two levels of operation to social identities – an individual level and a broader social level that relate to each other recursively.[9] This view is quite influential in allowing for a more complete application of Practice Theory to this study. The individual level is the subjective actor who simultaneously experiences, understands and is experienced in turn by the world around them.[10] The individual level is easily collected from living populations rather than archaeological material and as a result is not focused upon in a region where group solidarity equates with survival. The social level, on the other hand, is where identities are dictated by their wider context within social relationships.[11] These are found within the dialectical tension expressed by Bourdieu concerning Practice Theory. The individual actor experiences and expresses themselves in the subjective world while the broader social level is where occurrences that are more objective take place.

An individual actor within a group establishes their identity and to a lesser extent their concept of *self* through the utilization of goods and resources in unique methods and combinations. These are recognized as 'belonging' to a particular affiliation as well as actions and techniques that are associated in a similar manner. In general, identity is seen as being influenced in some way by childhood events as this provides the means of comparison throughout the rest of one's life, the basis for *habitus*.[13] There is some conscious choice

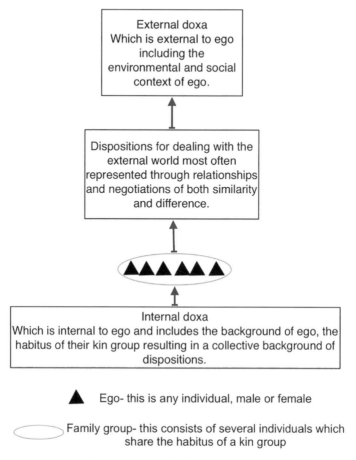

Fig 10. Schematic of individual interaction.[12]

on the part of the actors as to what the identity is formed from. Perhaps most importantly humans may concurrently hold multiple identities that may or may not be expressed at the same time. These identities may or may not interact with one another themselves. Modern considerations of identity are more likely to consider the individual as a primary subject of interest while archaeologically identity has been more concerned with that of groups.[14]

Microscale elements of identity in living populations are evidenced via the results of choices made under the influence of childhood and family experience. Results can be both intangible and tangible. Consideration of historic and prehistoric populations limits the evidence available to those that are tangible and have survived the effects of time. Archaeological evidence of daily social practice on the household level as well as that of the farm settlement provides much evidence for Norse microscale identity. These patterns of artefact placement, seasonal resource exploitation as well as midden location and utilization detail how a domestic household would function within the associated farm buildings, local landscape and when possible within the wider local network of associated satellite installations.

Textual evidence varies greatly depending on source type. For instance, sagas are unlikely to discuss domestic tasks such as daily cleaning, as it was a common task performed by women. Contemporaries would have assumed a farmhouse would have cleaning tasks. On the other hand seasonal farm activities were discussed as they provide a time scale for the saga audience. Legal treatises comment upon standardized concepts of the local farm network system. As such, this material is only used on the microscale level of analysis when the legal treatise in question is from a regional manuscript local to sites under consideration.

Groups may also concurrently hold multiple identities that may or may not be expressed at the same time and which may or may not interact with one another. At this level, we find the impact of wider kin groups within human populations. The impact of location upon several aspects of identity must also be considered, including but not limited to livelihood, subsistence and habitation. These are groups that are affected by and supporting of similar social norms, morals and ideals. Archaeologically this may be expressed in such ways as certain building construction practices and landscape utilization.[15] Evidence of communal activities must also be included in this as well including certain types of artefact utilization. 'Material culture […] plays an active role in the structuring of cultural practices, because the culturally specific meanings with which material culture is endowed as a result of former practices influence successive practices and interpretations'.[16] This is particularly relevant in the strong kin groups of the north Atlantic that became associated with certain farming regions. In written sources, this often expresses itself in the form of localized recorded place names and the promotion of localized history. Icelandic sagas, for instance, are regionalized in content and technique, particularly in reference to certain manuscript copies. This has much to do with the patron of the edition's relationship with the saga–scribe.

Macroscale elements of identity are those that are more broadly shared with a regional population. These are the aspects of identity that are influenced by external vectors such as religion, trade and exchange and socio-political organization. Archaeological evidence for this level of identity includes the physical evidence of formalized religion, artefacts available only via exchange and evidence for hierarchy. During the Viking Age and Medieval periods, most textual evidence is related to macroscale elements of identity. This is primarily due to the nature of authorship during this time as well as the influence of patrons. Although textual sources are available, some intangible evidence both internal and external in relation to the populations can be considered in relation to identity construction and maintenance.

Ethnic and national identities build upon this concept, as they are essentially group identities adopted by a wider group often across a larger physical region. These are identities that contain multiple groups and individuals, which share elements of common habitus. The adoption of certain ethnic identities is influential to intrapersonal and intercultural power relationships. This has become an increasingly powerful vector in the north Atlantic as the history becomes more embroiled into modern politics.[17] Identity has its roots in the anthropological concept of the family, a known form of group identity.

The family in an anthropological sense moves well beyond the biological definition to include all that is inherited by the individual actor otherwise known as the estate.[18] The symbolic estate of a group is an integral part of their identity and helps to establish the doxic practices described by Giddens and Bourdieu. This includes not only the family name but also their ancestors including the parent generation, family stories and myths. It can include recipes and cooking techniques as well as a wider body of elements as well such as family economic strategy. The symbolic estate of the family is core to their sense of taking in the world as it forms the basis from which to compare and contrast subsequent life experience.[19]

Ethnicity is a term that is often associated with identity but has a wider impact than an individual actor and so might be equated with a cultural identity which may or may not have a genetic basis.[20] According to Jones, '[…] ethnicity is a product of the intersection of the habitus with the conditions prevailing in any particular social and historical context'.[21] As such, it may be more advantageous for members of an ethnic group to promote their membership over others. Jones goes on to describe it '[as] both a transient construct of repeated acts of interaction and communication, and an aspect of social organization which becomes institutionalized to different degrees, and in different forms, in different societies'.[22] This is a much more complex process than simple cultural assimilation or blending as it involves the dynamic and active process of change of ideas amongst diverse fields rather than a perfect mix or cultural domination.[23] New cultures emerge from diverse elements via the creation and negotiation of cultural identities.

Medieval and prehistoric identities add another layer to this already complex concept. However, as researchers are working within a time period where nascent widespread cultural identities and medieval kingdoms were still consolidating and negotiating their power in the world while individual identity as an idea would not truly begin to arrive in Western thought until the Enlightenment.[24] Ethnicity and identity during this time is, if anything, in more flux than the modern period as the cultural norms, mores and associations were not firmly defined let alone being imposed. During this period, it was much easier to adopt regional identities and affiliations, as it was harder to prove individual identity beyond any doubt. An undoubted major influence on this is the impact of economic studies, which most often began their consideration with the onset of the modern period as this coincides with the large amounts of continuous written accounts which makes economics studies possible.[25] Due to this lack of formal definition during this period, an individual actor's ability to assume a secondary identity aside from their childhood identity would have been greatly enhanced.

Archaeology is an ideal method for studying the practices associated with the cultural expression of identities. Especially as a localized site that corresponds with the most basic and immediate level of society.[26] The idea here is that the identity that is displayed via the material evidence of an archaeological site is unique because certain contextual aspects of the site's placement in the physical, social, economic and political landscape are unique. It may not be possible to see the most telling of those unique aspects due to deterioration, subsequent land use or even the fact that some aspects of the site's unique nature was not physical at all.[27] This is equated to the type of information that can be derived from assemblages of human osteological material found on archaeological sites – individuality and unique aspects may have been lost with the flesh. Unfortunately, in this case those aspects intangible aspects of identity and ethnicity are lost. However, much can be done in spite of this through analysis and correlation of a variety of evidence types which shall be discussed below. There are individual aspects as well as group aspects of identity that co-exist in multiple layers. In relation to this study, north Atlantic identity is subjected to bipartisan consideration at microscale and macroscale levels discussed below. Actor choice and the responses to the context of both the individual and group levels result in a spectrum of responses. In this way the habitus, doxic practice, institutional influence and actor's choice can be seen as co-existing in such a way that the inter-play results in human identity creation and maintenance.

Levels of Identity

It is important to stress that this division of identity levels is somewhat arbitrary as the nature of the evidence shows that identity is in reality a spectrum ranging from the level of the individual ego (microscale) through to interregional groupings (macroscale). Determining one designation's space from another can be difficult and requires the corroboration of a variety of sources of evidence as well as a substantial data set for cross-comparison.

At the basis of these societal levels are individuals for which the physical evidence may be quite ephemeral in nature and the written record is often anachronistic in nature. Due to this, consideration of the individual is generally avoided in this work, utilizing family and farm groups instead. Hence, this level consists of many individuals. Microscale considerations focus upon evidence of the impact of the familial estate of the nuclear and extended family as well as the relative placement within the local hierarchy and exchange networks. Familial estates can include aspects of identity such as occupation, religion and physical location.

The microscale level of identity is the one that presents most often in the daily practice of living populations.[28] This study examines this through artefact placement diagrams that show space utilization, site maps and photographs as well as relevant written evidence charts when possible. Unfortunately, given the antique nature of the evidence for the north Atlantic settlement some of the greatest difficulties lie in recognizing archaeological material such as artefacts with their original cultural meanings and associations. Written evidence containing ethnohistorical details can be particularly useful for this. What has often occurred in past Norse north Atlantic studies is heavy interregional cross-utilization of archaeological and textual comparisons. This simultaneously reinforces the macroscale presence of a singular Norse culture and hence identity while obscuring the creation and growth of subsequent island identities.

The microscale level of identity in this study includes the evidence of choices and dispositions that relate to the success and decline of a small local population, i.e. that of a farm. Elements of microscale identity are composed of multiple local events and individual interactions that physically occur locally with a shared habitus of kin or employment group. The physical evidence of microscale identity includes artefact choices linked directly to the excavated site. This can be both domestically produced goods and trade imports shown via artefact presence in assemblages as well as evidence of onsite utilization. The interactions within a localized network of sites, as opposed to the wider north Atlantic network, can also influence microscale identity. Evidence includes those patterns and trends which fluctuate and change within a normal human lifespan. This can be the choice in construction material and architectural forms of buildings serving a local community, which are a direct result of the local environmental demands. These directly result in the adaptations unique to the local environment.

Macroscale considerations are possible due to evidence for long-term and far-reaching patterns best exhibited via continued production and emulation. Evidence for this includes the traditions related to architecture, subsistence and agriculture. These distinctive patterns of utilization and exploitation are passed generationally unchanged over the centuries. This includes the physical evidence of the long house, farm format and byre construction. For later sites under consideration, this may include church construction and the overall placement within the available landscape of the north Atlantic as well. In terms of language, macroscale elements can include language structure and format such as syntax and morphology as well. In order to do this, presence and absence charts can be used allowing for the more direct comparison of sites, maps of ecclesiastical placement in relation to secular settlements as well as site comparison directly via photographic comparison. The macroscale level of identity consideration includes evidence of broader cultural, and at times even national, aspects of identity as well as placements within international networks of trade and exchange. Childhood identities and the collective identity of archaeological sites as well as contemporary written evidence provide the final aspects of macroscale study.

Microscale and macroscale elements are not static but rather respond to social drivers and vectors that are explored by social theorists. Medieval textual sources are the most applicable to the macroscale level of identity as they make wide use of preceding and contemporary textual and oral sources as a means of both referencing as well as legitimization on many levels including social and political. In order to study this level of cultural identity, presence and absence charts allowing wider site comparison have resulted from the data found within this publication. Regional maps and site photographs as well as ecclesiastical maps have been included to better illustrate the specific aspects of identity being discussed.

Social Agency and Dynamics

Certain social theorists and philosophers have been particularly influential on the approaches and methodology followed in this research on identity. First is Weber who, perhaps most importantly in a consideration of identities, acknowledged the creative agency of individuals and attempted to account for the great diversity of human life without ranking according to a traditional scale of values and norms.[29] This attributes the option of personal choice and includes the particularly vital concept that identities themselves are of a fluid and dynamic nature, subject to boundaries of the same nature. This is vital for considerations of medieval identity in particular. Mauss is another who has heavily influenced conceptualizations of exchange and trade and the variety of impacts which may result for relationships between individuals and societies which was discussed at greater length in *The Gift*.[30]

Social relationships and institutions are intimately located in the all-pervasive economy of discourses of power that is inscribed in everyday life according to Foucault. Power in this social system determines different social forms throughout history.[31] Culture is emergent from the relations of power and domination as well as being a form of power and domination in and of itself. Culture and identity are also mediums in which power is both constituted and resisted. This presents in the archaeological records of many sites in the form of high status goods distribution and building construction techniques.[32] This may also relate to land choice and utilization techniques within the north Atlantic island archipelagos as well. In all instances, there is a high degree of inter-site comparison necessary in order to ascertain that the evidence presented is not a unique occurrence within the archaeological record but is rather more indicative of group identity practice and construction.

These ideas are quite basic to social theory, however, and allow for no true consideration of time and its impact on human society. They do highlight the fact that there are dynamic elements to the construction of culture that was a movement well away from the more static theories of the nineteenth century.[33] In order to consider the identity construction and maintenance within the north Atlantic more dynamic theory must be utilized. According to Braudel different historical processes known as structures are at work on different temporal scales in any society.[34] These are the levels of history where identity is practiced.

Many of the researchers who followed Braudel would and still do continue to use this tripartite breakdown of cultural time – one of the strengths of the approach when applied to living populations. The focus on long dead populations has resulted in a change in application for this work. This work also utilizes this time breakdown and focuses upon two groupings in particular. The relation to the conception of identity construction and maintenance utilized in the study is shown in Fig 12. This is a theory that is comparable to water referred to here as the Sea of Human Consciousness.[35] The *longue durée* relates to deep currents in this Sea, for instance. These structures are the stable elements found within a culture transmitted over many generations of society and like deep-water currents; they are fairly firmly set in course over quite long periods. This level of consideration is critiqued as being environmentally deterministic.[36]

To continue with the analogy the *conjecture* equate with tides that affect the Sea of Human Consciousness. These are the cycles experienced by cultures, including but not limited to the cyclical rise and fall of prices, politics and parties and other occurrences that are experienced in cycles.[37] The *événementielle* are the waves or other surface disturbances on the deep currents of the Sea of Human Consciousness. These are the everyday happenings of sociopolitical events.[38] One of the weaknesses of the Structure and Event approach is that the impact of micro-history, the *événementielle*, is de-emphasized however. This became a focus for theorists following Braudel although many of the basic units and terms utilized in the construction of the subsequent theories remained the same.

A key in the utilization of Structure and Event Theory, and one which is found amongst the strongest ideas following Braudel, is to examine the intersections of structures and temporal scales. Of those subsequent studies, two have particularly influenced this work. The first is the more widely impacting Practice Theory of Bourdieu[39] and Giddens,[40] which focuses on the idea that the cultural structures that exist in the mind are only actualized in the moments of practice. The second of these is Actor-Network Theory proposed by Latour[41] and advocated heavily in the works of Sindbæk.[42]

Individuals and groups constantly and continually respond to new situations. Sectorial interests outside of personal interaction also are taken into account. In this system, new opportunities and social relationships develop as a result. Choices are made to make sense of others as well as what best suits the individual's own sectorial interests and so in this way one is able to deal with ambiguity in the world.[43] In terms of the north Atlantic, this means that each constituent member carries the ability within them to effect the archaeological record by their choices – but just as likely may not.

Practice Theory
Practice Theory is based on the assumption that structures inherent to culture should be observable in daily practice. Giddens recognized the duality of social structures themselves as well as the dynamics of social structure. According to Giddens, structures exist in the process of being but they are also the medium and outcome of social practice itself. The practice of daily life builds structures and can be transformed in turn by encounters.[44] Practice Theory is more often associated with Bourdieu rather than Giddens, however. Bourdieu too followed in the tradition of Weber in the assumption and inherent belief that individuals create themselves during daily practice and the repetition of daily routines. Bourdieu has given a nomenclature to studies of cultural structures and practices that is detailed in Fig 11.

Term	Definition	Comments
Dispositions	The transposable habitual tendencies of individuals to act and react in certain ways.	The dispositions that are available to an individual or group will depend upon the constituent elements of the habitus.
Habitus	The embodied dispositions that are the domain of habit, which is at once individual and collective.	The individual habitus is dependent upon the collective habitus of the wider population to which they belong.
Doxa	The elements of culture which appear to be obviously self-evident and unchanging, essentially the known cultural world.	This is composed of the habitus and what is possible to be known.
Doxic Practice	The collective dispositions and choices that result from the habitus interacting with cultural doxa.	This functions upon the premise that habitus and doxa are recreated and reinforced through the dispositions of the individual and group.

Fig 11. Key terms associated with the Annales School.[45]

There is an emphasis placed on the day-to-day in this theory as this is the place where people play out underlying structures and identities and effectively serves as a microcosm of broader organizational principles.[46] In relation to the Norse north Atlantic Practice Theory lends some very important concepts. The first is that the individual constituents of a site or region's population contain a set of individually and culturally specific concepts within them that are expressed in all aspects of daily life from language used within the home to building construction and format to animal preference. Hence, although the populations of Norse and Hiberno-Norse are not the entirety of the Scandinavian population they carry within them the potential to have a very similar spectrum of doxic practices.

Practice Theory is a theory well suited to archaeology as it helps to bridge some of the gaps between consideration of social institutions and individual action. By excavating many types of sites, one can gain insight on the ordering of daily life and cultural constructs.[47] There are some critiques of its application however, which have resulted in some modification to the Theory of Practice since the works of Giddens and Bourdieu. Silliman poses the concept of practical politics during excavation analysis at Petalumá Adobe to address the fact that some daily practices speak of an outside intentionality and motivation.[48] Daily practices may become part of political practices through an element of daily negotiation. Practical politics is the negotiation of the politics of social position and identity in daily practices and, importantly, can alter doxic practice.

This assumes two things with reference to traditional identity and culture contact studies: the first that colonial domination includes the control of mundane day-to-day activities. The second is that daily practices of both the indigenous and the incoming population are pathways for exerting social agency.[49] In areas of known culture contact, it may be possible to see a reflected view of studied cultures in the actions and choices made. This is not a one-sided application, but is rather one that applied to both sides and thus enhances a more in-depth understanding of the site in general. The Norse north Atlantic presents a perhaps unconventional presentation of a colonizer in the eyes of modern research. The colonizing process is most often associated with a national colonizer, particularly since the fifteenth century. The primary colonizing base for the north Atlantic was consolidating into national identities at the time of initial settlement however. The majority of the nationalistic overtones found in sources from this region come from subsequent generations.

Actor-Network Theory

Actor Network Theory is represented in this study by the social theorists such as Latour and Sindbæk who focus upon the integration of such a wide variety of resources. Sindbæk summarizes this in the following way. '*Actor-Networks* are mixed assemblages of heterogeneous material, like pots, people, kingdoms, ships or seascapes. The character of the network cannot be reduced to any one of its properties'.[50] This theory assumes cultural boundaries to be singular moments within a wider framework of social networking formation and maintenance.[51] It is also based on the belief that archaeological artefacts were at some point active participants within cultural practices of the past and as such do more than merely exist in idealized categories.[52]

In this perspective, '[…] a trading-place is not primarily a political or economic structure, but a traffic junction – a point where certain networks of traffic convene. We can be sure that different traffic with different aims produced sites of different character, and that political and economic concern contributed even further to the variation'.[53] This is a view of particular relevance concerning the colonization and maintenance of the Scandinavian settlements in the north Atlantic. Due to the distance involved, this logically resulted in nodal points at certain locations in the north Atlantic. These were points where the deeper-drafted ocean going vessels of the North Atlantic zone network of communication and commerce connected into the central-place based localized networks. This formed the basis and continuation of exchange via established routes.[54] These routes were places not only enforced by culture. They also created their own context for culture in and of themselves, rather like aspects

Societal Scales	Scale Expression	Description	Evidence For
Macroscale	Over-arching	• Unique adaptations to local regional environment in terms of architecture, subsistence and agriculture • Language structure and format (syntax and morphology) • Aspects of maritime identity including local water knowledge, weather, boat construction and utilization etc which is passed generationally • Interactions between multiple sites occurs here • Trends and fashions (ie changes in execution of material assemblages but not changes in form) linked to economic and political market • Education externally imposed outside of the childhood identity • History becomes an important societal tool at this level	• Traditional patterns of landscape utilization and architecture • Local environment over long periods • In some cases oral tradition/ historical annals in certain situations such as folklore and poetry • Physical evidence of choices made for a group

Microscale	Externalized aspects	• Local changes to language structure and format which may result in regional dialects • Unique adaptations to the local environment • Dispositions relating to group success/decline is located here • History becomes an important societal tool at this level • Interactions between multiple local sites occurs here	Physical evidence of local choices made for a local group Architectural trends in material choice Artefact choice linked to trade What may be considered to be 'modern knowledge' Written history, works of poetry, different genres Patterns and trends which are more likely to fluctuate and change within the human lifespan
	Internalized aspects	• Composed of many events and individual interactions • Physically occurs locally, often within a shared habitus • This level consists of many egos • Dispositions occurring from physical situations found here • Individual innovations in response to the local context and environment	Domestic site utilization including space Artefact choice which is linked to the site directly including both domestic goods and trade imports shown via artifact presence in the assemblage
Individual	No societal aspects present	• The human animalistic needs and reactions without the mediation of childhood habitus • Basic innovation can occur here to meet these needs and reactions	Evidence for hunger, exhaustion, needs of shelter, fight or flight reactions [this evidence may actually come in the form of satiation of these] and hence by nature be secondary Ephemeral nature

Fig 12. Practice Theory as utilized in this work.

of individual and group identity. As Sindbæk has stated, in this period regional nodal points were partially chosen for their utility in transportation and the positive effects this had on long-distance trade networks.[55] This is associated with both physical and textual evidence. It is important to note that the reality of this temporal arrangement has much more in common with a continuum of time rather than clear demarcations. Power relations between varying cultural groups is one of these. The hierarchies and political structures of both the indigenous and incoming populations are considered as they directly and indirectly affect upon the construction of *habitus* and doxic practices.[56]

Social Space

It is important to consider the conceptualization of peripheries, frontiers and boundaries. They are an integral part to not only the theoretical background of this work, but also in much of the source material utilized as evidence. One in particular that must be discussed with reference to this maritime environment of island archipelagos and fjords is the ocean itself. Although the North Atlantic Ocean was an obvious boundary between the islands, it was by no means a barrier. Peripheries and frontiers, on the other hand, are more associated with the human colonization process.[57] The traditionalist view of frontiers is that colonists move into open or sparsely populated areas, pushing native populations aside or removing them when found. In this view, the colonists were seen as establishing a periphery for a core that is often portrayed as nationalistic.[58]

There are two concepts that affect this region in particular. The first of these islandscapes and the associated concept of 'island-ness'.[59] Islandscapes are determined in part by their physical location – islands are land which is in a dominantly aquatic environment, although in the past there have been practical islands conceived which functioned as islands but were not actually islands themselves.[60] Islands are often marginal in nature in relation to human habitation due to the reduced variety of species available; they may or may not contain a wide variety of environments. This relates to the effect of the northern latitudes, overall distance from continents for the initial colonization by species and the climate. In spite of all this, what species that represented may actually be quite high in comparison to similar sites on continents. This is due to reduced inter-special competition for resources. Islands inherently have liminal elements to them due to the constant water, air and land interactions. Island mentalities are often related to group identity construction as island locations form a commonality amongst populations of certain group members.[61] However, it is also a means of differentiating one's population and is a part of group identity affirmation.[62]

The second concept that affects the north Atlantic region particularly strongly is liminality. Liminal refers to threshold areas that may be tangible or intangible in nature. This is often relates to shorelines where there are interactions of air, land and water. Liminal actions can also be social and hence less tangible in relation to the archaeological record, however. Liminality can also exist in the worlds between the spiritual and the secular, between the world of the dead and the world of the living. Coastal areas are the physical interface between bodies of water and land; there are a series of implications associated. Physical implications include erosion, landing place availability and access to natural resources, whether this is through social restriction of goods or restriction through the ecology of the species themselves. The coastal liminal areas provide major resources for subsistence including, but not limited to, fish, marine mammals, seaweed, and birds. Social implications are involved with the fact that liminal areas are areas of forced interactions with more than one environment.

Islands and liminal spaces promote activities that require the inclusion of more than one individual in order to be as successful as possible and hence be of the most benefit to the entire group. At landing sites, this may also be areas of forced interpersonal interaction as well, whether local or long-distance in nature.[63] Culturally liminal areas are visible within the resultant culture in many ways: relationships between such areas and certain kinship groups may develop which are expressed within cultural practice and localized identity. Social liminality is highlighted in similar fashions. Liminal areas are highlighted through the efforts of cultural practice. They include place names, land utilization techniques, architecture, folk tales and legends as well as festivals, rituals and commemorations. The settling populations of the North Atlantic actively used the liminal nature of their respective island archipelagos to forge their own distinct identities. On the other hand, is this more of a case of indirect impact – the coastal sites are taken because they offer the most opportunities for subsistence resources and communication? The reality of this situation lies somewhere in the spectrum between these two. Liminality can refer to a particular type of marginality and relates somewhat to the concept of frontiers and boundaries, as it exists in the between space of frontier relationships across mutable boundaries.

The traditional perspective of frontiers and core/periphery interactions tends to be one of domestication. This is heavily influenced by Wallerstein's World Systems Theory.[65] This developed during consideration of the early and more recent modern world, not necessarily core and peripheries of the past.[66] In this case, however, one must ponder the questions: what occurs when those peripheries and frontiers are located on and around true marine environments?

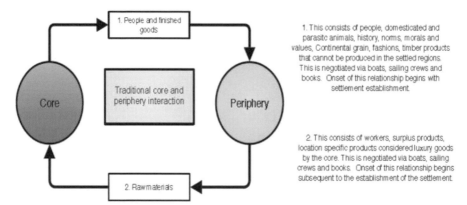

Fig 13. Generalization of Traditional Core and Periphery interaction; note the well-defined roles.[64]

What are the ramifications of forced human interactions within relatively contained spaces over time?

For archaeologists this theory has some recognizable strength including the establishment of a hierarchy with which to examine power relations. This theory makes an accommodation for the study of change over time as well as providing a structure with which to examine boundary situations. However, there are obvious problems with the traditionalist perspective of core/periphery interactions as well.

Frontier boundaries are portrayed as being distinct and the incoming and indigenous populations are often shown as being homogenous. This top-down approach utilizes mechanical models of indigenous acculturation where marginalization of natives occurs. Perhaps the most pressing problem with this theory for archaeologists, however, is that this view of core and periphery encourages macro-scale studies but archaeological sites by their very nature are areas of micro-scale interaction.

A new view began to develop during the 1990s that provided an alternative to the clearly defined traditional view. This alternative promotes frontiers as being comprised of zones of crosscutting over-lapping social networks. These are areas of dynamic multi-ethnic social and economic interactions. There are vectors of individual variation within this as well, including but not limited to kin, age, social relations, gender and political relations. Unlike the traditional view on core and periphery interactions in the alternative, neither the incoming nor the indigenous population is homogenous and alliances and identities crosscut between the groups.[67]

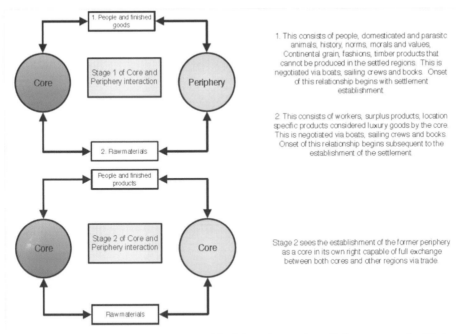

Fig 14. Diagram of Alternative Core and Periphery interactions. Roles are more flexible in this view as a mode and a medium for change is expressed.[68]

Forms of Evidence

A multi-scalar consideration of identity construction and maintenance such as this work requires input from a wide variety of source material. This includes but is not limited to archaeological material, textual evidence, ecological and climatic evidence as well as ethnographic and ethnohistorical evidence when available. Each of these sources adds their own associated problems as well which adds complications to the consideration. By such a variety of source material and discussion, conclusions concerning socio-cultural levels can be made.

Archaeological excavations and reports for those sites in the north Atlantic that had Norse habitation levels contribute greatly to the evidence for this study. Ideally, these are confirmed with radiocarbon or dendrochronology absolute dating techniques, but in certain areas this is based on typological and stratigraphic assessments of age. This material often involves viewing maps and site plans that have buildings typologically known to be Norse, including but not limited to bow-sided long houses and straight-sided house and byre combinations. Location choices can be determined from things such as artefact scatter, placement within a regional network and available natural resources.

This material provides an excellent and well-established means for the modern researcher to gain a glimpse of the level of individual and site – the microscale and the local identities aspects on the macroscale.

Actually being able to see the physical evidence for a people within their original contexts of social space greatly adds to the amount of information one is able to derive from a site.[69] Archaeological evidence can span the full range of physical human-impacted material, both direct and indirect, as well as human and animal remains. This includes everything from landscape utilization and household construction to artefacts and ecofacts that provide information concerning the surrounding ecosystems.[70] The archaeological evidence used within this consideration has come primarily from published works including, but not limited to, books, journal articles and excavation reports. Unpublished reports and personal interviews have been utilized when available. In some cases, personal visits to sites have provided photographic elements to the consideration as well. In those places that have not yet been excavated survey reports can tell of the general architectural format in many cases. Generally, such reports also have some discussion of any surface finds as well. It is also possible to make some consideration of location within networks.

Textual utilization has notorious associations in Viking Age Scandinavian archaeological sites, particularly in Iceland.[71] This has contributed to modern non-Scandinavian archaeologists largely divorcing their research from the most contemporary insular historical evidence provided by law-codes and sagas. This work seeks to make use of these sources within reason defined in an anthropological sense. Texts have been chosen based upon their contents as well as reliability and date such as the law-codes *Seyðabrævið* and *Grágas*. Sagas, with their widely recognized fantastic medieval elements, have been utilized only within regional contexts.

Here it is important to consider the texts as being social practices themselves for to take such work at face value has proven treacherous previously and distorts views of the past further.[72] It considers texts to be heterocosms of the ideas associated with the culture – written portions of *habitus*. Thus through this lens the potentially intangible emic aspects of identity may be commented upon. Through these means, texts are able to provide information on difference and similarity in relation to identity, ethnicity and personal interactions. These same values are found within contemporary written texts as well which provide etic views of the cultures under consideration. In some cases where the sources are of a specific ethnohistorical nature it is quite similar to the interviews that take place with living informants. These are qualities in lesser degrees found in all written and oral performance. By maintaining awareness of the existence of these aspects, more informed opinions can be made. References to cultural *habitus* as expressed through practice are sought after, including the utilization of space, traditional history and the maintenance of certain ideas concerning contemporary identity. Written evidence provides this consideration of identity construction and maintenance within the north Atlantic, a culturally internal perspective for early-medieval Scandinavian material. This is the only approach that provides this view on the pre-modern era, as the other available evidence inherently provides culturally external evidence. As such, it has been included with cautious consideration of the textual histories and contexts themselves.

The majority of the quoted Old Norse evidence included within this consideration of the north Atlantic has been personally translated into English and subsequently submitted to critique by medieval Norse specialists. This was done for several reasons. This allows for cross-textual comparison upon a consistent basis as of comparison as not all material has been translated with little in the way of subsequent editing. This also allows the written evidence to be considered more broadly than merely focusing upon the specific events of the individual people found within. It is in, its own way, a return to an older practice of research in the north Atlantic where land and text are analyzed by the same researcher. An additional benefit to this is the promotion of interdisciplinary research within Scandinavian studies.

Ethnohistorical accounts and ethnographic studies can also be incredibly useful in the reconstruction of identities, especially in areas of higher levels of cultural interaction such as distanced island archipelagos.[73] Ethnohistorical sources are mainly provided by the Norse written evidence that discusses the peoples encountered along the way. Examples which shall subsequently be studied in greater detail include *Grænlendinga Saga* and *Konungs Skuggsjá*. Ethnographic evidence, on the other hand, is gathered and made more widely available by trained observers. In certain cases, evidence from indigenous oral traditions is mediated through such source material. This type of evidence is incredibly ephemeral and may change due to context and the impact of subsequent peoples. It is subject to memory loss and story modification of any or all of the storytellers which have transmitted it over the years.[74]

The Traditional Norse North Atlantic *Habitus*
The traditional view of the Norse north Atlantic habitus is another important assumption, one with a particularly wide impact, which needs to be disclosed. The Viking Age and early medieval Norse have a long history as successful exploiters of maritime environments, both terrestrial and open water. Less often mentioned is the success of these groups with reference to other aspects

of maritime environment exploitation. This success was due to an intimate knowledge of maritime and coastal environments ranging from open ocean waters to the littoral zone to the seaside cliffs. It included observations on cloud and wind patterns, experience with localized currents, on the migratory habits of fish and marine birds. The stars, too, provided another means of associating a broader setting while the location of the sun in the sky both provided the means for many maritime cultures throughout history to journey with relative navigational security.[75] All of this knowledge linked intimately into the identities of these maritime inhabitants.[76]

As in other parts of the Scandinavian world water facilitated the wider exploitation of the medieval north.[77] It was the place where truly long-distance routes existed and where the safety of a crew and cargo depended on the social, ecological and geographic knowledge – the social practices – known by at least the helmsman and probably the rest of the crew as well. This formed an integral part of the internal *habitus* of the crew – every voyage would have been an affirmation of group identity in some way.

Terrestrial environment exploitation leaves the physical utilized by archaeologists as well as elements of identity. The early examples of excavation work conducted in the north Atlantic had also been involved in the major Danish settlements at Vorbasse, Fyrkat and the defensive fortification at Trelleborg – Bruun, Roussell, Brøgger and Shetelig amongst others.[78] Indeed cross-comparisons with the well-preserved and widely published longhouses at Vorbasse continued in the nineteenth century holdings of Denmark at archaeological sites in Iceland, Greenland, and the Faroe Islands. When these researchers travelled to the Northern and Western Isles of Scotland, they noted similar longhouse formats at the Brough of Birsay in Orkney and at Jarlshof in Shetland.[79] This became an archaeological affirmation of modern political land claims via the presence of Viking Age physical remains. A lack of known excavated sites and the homogeneity of artefacts found caused the cross-regional comparison early on that has obscured the study of island identity construction and maintenance with a heavy pan-Scandinavian element.

Aside from the physical remains of long house foundations, artefact placement, paleoentomological evidence, geophysical surveys and textual sources provide insight as to how the domestic space of the long house and to a certain extent home farms as well was utilized in a comparative manner. A long house would have existed within a complex of out buildings to form a farm within a family-based economic network.

Maritime identity construction and maintenance within the Norse north Atlantic presents an interesting situation. At this time, medieval identities were still in flux.[80] Due to the nature of their location, maritime identities are inherently in flux themselves although the physical location of sites themselves may often remain the same. No one type of source material presents a complete view of identity construction given the period. The utilization of long-term study allows the evidence considered to add different views and so make the resultant scales of identity more clear. This illuminates cultural considerations in higher detail and highlights their dynamic natures to greater effect.

Chapter 3

Settlement, Economy and Lifestyles in Zone 1
c. AD 800–1250

Introduction

The Zone 1 case study archipelagos include Shetland and the Faroe Islands. Unlike Orkney and the Hebrides to the south Shetland and the Faroes remained under the influence and control of Norway and Denmark for a greater period of time allowing for longer exposure to Scandinavian habitus. Each of the Zone 1 archipelagos is within a direct sailing voyage without layover from Norway and Denmark via the North Sea. The islands of Zone 1 all exhibit evidence of highly restricted wood resources at the time of Norse *landnám*.[1] In the Faroe Islands, the high salinity and reduced growing period have resulted in the lack of timber while further to the east over-exploitation by generations of humans is the cause. Both of these archipelagos are represented inconsistently by modern satellite imagery. Certain areas are as detailed in as much detail as more populated urban regions of the world while others are not represented with as high a resolution.

Shetland

Shetland was known as *Hjaltland* during the Norse period. This translates to potentially two place names. The first, 'Hilt-land', may hint at how these islands looked from the sea. The second, 'Hjalti's land', may show a social affiliation of the past via the utilization of the personal name Hjalti.[2] This island group had been continuously settled for more than four thousand years at the onset of Norse settlement resulting in an anthropogenetically derived landscape.[3] Areas where specific efforts at improving agricultural viability of settlements were sought as these were known production sites. Examples where this may have occurred include the multi-period sites at Kebister, Old Scatness, Underhoull and Jarlshof.

Shetland was subject to the elder law of the Gulathing, *Gulatingslova*, from western Norway until the revisions of Magnus Erlingsson [r.1161–84]. Following these revisions, Shetland continued to be subject to the *Gulatingslova* in the form of *óðal* law exercised in Orkney until the acquisition of the archipelago by Scotland in AD 1468 from the kingdom of Denmark.[4] The inclusion of *Gulatingslova* provides a further element of evidence for this study. Laws were

Sites Present

Da Biggins, Papa Stour, Cat-
pund, Jarlshof, Kebister, Upper
Scalloway, Old Scatness, Law
Ting Holm, Castle of Strom,
Sandwick, Hamar, Underhoull,
Clibberswick, Norwick, Hesta
Ness, Standibrough, Strobister,
Kirki Geo, Breckon Cullivoe, St
Ninian's Isle, South Whiteness,
Ward Hill, Setters, Watlee, Stoora
Toft, Soterberg, Gardie

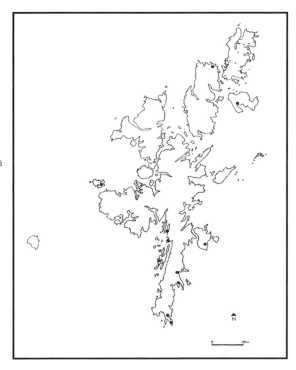

Fig 15. Shetlandic archaeological sites from the Norse period of occupation.

physically applied to Shetlanders via assemblies known as þings. Evidence for these survives as place names in the landscape. Tingwall on Mainland is the most famous for this island group.

Overall evidence for Shetlandic archaeological sites sits at a neutral position on the relative scale. This is linked to the amount of archaeological survey that has been done in the island group. When the rest of Shetland, with eleven known sites, is compared to Unst alone with thirty known sites where more recent archaeological survey has been conducted, it is quickly apparent the impact modern research has had.[5]

Shetlandic settlement sites follow a pattern of exploitation of previous settlement and utility. By far the best-known example of this practice occurs at Jarlshof that was excavated intermittently from 1897 but was only published in 1956 by Hamilton. Another example of this occurs at the steatite quarry of Clibberswick.[6] This was a conscious decision on the part of incoming populations as these were areas of previous proven utility. At sites such as Mousa the presence of broch ruins and Neolithic landscape features made the sites more prestigious. These were sites that were visible from sea and came to exist as landmarks in the Norse seascape, much as they had for earlier indigenous populations.[7] Other Norse sites follow a different pattern of land choice focusing instead on the presence of a shallow sandy beaching area, fresh water and relatively flat lands. Ideally, readily available areas of wild species exploitation are also associated with this. The conjunction of the presence of a landing area with previous regional utilization occurs at Sandwick on Unst, which was excavated from 1978–80 and subsequently published in 1985.[8]

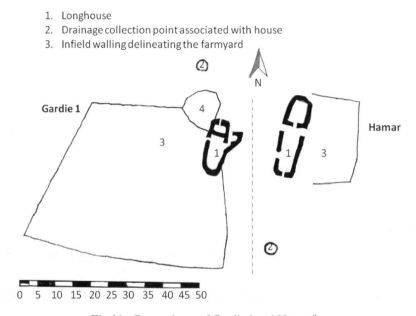

Fig 16. Comparisons of Gardie 1 and Hamar.[9]

To a certain extent, land choice dictates the type of site found in Shetland. A farm unit requires areas of relatively shallow graded land in order to construct buildings and enclosures upon. This consisted of a longhouse dwelling that was built primarily of turf. Longhouses and byres were aligned down slope in order to facilitate waste drainage and urine collection. As a freshwater source also exists on many farm sites this may have also contributed to the need for site drainage. At Hamar, signs of the original drain is present but as of yet is not fully excavated or published.[10] The turf used in the construction of these buildings has resulted in many Norse period drains going unrecognized in earlier excavations, however, drains were found in the earliest phases of Jarlshof excavated during the 1934–5 excavation seasons by Curle.[11]

In the earliest years of settlement, these buildings had bowed long walls and an internal measurement of around 20 m. Fig 16 shows the longhouse from Hamar on Unst that highlights the presence of a central long hearth, parallel rows of roof supporting posts and side benches within an end room. This format is also echoed in the slightly smaller longhouse found at Gardie 1.[12] Byres for the housing of cattle, sheep, goats and pigs were sometimes a portion of the long house. This would have added to the amount of biologically generated heat within a longhouse during the winter resulting in less fuel necessary to warm the human habitation. Other byres were separate buildings and as a result may be included amongst general outbuildings in publication rather than having the specific purpose recognized.[13] Also included in a farm unit are auxiliary out buildings which may be near the farm unit or away from it at a shieling or boathouse site.[14] All buildings would have been constructed utilizing local materials – turf, driftwood or imported timber for the roof and juniper branches also used in roof construction. Stone footings for wall foundations and internal wall facings occur in buildings dating from the late eleventh century on. At this time longhouses began to lose the more organic bow-sided longhouse shape becoming rectilinear in form and somewhat shorter in internal dimensions at c. 15 m.[15]

Farm sites have associated middens that have developed during the life of the working farm. Early Norse farms which were established in previously occupied areas will often utilize out of use indigenous buildings as middens such as at Underhoull.[16] In areas where there appears to have been no previous settlement midden deposits are made around the outside of the longhouse. This process of deposition resulted in the *heimrust* farm mounds under many modern farms of Shetland today.[17]

As initial Norse farms fell out of primary usage as human habitations they were repurposed as animal byres or storage until finally middens were established within the walls. The composted results of the midden process were used by farmers to improve the quality of the more productive infield area.[18] Early Norse burials were placed near or even cut into indigenous settlement mounds such as at Upper Scalloway and Kebister.[19] As time progressed, burials began to be placed on more remote portions of farmland such as at Breckon Sands.[20] Once Christianity became the religion of the majority of the Norse population, Christian cemeteries such as at Norwick developed.[21]

The early major excavation of the multi-period site of Jarlshof has heavily influenced consideration of the utilization of space in Shetland. Fig 17 illustrates internal utilization of space. This diagram is based upon artefact location maps generated by modern excavations at Da Biggins, Norwick, Stobister, Sandwick

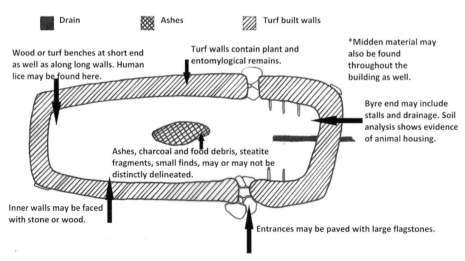

Drain   Ashes   Turf built walls

Wood or turf benches at short end
as well as along long walls. Human
lice may be found here.

Turf walls contain plant and
entomylogical remains.

*Midden material may
also be found
throughout the
building as well.

Byre end may include
stalls and drainage. Soil
analysis shows evidence
of animal housing.

Ashes, charcoal and food debris, steatite
fragments, small finds, may or may not be
distinctly delineated.

Inner walls may be faced
with stone or wood.

Entrances may be paved with large flagstones.

Fig 17. Generalized longhouse plan for Shetland.

and Catpund.[22] It is corroborated when possible with the older excavations of Underhoull, Jarlshof and Clibberswick.[23]

Artefacts relating to food preparation can be found near the long hearth of a Shetlandic longhouse. This includes steatite vessels and schist baking plates. Steatite lamps would have been used throughout the building for lighting as windows weaken the wall structure of turf buildings.[24] Small finds lost within hearth ashes and floor bedding may also be found around the hearth. Little in the way of artefacts is found on the side benches of a longhouse – these were for sleeping and sitting on.[25] They would have been easy to clear at the end of a longhouse's functional life as human habitation. End areas may produce some evidence of craft specialization such as loom or spindle weights used in wool processing. If the longhouse contained an animal byre in conjunction with human habitation areas, the central long hearth is shifted to the upslope end of the building. In the down slope end, a central drain leads to a sump beyond the exterior wall.[26] This as well as stalls may be constructed of local flagstones.

External use of space around a Shetlandic longhouse is based on the wider network of farming outbuildings and associated satellite institutions. It reflects the self-sufficiency required of a Norse farm during this period. It is reflected in the placement of names surrounding settlement areas.[27] *Gulatingslova* refers to the maintenance of a house's yard in section 73.[28]

A Shetlandic primary farm of the Norse period would have functioned seasonally. This was necessary due to the need to manage the restricted lands available within the archipelago. Hence, livestock were put to pasture well outside the area of growing crops during the summer months and brought back to the home farm as winter set in.[29] Collection areas for grass was necessary to collect winter fodder – the best evidence for this being locations for hay storage and the hand sickles utilized during collection. The relatively low numbers of this type of evidence in combination with the maritime climatic environment shows that this practice became more prevalent. Collection areas for other species were also held by prominent farms.[30] This could range from puffin nesting grounds to shoreline littoral zone species of fish and mollusks. It also included the rights to certain portions of any whale beached or landed within the farm's catchment area. *Gulatingslova* refers to fishing and hunting rights in section 93 of the code.[31] Although rights pertaining to the exploitation via hunting of wild animal exploitation exist within the code as well as the species named are native to the wooded areas of Norway. Whale claims, on the other hand, occur later in the law code in sections 149 and 150.[32]

Artefact choice as expressed within material assemblages is able to provide insight into microscale aspects of identity. Most are associated with meeting the requirements of daily existence within a remote area. Iron occurs in a wide variety of tool forms ranging from fish hooks to clinker rivets to patches for broken steatite vessels. Steatite occurs naturally in Shetland and those vessels found in Norse occupation layers are carved in a fashion recognizable as being distinct from that of previous populations. Steatite quarries active during the Norse period include Hesta Ness on Fetlar, Catpund at Cunningsburgh on the Mainland and Clibberswick on Unst.[33] Due to the local steatite sources as well as readily available Norwegian imports, pottery is traditionally seen as occurring rarely on Shetlandic Norse sites.[34] There is a very distinct possibility that this has been heavily impacted by the more rigid older concepts of what constituted a Norse site.[35] Reassessment of pottery assemblages from these sites throughout Zone 1 has been conducted primarily by Small and Stummann Hansen. Subsequently this has become an important way to attempt to date older excavated material found on Shetlandic sites, as a known typological sequence exists for grass-marked Norse platter style forms.[36]

Items of personal adornment so often associated with burials are not known from Shetlandic sites, save as midden finds. This is due to the relatively low number of burial excavations conducted in Shetland – many have already been lost to coastal erosion. Items of wood were common during the Norse period but given the organic nature of this material this is something poorly

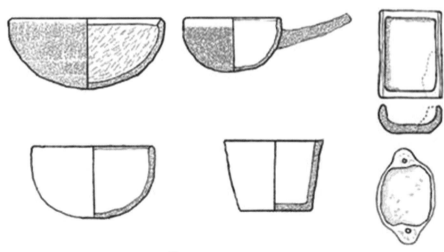

Fig 18. Shetlandic steatite forms.[37]

represented within the Shetlandic archaeological corpus. Sources of wood included driftwood, recycled wooden objects and imports of timber from the east and south, however, wood does not survive particularly well from known Shetlandic excavations.[38]

Biological evidence of lifestyle is heavily dependent upon the overall state of site preservation and the date of excavation as much of this evidence is organic nature. When soil acidity is low on sites bone preservation can tell not only of human health at time of deposition but also the strategy of animal husbandry practiced. Cattle were utilized in a dairy economy while horses were exploited for travel, light traction and as a source of fishing line. During the warmest years of the medieval optimal pigs were raised, however, this was later given up due to the detrimental effect pigs have on the fragile north Atlantic maritime eco-systems. Sheep and goats formed the majority of the domestic animal populations maintained by the early Norse. These provided wool, milk and meat and sheep at least still form a major part of the Shetlandic landscape. The amount of fish bone evidence which has been recovered from Shetland has been greatly increased since methods of wet sieving and 4 mm dry sieving of soil samples have become standard practice.[39] Excavations conducted during this earlier period have as a result promoted a species exploitation pattern for the Viking Age that is primarily terrestrial in nature. Other forms of biological evidence range from midden material to paleoentomological material as well as carbonized food and grain.

The Faroe Islands

The medieval Norse knew the Faroe Islands as *Farøy*. There are two reasonable translations for this; the verb form present in the place name may be more than one verb conjugation. The first name, sheep islands, has been linked in the past to the Papar introduction of sheep to the archipelago; however, the Faroes have maintained a sizeable sheep population since the Norse *landnám*.[40] If the word *Farøy* is broken down into its elements for consideration, *fé* and *ey*, the name is closer to 'islands of animal-based wealth' not necessarily just sheep. This may refer to the Faroes' available species for exploitation. The translation, on the other hand, appears to refer to the length of the voyage necessary to reach the islands' shores. This must be questioned given that there were much further settlements to the west. If the place name elements are derived from the second translation of the word, *far* and *ey*, the name is translated to 'the islands to travel to' which sounds like a marketing ploy.

The Faroe Islands, too, was subject to *Gulatingslova* until AD 1274 when Magnus Håkonsson lagabætir introduced the *Landslog* to Norway.[41] This was

Sites Shown

I Eingjartoftum, Vid Hanusa, Giljanes, Yviri i Trod,, Nidri i Toft, Kirkjubour, Havgrimsgrov, Tinganes, I Uppistovubeitnum, Toftanes, Argisbrekka, Vid Gjogvara, Nidri vid Hus, Noduri i Forna, Undir Junkarinsflotti, A Sondum, Vid Kirkjugard

Fig 19. Major sites in the Faroe Islands.

utilized until 1298 when the *Seyðabrævið* was written, supposedly by Bishop Erlendr at Kirkjubøur if *Færeyinga Saga* is to be believed. This was abandoned when Norway, and hence the Faroe Islands, were claimed by Denmark as part of the Kalmar Union. Laws were enacted and trials carried out on the Tinganes headland in Tórshavn on Streymoy.

The quality of archaeological evidence from the Faroe Islands is poor. It must be stressed that this is not due to poor excavation practice. It is due to the low sample number of excavated sites, both farms and burials. The textual evidence, on the other hand, is relatively poor. The law specific to the Faroe Islands is not instituted until AD 1298, subsequent to the period of this study. This source can be utilized for consideration of certain practices of species exploitation, but little else for this work. The saga evidence available for the Faroe Islands is limited to references within Icelandic sagas that were gathered together during the nineteenth century into a single work – the *Færeyinga Saga*.

The Faroe Islands are known for the cliffs and sheers sides of the majority of the archipelago. Due to this sandy shallow approach, landing areas protected from the wind have always been the areas of preferred settlement. Faroese farms

Fig 20. Medieval church and landing area at Kirkjubøur. Although there has been substantial erosion in the area the sandy approach is still partially visible. Just out of shot to the right is Mururin the cathedral.

are never far from the sea due to the nature of the islands themselves. Unlike Shetland, the Faroes had no previous substantial population in a biological sense. There is some debate concerning the presence of Papar in this island group that shall be discussed further in Chapter 7. What is most relevant here is that the two known Papar-derived place names from the islands, Papurhálsur and Paparókur, designate very remote cliff edges in Saksún and Vestmanna respectively.[42]

Also required for site choice was a fresh water source for domestic and farm use as well as relatively flat lands with a distinct down slope. Fig 20 shows the site of Kirkjubøur on Streymoy where the quality of the landing area, extensive agricultural lands and highly visible location led to the establishment of the Bishopric seat in AD 1152–3. In later years, a cathedral was also begun on the site. A series of churches have been associated with this site highlighting the farm's long-term prosperity.

The earliest phases of settlement are known from two sites surrounding the modern village of Sandur on Sandøy. At Undir Junkarínsfløtti a three phase farm mound with radiocarbon dates ranging from the ninth to the thirteenth centuries is currently still under excavation while across the bay is an apparent contemporary settlement site.[43] Examples of longhouses dating to the tenth century have been found at Toftanes on Eysturoy and Niðri í Toft on Streymoy, and Við Hanusá on Vágar.[44] Niðri í Toft is illustrated in Fig 21. At these sites bow-sided longhouses have been found with internal measurements of circa 20 m. Walls were constructed with interior stone faces, earth cores and turf exteriors. Roof supports ran in parallel rows down the centre of the building. Between these rows of posts lay a long central hearth – at Toftanes this feature was 5 meters long. Along the long walls were earth side benches.[45]

Faroese longhouses that also contained an animal byre were aligned down slope to facilitate drainage via internal stone channels and external sumps.[46]

Fig 21. Niðri í Toft at Kvívík. The erosion of the major site constructions are shown in relation to the nearby harbor in the background of the shot to the right and the retaining sea wall.

Byres that existed as outbuildings to a Norse longhouse were also aligned down slope for this reason.[47] At Niðri í Toft this process in conjunction with close coastal proximity resulted in the erosion and subsequent loss of the lower building ends.[48] Outbuildings constructed of turf with stone foundations accompanied the longhouses and byres. Many of these were used for the storage of fodder, however, at Toftanes evidence for craft specialization was found within the farm's outbuildings.[49] As time passed the bowed sides of longhouses became more rectilinear and the use of internal stone facings more regular. The overall internal length became much reduced – at Norðuri í Forna on Eysturoy as small as 9 m.

Sites which are not constructed in the coastal areas but rather on the cliff and hilltops of the islands' interiors provide evidence for Faroese farm practice and economy.[50] Outbuilding constructions of turf, clay, sand and gravel as well as the presence of stock pens were utilized seasonally during the spring and summer months to protect the infield crops from hungry farm animals. The best known example of this is Argisbrekka on Eysturoy which was excavated from 1985–7.[51] Other related place names are known, however, which also contain the bastardized Gaelic term _ærgi_ – for the Norse practice of sheep and cattle husbandry referred to as shielings.[52]

Relatively few middens have been excavated in the Faroes. The major cause of this is the continued utilization of farm sites into the modern period – modern farm buildings are located on top of the _heimrust_ which provides the most reliable evidence.[53] The effects of erosion must also not be overlooked. Early burials have only been confirmed at the site of Tjørnuvík on Esturoy.[54] The two other suspected burial sites at Giljanes on Vágar and Havgrímsgrøv on Streymoy have not been subjected to modern excavation.[55] A major reason for this is the long-term familial association with burial sites found within the Faroe Islands. Although pride in the historical heritage represented by longhouse remains is great, the potential that the remains

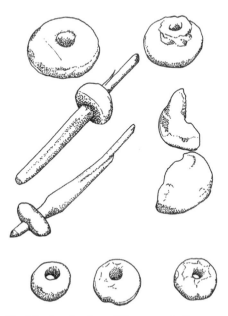

Fig 22. A collection of Faroese spindle whorls and wooden distaffs.

of a known great-great-great grandmother being disturbed would offend the modern farm inhabitants is even greater.

Consideration of space in the Faroe Islands has been heavily influenced by the excavation practices of Sverri Dahl who primarily excavated during the mid-twentieth century. During this period there was a greater focus on the interior of longhouses as being characteristically Norse in nature. Now research focus is more related to how the buildings functioned within the wider farm network and islandscape. In spite of this Dahl's excavations were conducted to a high standard for his day.[56]

The long hearth is a central focus of human activity, particularly domestic, within the Faroese longhouse. Around and amongst the hearth ashes finds of broken steatite vessels and schist baking plates have been found. Steatite lamps of a distinctive squared shape burned whale or fish oil for light. Other small finds and items of portable art may be found within the hearth ashes and floor bedding where they were once lost. Few artefacts are found in association with long wall side benches, although paleoentomological evidence for lice has been discovered.[57] During domestic use, these benches would have been used to sleep and sit on as the time of day dictated. The bedding and any cushions would have held any small finds for easy retrieval well within the primary utilization of the

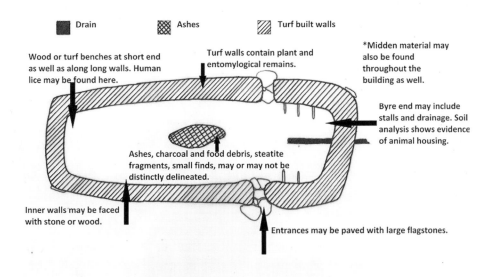

Fig 23. Generalized artefact placement for the Faroe Islands.

longhouse. End areas may also contain a raised bench area – potentially a prestigious sleeping location or craft area, or even farm storage although no artefacts have resulted from this area and soil samples taken.[58] A generalized format for longhouses is found in Fig 23. Drainage is provided for the animal stalls by paving, down slope location and channeling to an external sump.[59]

External use of space surrounding a Faroese longhouse is influenced by island location and is based upon a network of outbuildings for storage and farm activities as well as sites in other portions of the landscape. This system reflects the diverse ways that settlers in the Faroes exploited their marginal environment.

A Faroese farm of the *landnám* existed within a seasonally dictated

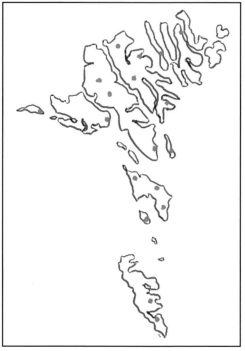

Fig 24. Shieling sites in the Faroe Islands.

physical landscape. Fields were improved when fallow utilizing midden material and seaweed. Crops were planted once the growing season commenced. Household plants such as angelica were grown in close proximity to the main farm complex.[60] During the height of the growing season, the farm's livestock were put on the high pastures to the interior of the island.[61] These shieling sites are often given the Gaelic place name element *ærgi*, i.e. Argisbrekka.[62]

Several types exist. Closest to the main farm would be the dairying shielings with both water source and the means of storing dairy products, generally as an outbuilding. A milking pen may also be present. The second type of shieling would be farther from the home farm. This would be where the livestock not being milked were pastured during the summer growing season.[63] These sites have a source of water for the animals and only occasionally have an associated outbuilding or natural feature utilized for human/animal shelter during poor weather. The third type of shieling is primarily utilized for the collection of winter fodder and the exploitation of local wild species. This type of shieling does not necessarily have a water source or building but instead may be a place name associated with a remote grassy area.[64] Other collection areas were

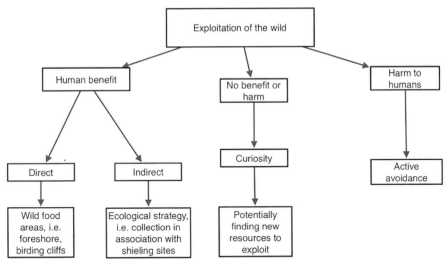

Fig 25. Choices involved in the exploitation of the wild.

associated with farms as well – littoral zones and birding cliffs being particularly important. Without these sources of food, the Faroese population would have been unable to maintain their numbers let alone their livestock. Due to this, rights to resource collection are closely detailed in the law code.[65] Choices about wild area exploitation are illustrated in Fig 25.

Certain recent excavations have been able to provide extensive artefact assemblages with good preservation in combination with reliable dating:

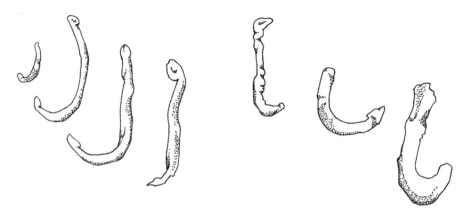

Fig 26. Iron fishing hooks from I Uppistovibeinum and Argisbrekka on display at Forøya Fornminnisavn.

Toftanes and the sites surrounding the modern village of Sandur on Sandøy.[66] Iron has been found in fish hooks, farm tools and ship rivets. Fish hooks are also known from Argisbrekka.

Steatite is found in forms know, from both Norway and Shetland.[67] Products of schist, i.e. whetstones, hones and baking stones were imported from Norway to meet the domestic demand.[68] Some Norse platter-style forms are also known from Argisbrekka, Toftanes and Undir Junkarínsfløtti as well as from re-assessment of excavated material from the earliest excavations. In spite of this ceramic evidence from the Faroe Islands is slight.[69] Items of personal adornment and portable art are relatively fewer, however, several items stand out. A ring-headed pin was discovered at Niðri í Toft while a portion of a lignite or jet arm ring was discovered during excavations of the longhouse at Toftanes.[70]

There is a substantial corpus of wooden artefacts being discovered in recent excavations of waterlogged sites in the Faroe Islands.[71] Many of these have been conserved and put on display at Forøya Fornminnisavn. From Toftanes there is an array of wooden boxes, tools and even twisted juniper boughs used as cording.[72] Wood requirements would have been initially met by trees indigenous to the Faroe Islands as well as driftwood originating from Siberia and Scandinavia.[73] As time passed, however, Faroese trees were over-exploited to the point of

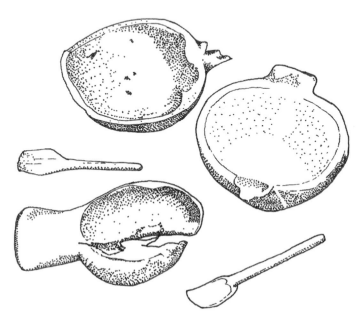

Fig 27. Steatite vessel forms and wooden implements.

extinction by *landnám* and Medieval populations and as a result recycling of wood, importation of timber and unquantifiable amounts of driftwood met this need.[74]

Biological evidence of lifestyle on an early Faroese farm comes from the examination of the *heimrust* of modern farms and palaeoenvironmental sampling of the floor layers.[75] *Heimrust* is the farm mound that has resulted from long-term midden practices.[76] At Undir Junkarínsfløtti an extensive osteological assemblage from the *heimrust* provided evidence of prolonged pig husbandry as well as the more common sheep and less common cattle.[77] This and other recent excavations in the Faroes have produced evidence of early-medieval fish exploitation. As time passed farms became more focused upon sheep husbandry for textile production as milk and meat could still be obtained as secondary production. The sheep was well suited to the varieties of the local Faroese island environment. Stuffed versions of this extinct species are found at Forøya Fornminnisavn in Torshavn.

The exploitation of sheep is evidenced not only directly via osteological material but also via the presence of paleoentomological evidence – wool parasites

Fig 28. Faroese sheep shot on the island of Litla Dimun during the nineteenth century. These sheep are descendents of the sheep brought by the initial Norse settlers. Both exhibits are on display at Forøya Fornminnisavn.

– within longhouse soil samples.[78] Indirect evidence of sheep exploitation includes a variety of artefacts from lamb bits to keep them from nursing when necessary to spindle whorls and loom weights utilized in wool processing.[79]

Discussion

The representative island archipelagos of Shetland and the Faroe Islands have had somewhat of a history of consideration within the same publication and study.[80] Much of this is linked to shared characteristics that the island groups share. These marginal regions with little in the way of agriculturally viable land as well as high relative salinity and shortened growing seasons has developed longer traditions of site reutilization than other areas in the north Atlantic and consequently both groups also share similar species exploitation strategies. By a comparison of the available evidence for the Norse settlement of these islands a more in depth examination of society can be made. This analysis has been assisted by the data tables described in Appendix D. In particular it has been possible to rate the evidence for the case study of Zone 1 in accordance to the relative scale presented previously. This is taken into consideration in the following analysis of microscale aspects of identity construction and maintenance in Zone 1.

House and Settlement

Examination of architectural trends expressed in Zone 1 has been impacted by the earlier techniques and practices of excavators. Perhaps the most lasting impact is the misattribution, and at times even complete lack of recognition of ninth and tenth century levels of occupation. This is due to the greater levels of preservation of the subsequent medieval period when the utilization of stone within longhouse construction became more popular. Recent excavation techniques that employ geochemical analysis and ground penetrating radar are increasingly able determine the presence of turf constructions in the landscape.

Case study evidence highlights the generalized nature of Zone 1 house features in terms of construction material, techniques and format noted by others.[81] Farm units throughout Zone 1 had supporting outbuildings both on primary farm sites and at secondary exploitation locations. The marginal environment and reduced growing periods of Zone 1 resulted in a resource strategy for settlements that distinctly integrated into not only the locally expressed seasons but also the natural environment of a variety of island locations secondary to the primary farms. In general, as with many farms prior to the Industrial Revolution, there is a pattern of self-sufficiency. This will be later be changed by the Continental economic market demands for fish and

Faroe Islands	Shared Characteristics	Shetland
Much of the region's coasts are actually cliffs and as a result settlement occurs dominantly upon the few bays with easy approaches (also good for of the time and for whaling)	Known Norse settlement expressed in the changes found to longhouses and other domestic forms	Confirmed habitation in the region for more than 4,500 years
Favorable layover location for north Atlantic trade and exchange networks (except for larger later vessels headed to Iceland directly from Bergen)	Political and legal structure based on the Gulathing Law as well as the Seyðabreiðr	Hilly and mountainous in comparison to Orkney which results in low levels of agriculturally viable land, less son in comparison to other regions.
Proven long reutilization of sites in certain areas	Available trade goods	Much of the region is shallow approach beaches
Seyðabræðr becomes the new law in AD 1298	Many wild resources including marine mammals, fish and wild birds	Local steatite and metal ore resources
	Domestic species including cattle, sheep and pigs as well as plant species	Favorable location for North Sea trade networks and North Atlantic, especially from Norway
	Norse 'culture/identity' as a dominant part of population	Complicated geology
	Prolonged period under direct Scandinavian rule	Oðal law derived from the Gulathing Law continues to be used until Scotland gains Shetland in AD 1468
Delicate balance between maintained subsistence and the local environment with little in the way of long term agricultural stores on the islands themselves to make starvation less of a concern in difficult years – this is compensated for by expensive and socially obligated food stores from Europe and Britain	Relatively few excavated and published sites most of the earliest of these having been excavated by a handful of Scandinavian archaeologists.	Delicate balance of the Faroes occurs here as well but there are much closer means of bridging the gaps include Orkney, Ireland, and the Baltic

Fig 29. Shared characteristics of Shetland and the Faroe Islands.

Viking Age (AD 800–1050) Longhouse	Medieval (AD 1050–1250) Longhouse
At least 16 x 4.5 m internally	No more than 16 x 4.5 m internally
Long hearth centrally located in human living area	Hearth is no longer centrally located which allows for a more open floor plan
Down-slope alignment of structure to facilitate gravity drainage of animal byre – early excavation techniques may not have recognized the associated signs of drainage at time of excavation and so at times early byres went unrecognized.	Down-slope alignment of structure to facilitate gravity drainage of animal byre – this is assisted with paving of at least the drain sluice within the animal byre but may also be entirely paved. Internal stone stalling does not impede this drainage in anyway.
Turf is used to construct walls – this may be stone-faced internally.	Although turf still occurs in construction more often stone-faced walls with earthen cores are cited in excavation. This may directly related to the highly acidic soils found throughout much of Shetland and the Faroe Islands.
Parallel-aisled roof supports with the exception of the byre-end.	Center-aisled roof supports with the exception of the byre-end.
Outbuilding association with longhouse	Very-close/connected longhouse outbuilding combinations.
Bowed long walls and rounded gable ends.	Straight-sided long walls and squared gable ends
Sleeping benches located along the long walls.	Division of the space human space adds a sleeping room at the non-byre gable end. Byre may also later be entirely removed to an outbuilding.
Benefits: This longhouse reflects more directly the traditional Germanic long house format. The utilization of turf as a building material would have been quick and local to gather as well as being an effective structure for many years although subsequent habitations would have been inevitable for a long-term installation.	Benefits: This longhouse is smaller and thus easier to heat as animal heat is more efficiently used. The construction techniques reflect the increased prosperity and technological innovations being introduced via both the Orcadian Jarls and Norway.

Fig 30. Changes to the Zone microscale identity over time.

wool products in combination with general global cooling which caused the north Atlantic shoals to come closer to archipelagos than they had during the warmer Medieval Optimal.

The generalized farm unit strategy as well as the assimilation of indigenous settlements, ruins and farm mounds into the Zone 1 cultural landscape highlights fluidity concerning the local environment's impact upon the socio-cultural habitus. Microscale elements expressed in farm strategy encompasses the local choices regarding building construction and maintenance that allowed the generalized longhouse and outbuilding constructions to better fit the environmental context. This includes material choice, design in relation to the surrounding landscape and intended primary utilization. Necessity, location, overall economic standing as well as the potential for secondary usage influence maintenance choices. The initial *landnám* period expressions of longhouses in Zone 1 directly reflect the presence of first generation settling populations who have not yet learned the most efficient adaptations for the local landscape. Also important to consider is the warmer climatic conditions during much of the Viking Age – certain elements of longhouse and farm format seem to highlight the cooling northern world. The

Orientation	Designation	Description
Terrestrial	A	Represented by active outdoor farm life
Marine	B	Represented by activities on water
Littoral	C	Represented by shoreline activities

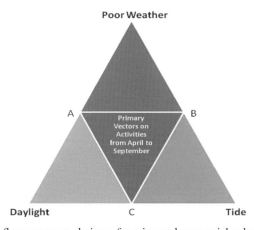

Fig 31. Influences upon choices of marine and terrestrial cultural practices.

reduction in internal length from more than 16 m to less than 16 m would require less fuel to heat during winter months. The addition of a connected outbuilding providing storage space or animal housing requires less building material than a separate farm building would, as there is a shared wall.

Identity was expressed in the practical modifications the Norse farm made to accommodate the limited access to timber resources within Zone 1 and the increased diversity in wild species exploitation reflects this. As *Gulatingslog* originated in Norway, littoral zone exploitation is only commented upon in section 93, and then only in relation to land uses fees that would have been due.[82] This is unsurprising as the larger Norwegian peninsula has greater terrestrial resources available – and indeed greater consideration is made regarding actions such as bear and deer hunting. The reality of this was to tie littoral zone gathering rights and other sources of subsidence to come under the jurisdiction of the local social hierarchy, as is expressed in the *Seyðabrævið* of AD 1298.[83]

Family and Gender Relations

Evidence of family and gender relations is best expressed via three forms of evidence: shape of the farm sleeping arrangements, the division of farm labor, and finally law codices. Not only gender but also overall hierarchy within the extended family influenced sleeping arrangements on the longhouses' benches as well.

The head of family and their consort(s) would have enjoyed the relative privacy of the upslope end of the longhouse.[84] Either a raised bench would have demarked this across the house end in a similar manner to the long-wall side benches or an internal partition wall of wood. Here family members would remove parasites from themselves leaving evidence behind of their presence.[85] The most favored of the farm's social hierarchy would have been closest to the head of family while the least would have been farthest from both the hearth and at some times closest to the animal byre – the two heat sources in the cold maritime winter.[86] During summer months, some lower members of the farm were sent with the livestock to the shielings. *Gulatingslog* makes provision for the sleeping arrangements of these farm workers in section 100.[87] In this section, responsibility for damage or burning of the shieling building was waived if the proper dimensions were not met resulting in the death of a farm hand by exposure. Infants would have slept with their mothers or wet nurses or else in a re-purposed container made suitable with blankets or raw wool that would have protected the infant's skin. Cradles are not common finds on Viking Age Norse archaeological sites as raw wool fulfilled this need without impacting the archaeological record.[88]

Labour Focus	Description	Intensity		
		easy	*moderate*	*difficult*
internal	associated with household practices	fuel gathering, food gathering, bedding gathering, child minding, crop maintenance, personal maintenance and hygiene	food preparation, food preservation, wool processing, milking, dairying, crop maintenance, sewing, harvesting	animal butchery, laundry, weaving, food preparation, shearing, harvesting
external	associated with farmyard and field practices	crop planting, crop maintenance, personal maintenance and hygiene	herd tending, fuel cutting, harvesting, hunting, local trade and other travel based commerce, coastal fishing	animal slaughter, ploughing, land clearing, bird catching, building construction and maintenance, field preparation whale processing, long distance trade and other travel based commerce, shearing, harvesting, open water fishing

Fig 32. Division of Labor. Intensity of activity is determined by the use of skill and/or physical effort. Items in red detail work only men could undertake.

Farm labor can loosely be divided into jobs associated with the internal working of the farmhouse that may at times occur outdoors and those jobs associated with the external working of the farm itself. These jobs all vary in intensity and who performs these actions is often determined by physical capability rather than being purely gender derived. This division is shown in Fig 22. These are divisions of labor found throughout the medieval Norse world and are reinforced by regional law codices as well as mythology. The physical evidence for this practice of farm labor is both direct and indirect in nature. Direct evidence of food preparation can include physical remains of the edible resources like fish and charred grain available from midden excavations such as at Undir Junkarínsfløtti.[89] Direct evidence of the gathering of food and fuel comes in the presence of partially burned wood, charcoal and wild food resources within midden and longhouse floor deposits.[90] At Toftanes, Old Scatness, Argisbrekka

Farm Unit	Feature	Function	Building material used	Species Exploited
Primary longhouse	Human and animal habitation year-round, although this may not actually be the pattern in true day–to-day practice, also secondary outbuildings separate from either the habitation or the byre, which housed a wider variety of activities such as weaving and smithing.	This is public and private at once as it is not only the domestic site for many in this period but also as the local node for trade and exchange in both economic and socially linked goods but also ritual and spiritual elements as well	Stone-faced walls with turf and rubble core; turf; drift wood; peat; rammed earth; stone	Secondary processing would take place here for a wide variety of goods from iron to milk to agricultural products
Daughter longhouse	Essentially the same features as home farm yet will be located quite physically close to the home farm's initial location if not actual structure. Still located within the initial infield.	The multitude of activities which occurred within the home farm can of course occur on a daughter farm but they are more likely to occur in the widest variety of forms in the home farm associated architecture.	Stone-faced walls with turf and rubble core; turf; drift wood; peat; rammed earth; stone	Secondary processing would take place here for a wide variety of goods from iron to milk to agricultural products.
Outfield	Buildings in the outfield depend on the utilization of the space – there must be a need for storage primarily and possibly shelter for animals and humans on a small scale.	These functioned as stations of procurement for the farm buildings, both home and daughter.	Earthen dykes; turf and earth built buildings; stone	Management station for domestically maintained species such as sheep, cattle and fodder fields for the same species for winter. Gathering areas for wild resources of plants, sea birds and eggs amongst other things.
Shieling sites	Buildings beyond the outfield depend on the utilization of the space – there must be a need for storage primarily and possibly shelter for animals and humans on a small scale.	These functioned as stations of procurement for the farm buildings, both home and daughter. This can be of dairy products, hay or even summer grazing to save the winter outfield crops.	Earthen dykes; turf and earth built buildings; naturally occurring caves and rock formations; stone	Gathering areas for wild resources of plants, sea birds and eggs amongst other things. Management station for domestically maintained species such as sheep, cattle over the summer season.

Landing sites	Natural features of shallow sandy bays which are suitable for the easy approach of shallow clinker-built shallow draft vessels.	This was a vial part of the system on a variety of levels. It provided the location for wider communication with the region and world. It provided the location for exchange to occur through. It provided a large number of relatively low-effort species – a vital part of a marginal environment's subsistence pattern.	stone; turf; drift wood; rammed earth	Whales and other sea mammals can be more easily accessed through here. Sea weed for fertilizer and animal fodder can be accessed on the shore as can littoral zone fish and crustaceans. On the land part of the shore marine birds can be found which is another vital source of protein.
Midden	This will be located within the home farm complex if not within former domiciles themselves.	This was integral for long term farm success in relation to land improvement practices. It was also integral for the short term of success of the farm due to the necessity of the removal of garbage from activity areas for the health and comfort of the farm inhabitants.	Organic and inorganic components of domestic and wider farm origin.	The contents of a farm midden includes anything that can be thrown away can end up in the midden area. Its deposition can be impacted by a wide variety of factors including subsequent redeposition by later site inhabitants.

Fig 33. Zone 1 farm progression.

and Á Sondum this material included evidence of marine fish exploitation.[91] Direct evidence for the exploitation of domestic species such as pig, cattle and sheep comes from the inclusion of skeletal material within midden deposits at sites including Í Uppistovubeitum, Undir Junkarínsfløtti, Norwick, Sandwick and Jarlshof.[92] Direct evidence for wool processing and textile production can be quite rare – not only is wool organic in nature but any tool which was more enduring would have remained within a cycle of use, maintenance and subsequent metal recycling once the tool was broken or too worn to repair on the farm. Indirect evidence such as sheep lice occurring within soil samples can also hint at wool processing.[93] Direct evidence for agriculture is provided by the presence of field boundary walls in association with Zone 1 farm units. In addition, finds of grain and pollen within midden and floor deposits can highlight a local practice of growing grain crops to add to a farm unit's economy, such as at Toftanes. The onset of this practice is somewhat under debate, particularly in the Faroe Islands; however, by AD 900 the practice of grain agriculture is present across Zone 1.[94]

Indirect evidence of food preparation includes containers used to store victuals as well as to cook in. Within Zone 1 this need was met by vessels of steatite as well as locally made Norse platter-wares. Both are known from several sites throughout Zone 1 – from Norwick, Catpund, Underhoull, Hesta Ness and Jarlshof in Shetland in Niðri í Toft, Toftanes, Undir Junkarínsfløtti, and Argisbrekka in the Faroe Islands.[95] Indirect evidence of the gathering of fuel comes from the presence of ash within longhouses as well as the loss of the presence of tree species pollen from the Faroese palynological record.[96] The presence of artefacts such as axes also provides evidence for local practices of fuel gathering.

Indirect evidence for the exploitation of domestic species comes from the provision of structures throughout the island landscape for the housing of these animals. Byres occur included in longhouses as well. They are also found as separate out buildings such as at Niðri í Toft, as well as at auxiliary sites to farms such as Argisbrekka. The byre of Niðri í Toft is illustrated in Fig 24. These buildings existed within an internal farm network that supported the maintenance and transhumance of domestic species to make the most efficient utilization of the island landscape. The provisions present within the laws applied to Zone 1 also indirectly evidence domestic species exploitation. Within *Gulatingslog* these include penalties for keeping stock in areas which are not claimed by the farm, for faulty boundaries which do not function properly thus allowing stock to damage crop fields, as well as the provisions necessary for farm workers housed off-farm with the herds at the summer shielings.[97] The gender of these farm workers is alluded to in the parses of the verbs utilized.

Sailors and long-term shieling workers/ slaves, i.e. those not affiliated with the dairying herd but rather the meat and wool herd are male. Domestic workers and slaves are more often referred to by feminine verbs and endings.[98]

Indirect evidence of agriculture is provided by the presence of provisions within *Gulatingslog* as well.[99] Indirect evidence of physical farms is best represented by the boundaries of fields discussed above as well as tools used in agriculture. Examples of boundaries are known from Gardie while agricultural tools are known from Toftanes and Niðri í Toft.[100]

What makes this evidence of the microscale level of identity is the expression of these practices within the local environments of Zone 1. Each local situation and combination of people within it would result in a unique distribution of farm jobs. In Zone 1 where archipelagos are a short sail between each other men of certain social standing or wider social connections would have been gone trading, harrying and fishing following the major spring activities of ground preparation, planting and lambing. Once the farm had moved into the stasis pattern of the summer months, many activities traditionally seen as men's work was taken up by the women of the farm through necessity. As the weather

Fig 34. Byre at Niðri í Toft, note the presence of stone stalling and stone lined drain.

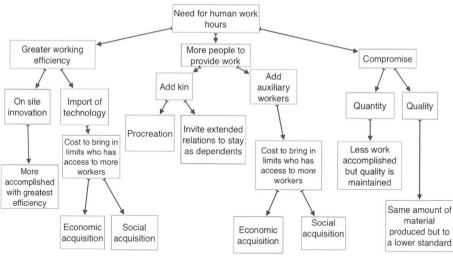

Fig 35. Need for human work diagram.

conditions of fall and winter made sea travel increasingly dangerous voyages abroad would decrease and men would return to their home farms in time for the harvest, fertilizing of the fields and winter animal cull. *Gulatingslog* makes provision for the maintenance of sailor's rights on land in sections 127, 148 and 310–5.[101] This highlights how common men's existence via ship was at the time. The ship became in social practice a farm unit in status, providing men legal security away from their home areas.

Social Status and Rank

Microscale evidence of identity construction and maintenance in Zone 1 is intrinsically tied into the concept and physical reality of Norse farms. Much of this is quite practical in nature. The location of farms and farm satellites conveyed certain common elements. These common elements include the close communication offered via a landing place. The farm complex allowed for multiple means of subsistence within the local environment and economy. This included wild and domestic species that were seasonally available. A high status farm would have more easily allowed for self-sufficiency as well as enough surpluses to make trade both possible and profitable. There is some debate as to whether sites were chosen because the founding family was particularly powerful or if the associated family subsequently became powerful due to the attributes of the site and its satellites however.

A high status farm in Zone 1 during the initial *landnám* settlement period would have been prominently situated on the shallow gradient areas near landing areas. A long, *c.* 20 m, well-appointed longhouse constructed of turf on stone foundations highlights the presence of a wealthy family. Wood paneling may have been utilized to provide an internal facing to the turf walls. The exterior turf was maintained to continue to provide optimal insulation during primary occupation against the changeable marine climate found throughout the Zone 1 archipelagos. Sites with continued use by several subsequent generations will have secondary longhouses constructed nearby to the primary house. These newer buildings developed as the family expanded and the turf of the original house began to decay beyond easy repair. A separate hall was included on particularly prestigious sites such as Jarlshof.[102]

At some sites there is evidence for an overlap in occupation, however, eventually the human occupation of the primary house would end shifting to the newer focus of the secondary longhouse. The original house would

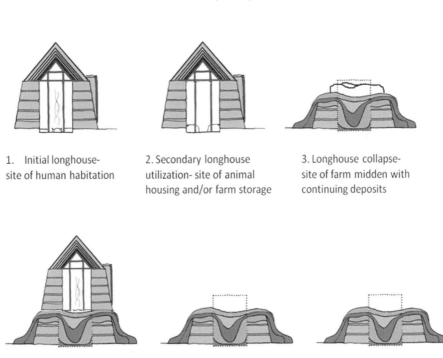

1. Initial longhouse-
site of human habitation

2. Secondary longhouse
utilization- site of animal
housing and/or farm storage

3. Longhouse collapse-
site of farm midden with
continuing deposits

4. Longhouse collapse- site
of new construction on top
of older building

5. Longhouse collapse-
Medieval abandonment

6. Modern ruins

Fig 36. General life of turf built longhouses in the North Atlantic.

subsequently house animals for a period but finally would contain the farm's midden containing composting efforts for field improvement. Several outbuildings would have accompanied the longhouse of a high status farm site. This is where storage of the farm's products, surplus and supplies would have been contained.[103] This would have been vital to the wealth and economy of the farm as this would have allowed the stockpiling of not only food and fodder but also products produced during animal processing, such as skins and wool. Outbuildings on high status farms also were used as activity areas themselves with iron working, wool processing and weaving being particularly well evidenced at sites such as Toftanes.[104] In order to make the most efficient use of the islandscapes several satellite sites were linked to a high-status farm. Shieling sites like Argisbrekka form one aspect of this that was primarily associated with the seasonal management of farm stock involving transhumance.[105]

The presence of multiple shielings highlights different elements of the overall animal economy that developed following the initial settlement of the north Atlantic archipelagos. A large, well-equipped dairy shieling implies a farm whose flocks and cattle are potentially very productive provided the size of the herd is still within the carrying capacity of the local environment.[106] This may be corroborated by the presence of broken and preserved containers and sieve as well as large amounts of animal osteological evidence found within midden assemblages of farms and shieling sites. This highlights the presence of domestic animals maintained for dairy production with a high number of young animals younger than six months in age occurring in the site assemblage.[107] A substantially sized summer shieling would have maintained the stock not being milked – those animals providing wool and meat, generally older females and neutered males.

Shielings primarily used as pasturage would have seasonally been utilized by a high status farm to house the animal stock away from growing crops. This system was maintained by the lower echelons of a Norse Zone 1 farm. These layers of society are discussed in sections 57–64 and 67–77 in *Gulatingslog*. These sections are concerned with slaves and handwomen, freedmen and freedwomen, contract farm workers receiving a wage, þing affiliates, farmers and their families and vagrants.[108] This evidence shows a hierarchy present on Norse farms in Zone 1 which can be placed in a relative order. Within each of these categories was a spectrum of hierarchy based upon functional utility both socially and economically. This division of labor is illustrated in Fig 39.

As is illustrated in Fig 37 the years of surplus on a farm can be followed by years in productivity deficiency linked to the wider environmental and climatic context. On a high status farm surplus can be stored while herd sizes can maintain a living

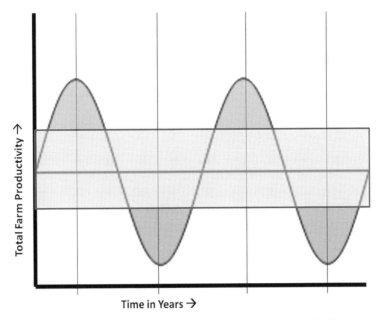

Fig 37. Farm productivity cycles presented chronologically.

surplus of domesticates. On a lower status farm, on the other hand, such a surplus might not be able to be gathered or stored in great enough quantity for any one of a wide number of reasons. Hence, when the environment and north Atlantic climatic conditions were poor there would be insufficient means to support the farm's family and domesticates. This situation had an array of cultural responses – from an appeal via already established networks of social obligation and hierarchy to the dissolution and selling of farmlands, stock and fodder. The methods of accomplishing this are discussed in sections 41–3 and 72 of *Gulatingslog*.[109] As the products provided by these animals, wool and meat, takes full seasons if not years to build up in comparison daily produced milk, the shielings upon which this type of stock was maintained had much less need to be kept in close proximity of the main farm unit.[110] Dairy shielings, on the other hand, were maintained within easy travelling distance to the farm to remove the dairy herd from the area of growing crops but so that they still would be accessible to provide milk and dairy goods for the farm's subsistence needs.[111]

A high status successful farm potentially may have more than one pasturage site, as this would have allowed utilization to be spread more efficiently. As with other farms throughout the world, one of the best indicators of continued high status is the ongoing management of resources. In the more marginal environments of the north Atlantic, this can mean the difference between life, death and overall economic success. The winter success of a high status farm also depended upon a variety of grass collection points as well – with the maximum possible amount of fodder being collected, dried and stored more stock would be maintained over winter into spring.[112]

Early familial burials are also associated with Zone 1 farms. The sample provided by Shetland and the Faroe Islands is quite small with examples dating to the period of Norse settlement having been excavated from Clibberswick, Breckon and Norwick as well as at Yviri i Trøð and Niðri við hús.[113] Following conversion to Christianity, burials no longer were accompanied by distinctive grave goods such as at Clibberswick or distinctive in shape such as the boat-shaped burial excavated at Breckon Sands.[114] Cemeteries associated with churches increasingly take the place of the farm burials. Examples of these are known from Norwick as well as Yviri i Trøð and a later cemetery was excavated at Niðri við hús.[115] Although the locations of cemetery and church sites are known several, such as at Við Kirkjugard and Kirkjubær, have not been excavated due to continued modern utilization. An illustration of the long house progression is found in Fig 36.

Finally, a high status Zone 1 farm may also have some local association with public spaces such as the sites of churches or those designated for the meeting of the seasonal things. Close proximity to the fields of a wealthy farm implies affiliation, although commonality of name elements between public spaces and farm sites can also highlight a particularly influential family member. A farm that also had affiliated public spaces for the wider island community implies the presence of hierarchy and social obligation on the part of the wider population.[116] Public spaces can be seen as obligation gifts to the entire local community in the system of total services. By providing and maintaining the local population with such spaces the family owning the high status farm not only proves they are wealthy enough to do such a thing but also that they mediate access to the social world of religion and the legal system. This is a statement of social power existing within both microscale practice as well as wider macroscale affiliation.

Lower status farms, on the other hand, were not as favorably located within the islandscape initially. This may have been through the availability of choice open to the settling family or even due to the cooling climatic trends associated with the Little Ice Age. These cooling trends would have made farm life within the marginal maritime islandscape extremely difficult. An example of such a site comes from Stobister, dated to the thirteenth century by typological consideration of format as well as the final place name element of *–bister*.[117]

Type	Description	Example
Supply and Demand	Exchange based upon the principle of supply and demand	Butter produced by one farm being exchanged for grain from another
Quality	Exchange based upon quality	Goods that you can make on site but someone else can make easier or better
Gift Exchange	Exchange of goods as gifts for the maintenance of social structure and hierarchy via social obligation	The exchange of luxury goods to maintain social obligation is documented in Orkneyinga Saga

Fig 38. Vectors on choice in the context of local exchange.

Without the resources of a larger higher status farm, lower status farms were more subject to the fluctuations of the north Atlantic environment. This means in good years the farm would be maintained, perhaps even building up a small surplus of available resources. However, in poor climatic years more marginalized lower status farms did not have sufficient stores to survive several such years in succession. An extended period of harsh or abnormal weather such as a drought or series of summers that were cooler would have been disastrous to a lower status socially marginal farm unit in Zone 1. When this occurred to a lower status farm, a drastic change in social practices could potentially result. *Gulatingslog* contains provisions for settling debt upon the failure of a farm

– many involving the sale or exchange of the farm unit as a whole or part in section 72.[118]

The structures associated with lower status farm sites reflect the reduction in available work force and resources from a higher status site. Longhouses associated with the *landnám* period of Zone 1 will still be over 16 m in internal length however; they rarely exceed more than 20 m internally. The walls are much less likely to be constructed of stone beyond the wall foundations unless there is a ready source of building stone nearby. The turf of lower status sites, particularly those with evidence of long-term occupation, may be more worn, repaired and dried out from prolonged utilization. This is due to the continued habitation of a building constructed of organic material – in optimal conditions turf constructed buildings, even those incorporating stone material, are still subject to decay. The prolonged habitation reflects the reduction in resources necessary to construct longhouses. The greater amount of degradation present in a longhouse of lower status sites is accompanied by fewer, one or two, outbuildings than its contemporaneous counterparts. As time passed the accompanying outbuildings increasingly became attached to the longhouse itself, such has been excavated at Setters and Hamar in Shetland and Toftanes in the Faroe Islands.[119] Small finds found with these farm structures are few in number and primarily associated with periods when the structure was used for farm middens. This may indicate that many of these farm structures were utilized for the storage of perishable organic goods such as winter fodder or drying meat.

The associated system of shielings and gathering sites is also reduced in comparison to higher status farms. This can be reflected in farms sharing pasturelands such as at Argisbrekka in the Faroe Islands. This allowed two or three smaller farms to exploit the high pastures that might have otherwise been affiliated with a larger farm complex and provisions for this practice existed within law.[120] Elsewhere lower status shielings were located in the more marginal areas where grasses were present but not in the quantities to support a large domestic animal population that would in turn create a surplus of animal product for later farm subsistence. Lower status farms were often more marginally placed in terms of coastal salvage rights, particularly during the medieval period. This may have in part led to such practices as communal division of whales that have continued to be practiced to this day in the Faroe Islands.[121]

Gender	Social rank	Outlook	Description
Female	Low/ unfree	Terrestrial, littoral	This level is associated with some of the most unpleasant tasks of the house and littoral zone gathering.
	High/ free	Terrestrial	This is associated with cultural taboos regarding women and marine productivity.
Male	Low/ unfree	Terrestrial, littoral, auxiliary marine	Any job not seen as women's tasks and many that were.
	Mid/once unfree	Seasonal change between marine and terrestrial for some, total marine for others	This level is most dependent upon the local economic context and much effort may be put for to gain profit.
	High/ free	Terrestrial and marine	Both outlooks are necessary to successfully and profitably exist within interregional networks of exchange.

Fig 39. Gender based consideration of identity orientation on Zone 1 Norse farm sites, including data from Gulatingslog.

Within a farm, there was also an existent social hierarchy. Simply put the larger the farm the more human working hours are required to maintain productivity and subsistence. There are three solutions to an increased need for human working hours: enhancement of working efficiency via technology, more people included in the farm unit, or a compromise must be made in the quality of work produced. This process is illustrated in Fig 35. Farms in Zone 1 were associated with extended family units and the auxiliary farm members according to *Gulatingslog*. Higher status farms were able to support greater numbers of both extended kin and their servants who may or may not have been slaves. *Gulatingslog* highlights the legality of slavery within the first centuries of settlement in Zone 1 in sections 57, 61–2, 64 and 67–9.[122] The physical presence of slaves on a site is impossible to tell from lower status archaeological evidence in Zone 1. There would have been enough surpluses to support the room and board for auxiliary farm members who otherwise would have been unpaid. These auxiliary members in turn facilitated a farm's success.

The presence of slavery on Zone 1 Norse north Atlantic farms is difficult to find. Archaeological evidence has a notable lack of items associated with slaves elsewhere in contemporary Europe that makes slaves unable to be discerned from the other landless poor of society. *Gulatingslog* also acknowledges the presence of vagrants within Norse society of Norway and by extension Zone 1 in section 77.[123] The fact this status is given a full description within the law code shows how anathema the concept of living outside the delineated network of Norse culture would have been to many of the early twelfth century. Living outside of the law, for whatever reason, would have been a difficult existence in the marginal environments of Zone 1. The lack of physical evidence hints at either slavery not occurring in the same manner as it did in latitudes to the south or else the evidence itself was not preserved on the sites now known. In relation to farms in Shetland and the Faroes slavery can be seen as being impractical in the marginal archipelagos for the majority of family farms. Farm slave labor had to be fed out of the farm's produce and stores. Since agriculture is not as productive a utilization of northern island resources as animal husbandry, this would have quickly become a real concern. An exception to this may have been female concubines who also performed domestic duties in the house, as these would have been a sign of status.[124] Potentially a concubine might be either slave or free.[125] This will be further examined in Chapters 6 and 7 as slavery as both economic and social concept relates to macroscale elements of identity. Lower status farms would have less or potentially no auxiliary members resulting in the extended family taking up the totality of farm work. The actions of the lower levels of this social system are visible on farm sites through Zone 1, however direct evidence aside from that provided from completed and abandoned tasks for this level of society can be quite difficult to find and must be considered within singular sites at this time as opposed to this regional consideration. This reflects both the long term archaeological practices used throughout Zone 1 as well as the more marginal nature of sites in the north in general as it was increasingly difficult for solitary and extremely poor people to exist successfully without the support of a larger farm particularly as the Little Ice Age advanced.

Orientation

Microscale evidence for the orientation of identity in Zone 1 highlights a seasonally dictated fluctuation between marine and terrestrial loci. These loci are expressed in a number of practices. The balance maintained in the spectrum between these two is heavily affected by the availability of day light in combination with available technology, particularly boats.

Between April and September a Zone 1 Norse farm would experience the greatest pressure from marine and terrestrial vectors. There are three practical drivers to the choice of activity on Norse settled islands of Zone 1: the amount of daylight, the type of weather and the tide. Terrestrial activities in this period before electric lights are dictated by daylight and to an extent by poor weather

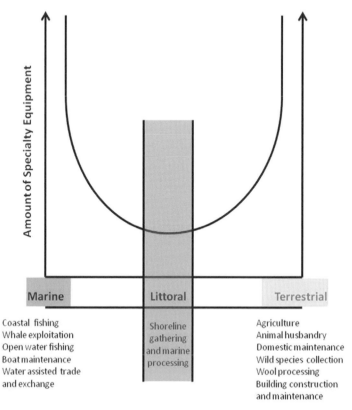

Fig 40. The amount of specialty equipment required for exploitation in relation to productivity of marine, littoral and terrestrial areas.

and the tide. These activities include the majority of outdoor work on the farm including ground preparation, building construction, as well as management of farm stock. Littoral activities are dictated by the tide and amount of daylight but the weather also plays a part to a lesser extent as well as this can affect the amount the tide effects access to the littoral zone. Littoral zone activities centre on obtaining coastal marine resources both by collection of shoreline species when exposed during periods of low tide as well as shoreline fishing. Although daylight is useful, marine activities are dictated by both the weather and the tide. This type of activity includes open water fishing; water assisted trade as well as water born transportation. Fig 40 illustrates the amount of specialty equipment required for relative success in the different areas of a Norse Zone 1 farm.

Labour Focus	Description	Intensity		
		easy	*moderate*	*difficult*
internal	associated with household practices	fuel gathering, food gathering, bedding gathering, child minding, crop maintenance, personal maintenance and hygiene	food preparation, food preservation, wool processing, milking, dairying, crop maintenance, sewing, harvesting	animal butchery, laundry, weaving, food preparation, shearing, harvesting
external	associated with farmyard and field practices	crop planting, crop maintenance, personal maintenance and hygiene	herd tending, fuel cutting, harvesting, hunting, local trade and other travel based commerce, coastal fishing	animal slaughter, ploughing, land clearing, bird catching, building construction and maintenance, field preparation whale processing, long distance trade and other travel based commerce, shearing, harvesting, open water fishing,

Fig 41. Division of Labor. Intensity of activity is determined by the use of skill and/or physical effort.

The widely accepted view of women's roles on Norse farms are influenced by ethnographic evidence provided by later Icelandic textual sources and Danish longhouse excavations linked to the traditional triad of farm, livestock and hearth.[126] However, when the microscale evidence for identity orientation is considered with reference to gender this view is dramatically changed. The littoral zone functions as an intermediary neutral area for identity as well as being a physical intermediary between marine and terrestrial elements of Norse society. The breakdown reflects levels of farm hierarchy including the freeborn, the un-free and the once-un-free. These elements are certainly aspects of identity construction and maintenance in the north Atlantic.

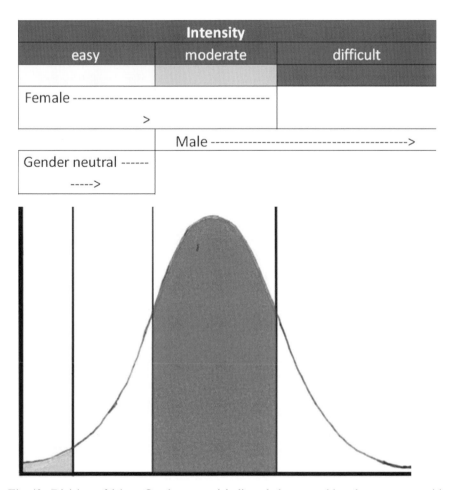

Fig 42. Division of labor. Gender neutral indicated the very old and very young with reduced capacity for work. Chart indicates the peak period of labor capability during human life. X indicates increased age while y represents capability.

Conclusion

The analysis of case study evidence from Zone 1 has highlighted a highly practical element to the microscale aspects of identity construction and maintenance present on Norse sites. This element was highly adaptable concerning local environments. This resulted in a reliance on turf and stone construction techniques but also the exploitation of a wide variety of wild species as evidenced at Undir Junkarínsfløtti on Sandøy.[127] A four-part social hierarchy maintained this local system. This social hierarchy also expressed and was impacted concurrently occurring macroscale elements of identity construction and maintenance. These wider reaching elements are discussed in detail in Chapters 6 and 7.

Chapter 4

Settlement, Economy and Lifestyles in Zone 2
c. AD 870–1250

Introduction

The case study for Zone 2 utilizes evidence from the Easter and Southern Quarters of Iceland in corroboration with the most recent of farm sites from the rest of Iceland. As these Quarters are less well represented by modern excavations, the region of Mývatnssveit located in northern Iceland has been included. This area has been subject to intense archaeological survey, excavation and publication.[1] Much of this work has been widely published, primarily by the international research group NABO. The Quarters were legally established in AD 930 as the physical areas for the Spring and other seasonal assemblies. These in turn supported and carried out the decisions made by the national assembly the Alþing held later in the year at Þingvellir.[2] In this fashion, the period of Icelandic medieval independence known as the Free State was able to function as a parliamentary political unit sans a singular ruler within the Continental networks until Iceland's submission to Norway in the 1260s.

Iceland, Zone 2, is physically located over the mid-Atlantic ridge where the North American and European continental plates meet.[3] Due to this, there has been ongoing volcanic activity throughout much of the area. This can be incredibly useful in terms of dating archaeological sites. Studies that have successfully associated tephra layers with archaeological sites from both Zone 1 and Zone 3 have also utilized this dating sequence as winds cause the pyroclastic clouds to spread beyond Iceland's shores.[4]

The case study sample for Zone 2 is derived from the Southern and Eastern legal Quarters of jurisdiction in Iceland, which were established during the early tenth century, as well as the modern excavation of a northern local network at Mývatnssveit. This selection, except Mývatnssveit, is warmed by the water currents to the South of Iceland. These currents reduced the impact of sea ice accumulation that influenced areas to the north. This allowed some grain production to occur during the climatic Medieval Optimal that coincided with much of the timeframe under consideration. This warm period also influenced the amount of open and coastal oceanic travel that was able to occur annually.

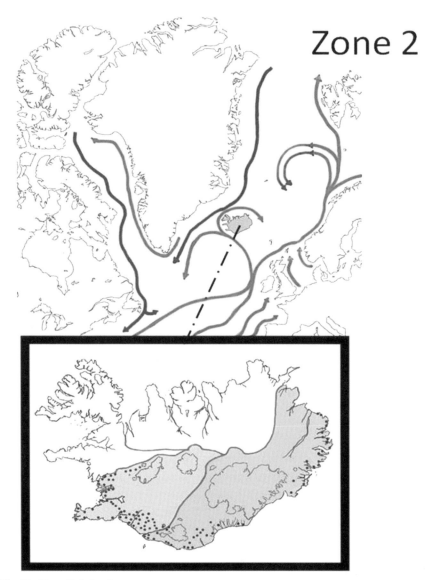

Fig 43. Zone 2. Atlantic currents.

Zone 2 was known to Atlantic populations prior to the arrival of Norse *c.* AD 870 although whether they were settled is subject to debate.[5] Within contemporary ecclesiastical sources, reference is made to hermetic priests originating in the British Isles inhabiting the remote north Atlantic islands. Their presence in Zone 2 is potentially evidenced by Papar associated place names in the landscape. This is discussed further in Part 3 concerning external vectors of identity change. The corpus of Icelandic textual sources has heavily impacted not only archaeological research in Zone 2 but also in the field of medieval Scandinavian studies in general.[6] Zone 2 has produced and maintained a substantial body of vernacular written evidence since the medieval period detailing such topics as history, law, religion, politics and economics. This is what other western European political units had been doing for centuries creating a public group history that can be utilized as a social tool. Iceland's peripheral location resulted in a strong adherence to the sagas in particular as nationalistic historical tradition following Norway's acquisition of Iceland in AD 1263. This has been recognized in both Icelandic and Scandinavian archaeology.[7] In spite of this aspect of Icelandic textual sources they allow insight into what day to day actions were associated with living on farms in Zone 2 and how those actions were socially viewed in short a literary snap-shot of daily life. This can be invaluable for considerations of microscale levels of identity, as the local microscale aspects do not always survive archaeological excavation of the site. Recognized saga sites are illustrated in Fig 43.

Overall, the widest variety, i.e. different types, of evidence has been either discovered or preserved in some way in affiliation with Iceland, Zone 2. This

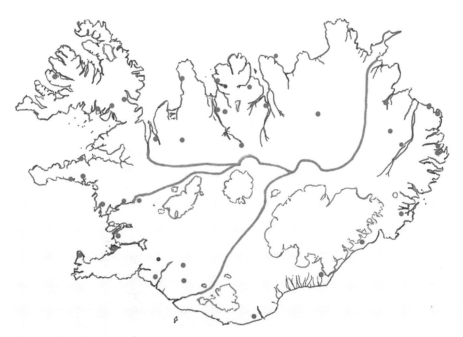

Fig 44. Zone 2 saga sites[8]

material has influenced not only studies on early Iceland but also the wider field of medieval Scandinavian studies in general by causing a generalization of the elements of identity construction and maintenance resulted in a blending of identity elements. This case study is intended to highlight what elements are present within the Eastern and Southern evidence. Many of the sites in this Zone were excavated during the early twentieth century, which has necessitated the inclusion of Northern Quarter evidence that has been more consistently excavated. This has been drawn from the modern regional surveys and excavations of Mývatnssveit.[9] This area contains well-published evidence for a localized network including coastal and interior valley sites. This material is presented separately from that of the Eastern and Southern Quarters, so that this process of cross-consideration can be critiqued.

Biases Associated with Zone 2

There are several archaeological biases associated with Zone 2. Turf construction techniques are mostly organic in nature that can be difficult to find within a long settled landscape. There has been a heavy reliance upon textual evidence taken as historical fact in the past which was used to locate, name and at times even associate with certain unique historical events. This practice has been recognized and explored more fully in academic research, first by Friðriksson with regards to Iceland,[10] then Svanberg who applied the concepts to the wider Scandinavian world.[11] In spite of this there continues to be a strong popular association between physical sites in the Icelandic landscape and saga. There was also a heavy antiquarian influence upon site choice in excavations, i.e. burials chosen for excavation over farm sites, the more impressive longhouses chosen over smaller auxiliary buildings.[12] This has resulted in a divorce of the buildings and burials of Norse north Atlantic sites in publication.

The preservation of medieval farms in Zone 2 is dependent upon the effects of erosion, volcanic and Aeolian activity that affects Iceland. Several sites have been subject to subsequent utilization, which may be continuous. Many sites located away from the settled coastal areas were less likely to be found until quite recently. The preservation of turf and soil constructions in particular has added to the difficulty in site location and recognition. Modern technology is somewhat able to compensate for this: soil sampling for palaeoecological evidence as well as less invasive methods of ground-penetrating radar and magnetometry. Ideally, this would be considered in conjunction with satellite imagery from Google Earth and aerial photography provided by Landmælingar Íslands however, the entirety of Zone 2 is not yet available in the same amount of detail due to the presence of cloud cover within the satellite image that obscures the detail. This situation is rapidly changing and will form an easy way to further the number of known sites.

Artefact assemblages are often quite small in comparison to the size of the building and farm complexes although there are certain anomalies to this such as Stöng, Hólmur and Hófstaðir.[13] Perhaps unsurprisingly these assemblages are primarily inorganic in nature with stone and iron being present but also organic elements as well such as wood and bone. The small amount of material in combination with the homogenous nature of the assemblages has contributed to the later focus on farm mound and midden locations that provide greater environmental detail.

Textual sources by type are illustrated in Fig 45. The preservation of evidence for identity construction and maintenance is also subject to its own biases. Some locations are represented more completely than others as certain locally powerful families were the patrons of the medieval authors and scribes. The physical preservation of medieval manuscripts is also a concern. The major medieval legal source *Grágás*, for instance, is only known directly from the manuscripts of *Konungsbók* [*c*. 1260] and *Staðarhólsbók* [*c*. 1280], but had been codified in the early twelfth century[14]. Two of the main textual sources that discuss the settlement of Iceland – *Islendingabok* and *Landnamabok* – have been linked to the efforts of a single author, Ari Þorgilsson.[15] Other sources

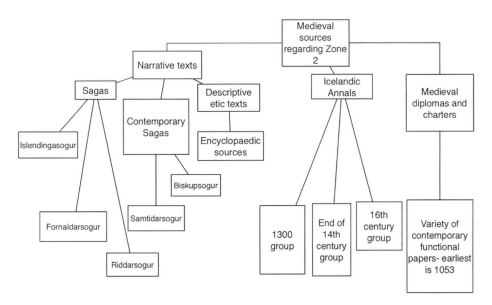

Fig 45. Zone 2 Textual sources by type.

are represented only by quotations via later medieval authors, the most famous of these being Snorri Sturlusson. This work does not employ such evidence, however, fragments of poetry in particular has survived in this manner and has influenced other researchers in the past.

During the nineteenth century, Icelandic medieval sources were accepted as a true representation of the period from settlement immediately prior to the Reformation.[16] Since the late twentieth century, a trend of focusing less on historical events presented and more upon cultural values and practices represented within saga material in particular.[17] Although this is no longer the case the impact of this reasonably accessible corpus of material for speakers of modern Scandinavian languages cannot be underestimated. Sources that discuss the initial period of settlement *landnám* date from three to four hundred years later than the events they discuss.[18] For the subsequent Commonwealth Period the textual evidence of identity construction and maintenance is more often contemporary to the thirteenth and fourteenth century. However, this may have been edited during the subsequent recopying prior to modern printing. These texts also provide a sense of the patron/author relationship, international politics and trade networks. This is a view influenced by the habitus of the writer and previous oral transmission practiced even in works which claim no affiliation other than knowledge and religion.

Eastern Quarter

The Eastern Quarter of Iceland is located the closest physically to Zone 1. Settlement of this Quarter occurred primarily on the coast, including two island sites at Goðatættur and Hérjólfsdalur. The Eastern Quarter has been subject to fewer farm excavations in the past. This is not a pattern continued with reference to excavated medieval burials, however, as evidenced by the work of Eldjárn which compiled the vast majority of known Icelandic material from throughout the area.[19] As much as is possible Eastern adaptations of identity construction and maintenance in practice shall be highlighted. Some of the reasons for this lacuna in evidence will also be considered.

The oldest excavations within this area were conducted on sites now being acknowledged as being late twelfth to thirteenth century in date through reanalysis. This may reflect the nature of preservation with regards to the physical evidence or possibly that these were just the easiest sites to locate. Erosion is the dominant means of finding sites in the Eastern Quarter of Zone 2. Modern construction efforts, particularly road construction have been another major means of locating sites. To a lesser degree field levelling carried out by modern farmers to alleviate some of the effects of glacial runoff, derived erosion has located sites within more marginalized areas. These archaeological sites are unprotected by farm boundaries and are intensively drained when necessary. Antiquarian efforts of both later farm owners and foreign researchers also discovered a number of sites. In every one of these cases antiquarian efforts were associated with eroded burials found near farms rather than farm sites. The corpus of burial material from throughout Iceland was reconsidered and dated during the late 1990s by Eldjárn and Friðriksson.[20] Due to this, it is possible to consider a more complete view of medieval Icelandic familial identity, however, a discussion on the initial period of settlement is difficult to make due to lack of dated evidence.

Fig 43 illustrates the area of focus for this section as well as site locations utilized as evidence. Several glaciers have resulted in, series of glacial moraines dominate the interior of this Quarter and runoff derived rivers. There are also three volcanoes in this Quarter. These features have influenced not only the amount of farms initially established but also the amount of modern excavations conducted, as conditions for travel have been poor.

Eastern Quarter farm sites are poorly represented within the Zone 2 archaeological record. They can be placed into a relative chronological grouping of early and late sites. Early sites are represented by Hérjólfsdalur, Stóraborg, and Hólmur.[21] These are also the most recently excavated settlement sites, with the excavation of Hérjólfsdalur being both the oldest and most complete beginning in 1971 and continuing every excavation season until 1983.[22] There are some commonalities between these three sites, which potentially may be corroborated by greater archaeological survey and excavation in the Eastern Quarter.

Norse settlers exploited a variety of landscapes for the establishment of their farms. Wetland areas were less covered by trees at the onset of settlement that required less land clearing prior to construction of buildings. A variety of food and material resources such as fresh water were nearby. This meant less time had to be spent devoted to resource procurement and more could be devoted to construction efforts. Many of these sites held rights over adjacent shores, highlighting the method of site discovery being via open water marine vessels. This is sometimes alluded to within textual sources as well. Turf constructions of the medieval period were damp places due to a lack of a roof runoff system to cope with the rainy north Atlantic climate. This, in combination with damp foundations laid upon wetland areas, would have resulted in a damp house more difficult to heat.

Farms were also established on smaller islands as well such as at Hérjólfsdalur on Vestmanna.[23] The site of Hólmur hints at the presence of a low-lying island nearby as well in its place name.[24] Island and coastal sites are both subject to marine derived erosion. A marine orientation is expressed more often in such areas. Hólmur, dated to the late ninth to tenth century, reflects a descriptive toponymic from nature which translates to 'low islet'. Hérjólfsdalur, on the other hand, reflects a tenth to eleventh century date with the personal name of Hérjólfr in combination with a natural name element – valley.[25] The early island utilization in combination with the osteological assemblages of these sites highlights the presence of great auk exploitation.[26] Low lying islands were the preferred location of auk colonies and formed a substantial portion of protein derived from wild sources.

All three of the early sites within the Eastern Quarter of Zone 2 provide evidence of pithouse construction and early utilization. At Stóraborg, this was a quite small area – en a wattle and turf-covered roof had covered excavated pit of 2.1 x 2.3 m. It contained evidence of a small hearth as well.[27] This pithouse was dug into a low-lying hill, perhaps to reduce the effects of a high local water table.[28] At Hólmur, another pithouse was excavated in 1999 from another low-lying hill near an abandoned farm. This particular structure was cited as an area of cult focus, a *blóthus* or 'sacrificial-blood house' within site publication.[29] At Hérjólfsdalur a third, pithouse was also discovered dug into a low-lying hill around which a subsequent farm was constructed.[30] Stóraborg and Hérjólfsdalur both developed farm mounds that were associated with the later farmsteads.[31]

At Stóraborg, a singular longhouse was constructed following this initial phase of pithouse.[32] The longhouse was between 16 and 25 m in length.[33] Unfortunately, subsequent continued site utilization has made it difficult to determine long house details on this site. In the case of Stóraborg, this continued to the modern period and a farm mound developed.[34] Partial site excavations in combination with older excavations have made discussion of early longhouses other than these much more difficult as turf remained the primary method of construction for settlement and medieval Zone 2. Evidence provided at some sites continues to overlain by modern buildings which has resulted in a reduced amount of evidence for analysis.

At Hérjólfsdalur, on the other hand, two contemporaneously utilized longhouses were built following the pithouse.[35] At Hólmur a longhouse and farmyard was discovered some 250 m away from the presumed *blóthus* – this was excavated in 1997.[36] Hólmur is illustrated in Fig 46. All of the initial longhouses constructed share the characteristics of bowed sides and longhouse dimensions. At Stóraborg the dimensions of this longhouse were between 16 and 25 m.[37] Unfortunately, subsequent continued site utilization has made it difficult to determine long house details on this site. In the case of Stóraborg, this continued to the modern period and a farm mound developed.[38] Milek utilizing both morphology and geochemical analysis of microsediments has recently considered transitions of house types over time.[39]

There are two farm sites that date to the later phase of medieval construction in the Eastern Quarter. The earlier of these is Goðatættur that has been typologically associated with the eleventh and twelfth centuries.[40] It consists of a singular longhouse and byre. This site is located on an island, maintaining some continuity with earlier centuries[41]. This longhouse has straighter internal sides shown by the presence of stone foundations for the turf walls. The later site of Bergþórshvoll was initially occupied during the twelfth to thirteenth century.[42] This is represented by a byre underlying a later medieval longhouse and associated outbuildings.[43] A farm mound developed during the subsequent occupation that overlaid the site. Unfortunately, this site has been incompletely recorded over its excavation history. This has made it difficult to consider such topics as space utilization in relation to microscale elements of identity presented in the Eastern Quarter of Zone 2.

Space utilization within the Eastern Quarter is incredibly difficult to comment upon due to the small sample size – no generalizations can be made because of this. Relatively few internal features can be commented on in any depth. Central hearths are included on site plans indicating a central focus within the longhouses themselves. Hólmur is somewhat of an anomaly to this group.[44] Although the pithouse here was within 300 m of an abandoned medieval farm site it was more directly in association with accompanied pagan burials which contributed to the excavator's designation as an area of cult focus.[45] This is a unique site at the moment which potentially highlights the presence of a pagan element to the local population. As there is no way to average such a small sample and have it be considered representative data from other areas of Iceland, in particular the region of Þjórsádalur, are utilized.

The burial evidence from the Eastern Quarter, however, shows what is possible with a greater sample.[46] Located to the outer edges of the outfield to the north and northeast of a farm were placed family burials. This was in association with the main farm unit yet not within the area of heaviest daily utilization. Both accompanied and unaccompanied interments have been excavated from mounds in the landscape.[47] The excavated and documented burials are primarily accompanied by grave goods including items of adornment and practicality. When animals accompany human burials they are primarily horses although evidence of dogs has been found at Brú and Rangá.[48] The burials are often covered first with a mound of stones then earth which accentuated the presence of the low mounds in the landscape. These are not always singular interments as cemeteries have been located and excavated at Vað, Straumer, Reykjasel and Hrífunes.[49] These sites are located near rivers.

The amount of direct evidence provided by the material culture of an excavated farm site from Iceland is actually quite small in comparison to the physical size of these farms. When this is considered in conjunction with burial evidence, however, certain elements of microscale identity practice can still be seen. This material is presented first in relation to domestic practices and subsequently wider farm practices.

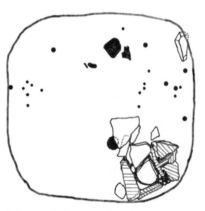

Fig 46. Hólmur sunken feature building.[50]

Fire utilization in the domestic longhouse took place in central hearths; however, evidence from Hólmur shows other forms of fire manipulation. Earth and local stones were utilized within Norse medieval constructions to assist with cooking in daily life. At Hólmur an example of both an oven as well as a cooking pit were excavated.[51] Both of these constructs allow for the more specific application of heat than was available via the central hearth of the longhouse. The central hearth contributed to the general atmospheric heating and lighting of longhouses.[52] Cooking which required open flame, a vessel or even smoke produced by burning fuel also would involve the central hearth.

Imported steatite was utilized in vessels that were able to withstand the heat of nearby flames, similar to ceramic vessels in later periods in Zone 2. This soft stone is easily carved into a variety of forms including lamps used to light the dark interiors of longhouses and other human habitations. Unlike Norwegian lamp sequences, however, north Atlantic steatite forms are less distinct.[53] At Hérjólfsdalur on Vestmanna off the southern coast of Iceland, steatite was 13% of the assemblage.[54]

Evidence for the smelting of iron is known from Bergþórshvoll where bog iron was converted into iron blooms.[55] Iron was also imported both as iron ingots as well as completed products such as knives and fish hooks. The need for iron within Zone 2 was greater than the supply of raw iron in the area that led to a practice of recycling and reuse of iron.[56] This method also required much less fuel than the full smelting procedure. This also led to a practice of utilizing animal bone as a replacement material for iron and wood items.

Personal items of adornment from sites such as Hrífunes, Einholt, Ormsstaðir and Ketilsstaðir appear to largely be designated as female – particularly the tortoise brooch.[57] This may be due to several causes – a change in fashion where tortoise brooches no longer held any use save as heirloom, conditions of preservation better suited to non-ferrous metals, and even misidentification of male graves. Six of the recognized thirty-one burials considered for this case study contained evidence for burial with horses and one of those had evidence of dog interment with human as well at Rangá.[58] When ferrous items have been found they range from common knives to axes and strap ends. These are rare due to the conditions of preservation and of excavation. Many of the burials in the Eastern Quarter were discovered over time as land eroded or was moved with human intent.

Southern Quarter

The Southern Quarter experienced heavy settlement during the initial *landnám* according to a variety of evidence. Major modern excavation and survey efforts have been conducted at Aðalstræti and regionally at Mosfellssveit.[59] This area also contains the first bishop's seat at Skáholt, which has also been subject to recent archaeological research, as has the site of the Icelandic National Assembly at Þingvellir. The most famous excavation efforts in Zone 2 were carried out during the early twentieth century in the interior valley of Þjórsádalur at Stöng that have been influential throughout the subsequent studies of the medieval Scandinavian world.[60] Since that time famous conservation efforts have been undertaken within Reykjavik itself.

This Quarter contains Reykjavik, the modern capital of Iceland. Settlement of this Quarter of Zone 2 occurred initially on the coast, although the rich river valleys of the interior such as Þjórsádalur were being exploited by the mid-tenth century.[61] Erosion as well as road construction is often associated with the discovery of sites in the Southern Quarter. To a lesser degree farm activities, such as field levelling or gardening, have been associated with the discovery of archaeological sites. Antiquarian efforts do appear to play a greater role in the discovery of archaeological material, when considered in light of the higher number of known archaeological sites, however, the proportion remains similar.

The Southern Quarter has some of the most favourable environmental conditions of Zone 2. These are fewer glaciers and they are farther inland resulting in greater amounts of land being available for settlement exploitation. Glacial runoff figures heavily in the drainage system of the region. Norse settlers exploited a variety of landscapes for the establishment of their farms in the Southern Quarter. Wetland areas were less covered by trees at the onset of settlement that required less land clearing prior to construction of buildings. A variety of food and material resources such as fresh water were nearby. This meant less time had to be spent devoted to resource procurement and more could be devoted to construction efforts. Examples of this in practice are the sites of modern Reykjavik: Aðalstræti and Suðurgata.[62] Many of these sites held rights over adjacent shores, highlighting the method of site discovery being via open water marine vessels. This is sometimes alluded to within textual sources as well. Turf constructions of the medieval period were damp places due to a lack of a roof runoff system to cope with the rainy north Atlantic climate. This in combination with damp foundations laid upon wetland areas would have resulted in a damp house more difficult to heat. Sites that existed in such conditions can be incredibly well preserved such as at Aðalstræti.[63]

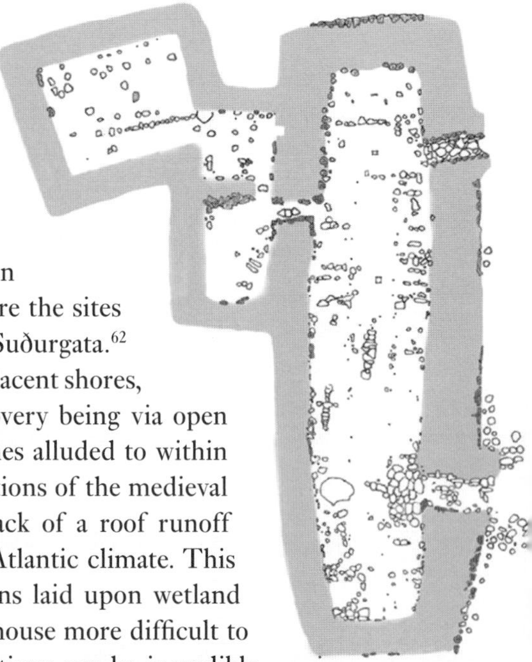

Fig 47. Skallakot.[67]

The earliest phases of construction in the Southern Quarter are sometimes linked to sunken feature buildings. This does not always hold true however as at Aðalstræti no evidence for one was found, perhaps do to the presence of a spring mistakenly included into the long house walls. At Gjáskógar, the sunken feature-building phase was followed by a longhouse and associated outbuilding.[64] At Bessastaðir, a longhouse was excavated in association with the sunken feature building – both constructions were overlain with more recent constructions of modern Reykjavik.[65] At Hvítarholt, the five sunken feature buildings were discovered in association with two multiperiod longhouses and outbuildings.[66]

The main building, the longhouse, was constructed next. At Skallakot in Þjórsádalur, the farm's longhouse was 26 x 5 m internally at Hvítarholt the longest farm building measured 19 x 6 m internally.[68] Skallakot is illustrated in Fig 47. At Aðalstræti, the initial phase of the longhouse measured 16.7 x 3.7–5.8 m with a well-defined central hearth.[69] The smaller site of Áslakstunga fremri is illustrated in Fig 48, the famous site of Stöng in Fig 49.

Interior forest areas also became chosen as time passed, as there was a ready supply of timber, fuel, forage and wild resources.[71] Wooded areas such as Þórsmörk were also sheltered in the landscape from bleak maritime winds and

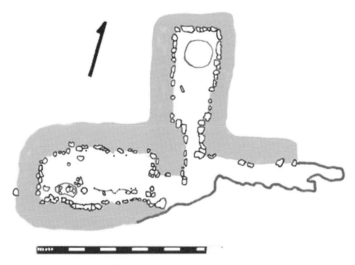

Fig 48. Aslakstunga fremri.[70]

hence were better suited for house establishment.[72] Land clearing is necessary which reduces the amount of time available to construct buildings. As a result, farm establishment in these areas would have been a multi-year process in particularly densely wooded regions. Interior regions in general were more removed from the direct lines of water-borne communication. In this period before roads had been constructed in Zone 2 internal travel by foot or by horse would have been quite slow and potentially dangerous depending on the number of glacial runoff rivers in between origin and destination. Forest areas were also maintained to provide a source of charcoal necessary for metal working.[73]

Construction material types utilized in Zone 2 are primarily organic in nature. Turf blocks remained a major building material in the rural region from initial settlement past the nineteenth century.[74] At Hrísbrú diatom analysis has shown that, more robust wetland species of grass were cut for turf blocks to build longhouse walls.[75] Dryer meadow species were cut to cover the roof. This was also confirmed via paleoentomological identification at Holt.[76] Timber was also an important construction material utilized in roof supports and internal planking as well as a variety of domestic and farm implements. Initially the need for this material was met by local forests of birch, *Betula pubescens*, evidenced by pollen, and driftwood.[77] This practice continued throughout the Commonwealth period via provisions in law.[78] *Grágás* section 199 deals explicitly with ownership of woodland areas. The fact that this section is quite long in comparison to other portions of the land law highlights the importance of this resource within

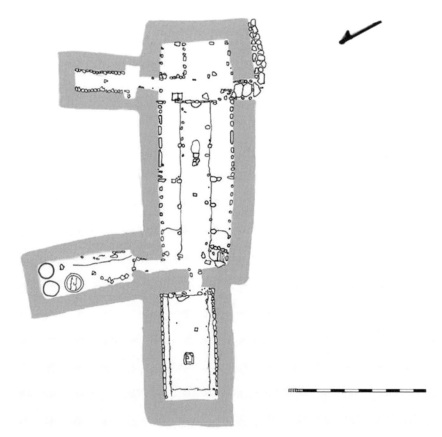

Fig 49. Stöng.[84]

eleventh and twelfth century Iceland.[79] The first chapter of *Íslendingabók* also confirms that Iceland was a forested land at the time of settlement.[80] *Grágás also* deals specifically with driftwood and establishing claim upon it in sections 209–11.[81] Timber was also imported later as the woods of Iceland became over-utilized subsequent to the thirteenth century.[82] Smaller branched woody plants such as dwarf birch were utilized within roof construction. Straw was also a form of construction material, particularly in the south where barley and later lyme grass could be grown.[83] This was used as thatch and in rope production for a variety of tasks.

In the Southern Quarter, the Þjórsádalur excavations represent this later period. This inner abandoned region was subject to early antiquarian survey and excavation such as at Undir Lambhófða, Áslakstunga innri, Áslakstunga fremri, and Sámsstaðir[85]. Immediately prior to World War II, major Scandinavian efforts at Áslakstunga fremri, Stórhóshlíð, Snjáleifartóttir, Skallakot, Skeljastaðir and Stöng resulted in *Forntida Gårdar I Island.*[86] Of all of these Stöng, occupied from the eleventh to the thirteenth century and abandoned because of volcanic activity, is the most famous.

Associated with longhouses were outbuildings that housed farm activities unsuited to storage within the longhouse. These activities include iron-working and weaving discussed above. These vary in form but include sunken feature buildings and smaller sub-rectangular turf builds. Barns for the storage of fodder indirectly highlight the presence of domestic farm stock as do byres for the housing of cattle.[87] Outbuildings that are auxiliary to the farm but are removed from the home farm exist in similar forms.[88] Outbuilding construction continues utilizing turf blocks through time that can make determining the presence of early-medieval shielings quite difficult. Although several regions to the interior have been surveyed, no excavation of shielings has provided radiocarbon dates.[89] Berson published a survey of the medieval evidence for barns in Iceland in 2002.

There are changes to the house format over time, although the use of turf blocks continues. Bow-sided longhouses of varying lengths are the earliest.[90] As time passed middens and farm mounds began to develop in the landscape a straight-sided form of longhouse became prevalent. At some sites, such as the second phase of Aðalstræti and at Stöng, outbuildings for storage and animal housing are attached to the farm's longhouse. Finally as the world cooled and the thirteenth century ended leading to more of the farm's auxiliary outbuildings being incorporated into the passage house form.

Domestic use of space focused upon the central hearth present in all medieval longhouses known. This is shown in the physical location of the hearth, evidenced by ash deposits, soil samples and charcoal. Examples include Hrísbrú and at Aðalstraeti amongst other sites.[91] As time passed, the format of the longhouse in particular began to change, incorporating outbuildings onto the longhouse form. The main structure of the longhouse became straighter along the long walls as well.

At four of the earliest farm sites in the Southern Quarter of Zone 2 sunken feature buildings were discovered which predated or were concurrent with longhouse utilization in the area. At Gjáskógar in Þjórsádalur, an early sunken feature building was associated with iron-working activities. This was a multiphase site that was occupied from the tenth to the thirteenth century when the site was abandoned along with many others in the region.[92]

Immediately beyond the environs of the farmyard were the protected infields and domestic gardens. Beyond the inner fields of a home farm, the outfields were located. The use of walls of turf and earthworks to help protect areas from livestock as well as to delineate the physical boundary of the main farm area is known from many sites. One of the best-preserved and conserved examples of this is located at Aðalstræti.[93] The physical delineation of farm boundaries and the manner of having this recognized by the local legal community became incorporated into Icelandic law by the eleventh to twelfth century, being discussed in section 181 of *Grágás*. At this time a '[...] legal wall is five feet thick down at ground level and three at top. From the base it should come up to the shoulder of a man whose arm-size gives valid ells and fathoms'.[94] These were required to be maintained by both neighbours in most cases and were walked upon land transactions such as selling and purchase.[95]

The burials are often covered with first a mound of stones then earth which accentuated the presence of the low mounds in the landscape. The only fully excavated farm with auxiliary burials is located at Skeljastaðir. This site is part of the major early excavations at Þjórsádalur in the Southern Quarter. Cemeteries containing multiple burials have been found located near rivers at Vað, Straumer, Reykjasel and Hrífunes rather than being located to the outer areas of a singular farm.[96] Beyond the main farm unit were auxiliary aspects of the farm that were integral parts of the farm economy. This includes collection areas for wild and natural resources such as shorelines, marine bird nesting areas and fuel wood.[97] These areas are incredibly difficult to find within the landscape, as they do not necessarily require substantial human constructions or land manipulations to exploit. These sorts of sites may be located via ecological survey in combination with legal descriptions of common rights provided by the *Grágás*.[98]

Evidence of lifestyle from Zone 2 is greatest in the Southern Quarter, largely due to the early Þjórsádalur excavations.[99] However, there have also been modern excavations in the region as well, particularly in and around modern Reykjavik as the city has expanded.[100] Because this sample includes both modern excavations of waterlogged site as well as those which were abandoned due to volcanic action, the variety of evidence is broader than in other parts of the North Atlantic. The site of Stöng in the Þjórsádalur and its range of artefacts have had the greatest impact on not only North Atlantic sites but also contemporaneous sites in Scandinavia as well.[101] There is a large amount of material that can still only be discussed indirectly as the material is organic in nature, such as textiles. Evidence for a wool-based economy rarely comes in the form of the finished textiles, however; loom and spinning weights as well as the remains of the sheep themselves can survive deposition much better. The excellent conditions provided by the Þjorsa valley allowed the evidence for much of the region's wool economy to be preserved.

Iron finds are most often associated with burials although evidence for the shaping of iron is known. A prosperous farm might have a smithy present to fulfil the need for iron within the material assemblage. Evidence for this was found at Bergþórshvoll as well as at Gjáskógar.[102] The past recycling of iron has impacted the amount of evidence known for iron utilization as broken and worn tools were re-shaped.[103]

Wood was much easier to shape into useful forms than many of the materials discussed here. Domestic items of wood ranged from the handles of farm tools to entire constructions such as upright looms.[104] A whale bone weaving sword used to tighten the weave. Sites and regions which have been waterlogged, such as Aðalstræti, or abandoned due to volcanic action, such as the region of Þjórsádalur, produce some of the best assemblages. Dating this material is most often accomplished typologically due to the variable absolute dates associated with driftwood that has been incorporated into wooden and timber goods.[105]

Like Zone 1, finds of steatite are also known from the South Quarter.[106] A major advantage which steatite vessels have over ceramics is the ability to recycle the vessel.[107] If the object can be repaired with a patch and rivet, it continued in its original role – particularly if it is still able to hold fluid. If the object was damaged beyond repair, however, the sherds may be reshaped into spindle whorl and loom weights.

Marine mammals were exploited as well; however, they are not as well represented within the archaeological record. Part of this is due to the size of these animals – ethnographic practices from several whale exploiting cultures highlight the fact that whale meat and blubber were brought back to human settlements. Skeletal elements of larger species such as whale, particularly when freshly dead, were not brought back because of weight and low utility.[108] After the skeleton had weathered for several seasons thus reducing the amount of total bone fat present only those elements that would be useful such as large strong ribs, scapula and vertebrae.[109] Evidence for walrus has been produced from excavations at Aðalstræti showing a period when the north Atlantic walrus maintained breeding populations on the southern Icelandic coast.[110] Walrus is eventually hunted to regional extinction in Zone 2 waters.[111]

Mývatnssveit

Excavation and survey work in the Mývatnssveit region of northern Iceland has provided great insight into a regional network.[112] This has been possible due to the efforts of Háskóli Íslands, Fornleifastofnun Íslands, and Þjóðminjasafn Íslands in combination with international research groups. These groups include

NABO as well as foreign university departments and research initiatives. This area shows the wealth of material available when a wider local network approach is utilized in data collection.

At Hófstaðir to the north tephrochronological and radiocarbon samples showed the sunken feature building co-existed for maybe twenty years, with the dual phased timber and turf hall of bow-sided longhouse format and a sunken floor outbuilding.[113]

A sub-rectangular sunken feature building approximately *c.* 5 x 3.4 x 1.1 m was discovered and excavated by Bruun in 1908 during Iceland's first major archaeological excavation.[114] This feature was later re-excavated, twice, and documented using more modern techniques from 1991–2001.[115] In the northwest corner of the structure was located a small hearth while access and potential side benches were negatively evidenced during geophysical analysis.[116] Subsequent to the sunken feature building's initial utilization once the *c.* 1 m high roof had collapsed it became the location of a midden.[117] Tephrochronological and radiocarbon samples showed the sunken feature building co-existed for a short time of twenty years, with the dual phased timber and turf hall of bow-sided longhouse format and a sunken floor outbuilding.[118] The Hofstaðir hall itself consisted of two entrances, four rooms with a central hearth in the largest of these.[119] All of the initial longhouses constructed share the characteristics of bowed sides and longhouse dimensions. The largest of the early Zone 2 longhouses is that at Hófstaðir with internal dimensions *c.* 38 x 8 m.[120]

Domestic use of space focused upon the central hearth present in all medieval longhouses known. This is shown in the physical location of the hearth, evidenced by ash deposits, soil samples and charcoal. Examples came from midden material at Hofstaðir. Midden material was thrown to the outside of the human and animal habitations contributing to the development of farm mounds. Modern Zone 2 excavations have located and made good use of midden evidence. This evidence is more abundant than other forms of site deposition and material assemblages, particularly on sites excavated previously. Excavation of midden features allow greater insight and discussion to be made concerning both human patterns of species exploitation and material usage as well as environmental contexts. Mývatnssveit in particular has provided several representatives of middens from not only Hófstaðir's phases but also the less well-known sites of Brenna, Hrísheimar, Selhagi and Steinbogi that have occupations from the ninth to the thirteenth century.[121] Any outbuildings that deteriorated to the point of being unsuited to their original purpose may also have been utilized as midden locations or had been dismantled to provide turf fertilizer for the fields.[122]

Beyond the main farm unit were auxiliary aspects of the farm that were integral parts of the farm economy. This includes collection areas for wild and natural resources such as shorelines, marine bird nesting areas and fuel wood.[123] These areas are incredibly difficult to find within the landscape, as they do not necessarily require substantial human constructions or land manipulations to exploit. These sorts of sites may be located via ecological survey in combination with legal descriptions provided by the *Grágás*.[124] The most direct form of archaeological evidence for this practice comes from the excavation of midden as the refuse from wild collection efforts is deposited with the rest of the farm refuse.[125]

Imported steatite was utilized in vessels that were able to withstand the heat of nearby flames, similar to ceramic vessels in later periods in Zone 2.[126] This soft stone is easily carved into a variety of forms including lamps used to light the dark interiors of longhouses and other human habitations.[127] Steatite is not represented in the same amount of every site. For instance steatite composes some 17% of the total assemblage at Hofstaðir.[128]

There are many provisions for the keeping of animals – in particular sheep but to a lesser extent of horse, cattle and pig as well. Sheep form the basis for the medieval vaðmal industry of Zone 2.[129] There is physical evidence for their over-wintering in byres and other farm outbuildings. Evidence for the seasonal transhumance of sheep is mostly completely explored at shieling sites.[130] There are extensive provisions regarding common grazing lands in the *Grágás*.[131] Horses are evidenced not only by the inclusion of their harness fittings in burials but also by inclusions of the horses themselves.[132] Horses would have been vital to rapid transport in the interior of Iceland – the land was too rough and too sparsely settled to warrant the construction of road networks. Indeed horses were used as a primary means of transport throughout Iceland until the twentieth century.

Wild species are also represented within osteological assemblages, highlighting the contributions these resources made to the overall economy of Zone 2 farms. Evidence for marine birds including but not limited to the great auk and puffin have been discovered. Evidence for marine fish has been recovered from both coastal and interior archaeological sites. Eggs were gathered seasonally. Egg shell has been recovered from midden deposits at Brenna, Hofstaðir, Hrísheimar, Selhagi and Steinbogi whose occupation date from the ninth century to the early thirteenth century.[133] This highlights both some of the wild species exploited as well as the results that can be provided by soil processing techniques on modern excavations.[134]

Discussion

As has been shown the evidence provided, Zone 2 has been heavily impacted by its history of excavation. The influence of the early twentieth century excavators is felt in lingering patterns of thought concerning settlement as well as directly through their excavation practices. Systematic survey was not the primary means of locating archaeological sites in Zone 2 at this time.[135] Sites were located by farmers who saw burials and farms eroded out of the landscape because of glacial and winter runoff – those sites more exposed to the elements. Field levelling by farmers using modern, i.e. not animal powered, equipment has also led to the discovery of early-medieval material in Iceland. Construction of roads such as the Hringvegur has also been linked to site discovery. Major modern excavations, particularly those which focus on regional networks focus upon environmental impact and to a lesser extent than in the past seek a description of the development of a people.[136] Sites which have been discovered since the formation of the Fornleifastofnun Íslands are much more likely to have been discovered via systematic survey. Several sites located by earlier efforts were initially excavated while other sites such as Hofstaðir were re-excavated utilizing modern techniques.[137] The history of excavation practices has greatly impacted the amount of microscale evidence derived – particularly in reference to evidence immediately outside of longhouses and other buildings.[138]

Microscale evidence highlights the arrival and continued presence of a population that had to adjust to several contexts quite quickly. Producing and managing multiple lines of subsistence became imperative in this area removed from established and well-travelled trade networks. This was accomplished by group interactions at the farm unit level that established and maintained these multiple lines of subsistence within the realm of farm life. This in turn occasionally created a surplus of resources that promoted the economy of the farm unit on a regional scale.

House and Settlement

Discussion of elements of both the household and settlement of Zone 2 has been heavily impacted by excavation and survey work conducted during the early twentieth century.[139] This earlier phase of research focused on quite specific elements of Icelandic existence – namely the internal aspects of longhouses, furnished burials and items of portable art and personal adornment. By focusing on the evidence in this manner, however, a disconnection appeared within consideration and publication of Zone 2 farm sites. Longhouses were not considered in conjunction with any associated burials in spite of the greater presentation numerically of excavated burials.[140] There are only two fully excavated farm burial complexes excavated during this time, Skeljastaðir in Þjórsádalur that was published in 1943 and Hofstaðir in Mývatnssveit that was published in 2009 after a century of periodic excavation.[141] The excavation of Skeljastaðir was conducted to internationally high standards for its day – the Scandinavian excavators who led these efforts were some of the best known in Europe at the time. At Hofstaðir a modern confluence of regional experts have conducted a re-excavation and assessment of the entirety of the available material assemblage from the site.

Eastern Quarter	*Southern Quarter*	*Mývatnssveit*
Gap in farm evidence due to survey practice – a part of the Zone 2 hiatus in evidence	The excavation of Þjórsádalur has resulted in an over-reliance on these farms as type sites, the most famous example being Stöng	Modern excavation and re-excavation of regional network has produced a substantial body of evidence in relation to the local environment
Burial evidence highlights the presence of a larger population	Access to both walrus and auk populations	Represented at the Alþing by the Northern Quarter Court
Trees evidenced via presence onsite, law codes such as *Grágás*, and place names	Trees evidenced via presence onsite, law codes such as *Grágás*, and place names	Trees evidenced via presence onsite, law codes such as *Grágás*, and place names
Coastal access	Coastal access	Lake access
Early antiquarian efforts associated with burials sites	Early antiquarian efforts associated with farm sites	Early antiquarian efforts associated with farm sites
Grain agriculture initially possible	First bishopric established at Skáholt	Direct saga reference
Potential pagan religious element at Hólmur	Several direct saga references	Potential pagan religious element at Hofstaðir
Preceded at the Alþing by 3 local Spring assemblies	Preceded at the Alþing by 3 local Spring assemblies	Reliable radiocarbon and tephrachronology used to dated the site
Relative quality of the evidence is low due to the number of excavated sites available	Relative quality of the evidence is high and has been so for the past 70 years	Relative quality of the archaeological evidence is good, the textual evidence is less so

Fig 50. Major Characteristics of Zone 2.

Buildings on Zone 2 sites were most often constructed from turf with internal wooden supports until the twentieth century.[142] This includes not only the widely known longhouses but also the earlier sunken feature buildings and outbuildings as well. In the past, this fact has been used to promote ideas of a tree-less Iceland that corresponds to the modern environmental condition. However, when considered in light of the climatic nature of the marginal Zone 2 environment the thick turf walls of a medieval longhouse were much more insulative than timber walls alone, if not as impressive within the natural landscape.[143] Turf blocks were cut and laid in a variety of patterns dependent upon location in the final structure as well as the type of grass species being utilized.[144] Blocks utilized for the lower walls were cut from dense wetland grasses.[145]

Turf itself was insufficient to maintain the form of a longhouse's roof. For this, internal supports of wood were utilized. This may have been local timber cut for the purpose from local stands of trees, driftwood or even recycled internal supports from earlier buildings following the Settlement period.[146] Each portion of this internal support system was given a specific name.[147] This internal network of timber supported a covering of branches that was subsequently covered by a layer of lighter, drier meadowland turf.[148] This allowed less vertical stress to be put onto the roof itself. According to later ethnographic evidence from the area, these turf blocks were cut to a larger size and laid in an over-lapping pattern, producing a roof that is quite similar in pattern to the tegulation found on eleventh and twelfth century hogback sculptures.

As time passed, some farms began to utilize a foundation course of stone and earth within building construction. The earliest phase of Aðalstræti, dated to the mid-tenth century is an early example of this practice.[149] This not only protected the first courses of turf block from ground damp which would result in more rapid block deterioration but also is much easier to locate within the landscape during later archaeological efforts because the walls are more distinct initially.[150] These organic construction techniques were employed in most constructions in Zone 2, but are the best recognized in relation to longhouses.

Name	Length	Other Information
'corse' seal	< 4 ells	–
'erken' seal	5–6 ells	–
'flett' seal	4–5 ells	–
'bearded' seal	6–7 ells	–
'saddleback' seal	<4 ells	Swims on back or side
'short' seal	2 ells	Can blow through ice 4–5 ells thick

Fig 51. Seals described in Konungs Skuggsjá.[151]

Longhouses did not exist alone in the Zone 2 landscape, nor were they always the first building constructed. Initially a Zone 2 farm unit concentrated efforts towards self-sufficiency in subsistence. This is unsurprising as establishing settlements in wilderness areas by its very nature places a group beyond an area where deficiencies in farm production and collection strategies were alleviated by trade and exchange. The networks have not yet been established to do this. As a result, practices that evidence pragmatic aspects of life are present with the archaeological and textual record. Only by exploiting resources in a general manner rather than focusing on a singular means of specialized subsistence were the settlement populations of Zone 2 able to establish themselves. During the *landnám* period, the specific niches within the ecology of Zone 2 were not yet known and so species that were exploited were those which were the most recognizable and substantially sized. By exploiting larger species such as walrus and great auk allowed domestic stock to be used for breeding rather than for subsistence.

Fig 51 illustrates the seals associated with the north Atlantic in contemporary sources. The gathering of fresh food to eat and store would have been a priority, as would provision for long-term subsistence such as grain production by clearing land and preparing fields for planting in the first spring. Local grasses such as lyme grass may have been gathered at this time to supplement both domestic farm stock and man.

Family and Gender Relations

In Zone 2, evidence for family and gender relations comes in a variety of forms. This includes microsediment analysis for paleoentomological evidence, the division of labour and the substantial corpus of textual material. Sleeping arrangements that illustrated some of the microscale relations internal to the farm are described in passing in saga texts – archaeologically evidence comes from environmental analysis of soil samples taken from longhouse and passage house interiors that have produced concentrations of human lice. Gulatingslog also discusses provisions for the sleeping arrangements of farm workers in section 100 and this continues when *Grágás* are adopted following the establishment of the Althing.[152] The format of the Althing is illustrated in Fig 52.

Textual sources, particularly those that are not law codes, record material that is contemporaneous to the time of writing. This means that it is an element of microscale identity that cannot be discussed utilizing textual sources until the twelfth and thirteenth century. By this point *Grágás* stipulate provisions of sleeping arrangements for farm auxiliaries and for shared public space.[153] Sleeping closets with lightly built internal walls of wood line a large room. For

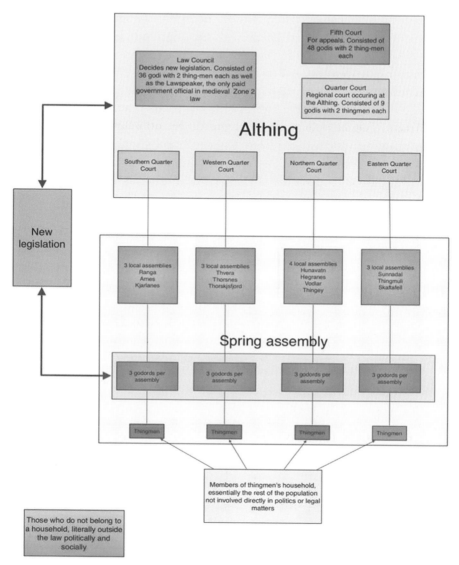

Fig 52. Format of the Althing.[155]

many years these views were primarily based upon the finds from Þjórsádalur, with the greatest reliance being on Stöng which was abandoned during the thirteenth century.[154]

Another way to examine family and gender relations is to consider farm labour. As in Zone 1 the efforts undertaken by family and gender linked work units can be split into internally oriented house tasks and externally oriented farm tasks. Physical evidence for farm labour exists in the form artefacts and ecofacts on site, in the remains of buildings constructed and lived in. Zone 2 artefact choices are illustrated in Fig 53. Collection of goods, such as eggs, is evidenced by eggshells found within middens in Mývatnssveit but also wood collection in the form of charcoal found in the hearths of Hólmur and Aðalstraeti.[156] Other evidence for fuel and timber utilization comes from the lack of extensive woodland in modern Iceland in spite of palynological evidence for trees at the onset of *landnám*. Provisions existed within the Norwegian Gulatingslog for the process of land naming including taking hold of lands with woods.[157] Provisions exist within Grágás to protect such areas as valuable natural resources – this is unsurprising given the time when Grágás were first written down, following the establishment of the Althing.[158] Much of the activity linked to natural resource exploitation is initially male in the sagas – the felling of timber for instance being labour intensive. Even collection of large driftwood may have been primarily male and lower status. Once larger pieces of wood had been portioned into sections of more manageable sizes then female members of the family – again probably of lower status due to the low skill needed.

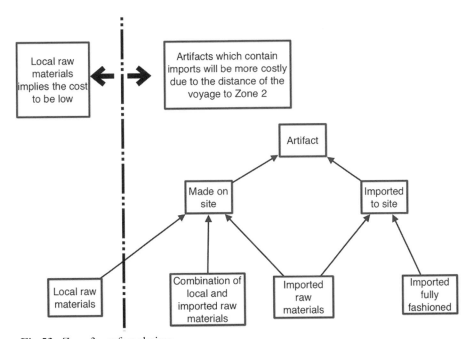

Fig 53. Zone 2 artefact choices.

Evidence for wool processing and textile production in general is quite good with many levels of processing being evidenced. Parasites including sheep lice, *Damalinia ovis L*, have been found in concentrations not only from outbuildings but also from within longhouse and conglomerate houses themselves when subjected to microsediment analysis.[159] Loom and spindle weights constructed from broken steatite vessels have been discovered in quantity from Þjórsádalur but also from the rest of Iceland as well. In rare cases samples of textiles produced have survived, particularly vaðmal that was the basis for Icelandic medieval and post-Medieval terrestrial exports.

Zone 2 maintained the marine gender biases with regards to work. This is something that can only be discussed indirectly, however, as the artefacts themselves are largely gender neutral. A gender bias affiliated marine activities with Zone 2 males. This is expressed indirectly within surviving evidence. Marine activities were primarily group ventures for medieval Norse due to the size of their vessels. No single person vessels aside from auxiliary ship's boats being known. These are only from burials[160]. Marine oriented practices were inherently full of risk yet they had the potential to be very beneficial to the maintenance of a settlement. Those that undertook these voyages – particularly the trips to Europe – were making a gamble against that risk that the skill and ship belonging to the crew would alleviate the effects. The success of these marine oriented groups translated terrestrial elements across the north Atlantic. The success of this network is evidenced not only by the presence of Zone 2 products on European sites and within collections but also by the very presence of laws which guaranteed landsmen rights to Icelandic sailors landing in Norway. As this was a group venture, the exclusion of females must be considered in light of the reduction of risk. In this sense, the female population were largely untrained in marine tasks such as manoeuvring large, square sails. These open water practices could be potentially deadly if not performed correctly on the open water.

Social Status and Rank

While Zone 2 was initially settled location became associated with a certain level of rank. Iceland is more than a few days west of Zone 1 and was unsettled by human biological populations.[161] Due to this, any initial status/rank would have been imposed as a part of the Scandinavian habitus carried by the settling populations. Those farms established by high-ranking members of that system had the benefit of a larger amount of physical and social capital from which to establish themselves on new farms. These had faster, larger ships to bring them to Zone 2 that resulted in comparatively earlier arrivals meaning that the richer areas were free to be settled. Some settlement groups appear to have pooled resources to have a greater amount of capital to draw upon – an example of this occurs at Stóraborg where a pithouse was found to precede and coexist in use with two longhouses.[162] Large sized farms required many hands to construct and maintain the buildings as well as the stock that was affiliated. They also had the resources to support writers and ecclesiastics. Writers were able to take down the local traditions – elements of microscale identity – which promoted the local power interactions occurring in the area in relation to the rest of Zone 2 as well as the wider north Atlantic economic network as well – macroscale statements. The presence of a church on site can also highlight a microscale expression of a macroscale statement.

Another way to determine relative status and rank is to examine affiliated coastal wild resource exploitation areas. There are several sections of *Grágás* that are linked to the negotiation over common held collection areas.[163] There is some concern utilizing just farm size as a determinant of relative rank as phasing and dating is inconsistent on older excavated sites.[164] The ability

Fig 54. Reconstruction of vertical loom utilized in the weaving of vaðmal from Þjóðminjasafn Íslands. Reconstruction made utilizing ethnographic and archaeological evidence from throughout Zone 2.

and necessity for Settlement Period auxiliary unit construction was dictated largely by availability of resources. The need for common lands to the interior of Zone 2 where glaciers and volcanic fields dominate the landscape became more necessary after the land of Iceland had been fully claimed by a century of incoming settlers.[165] Artefact quality and presence can also be an indicator of social status. Initial presence on site implies either construction of the piece on site or importation. This develops specifically because of the distance inherent to the North Atlantic system. When this is considered in conjunction with the amount of human effort a relative idea of artefact worth sans sentimentality can be made. Artefacts that were initially constructed from high quality resources are costly, and more likely to be afforded by those of higher status. Those artefacts had the potential to be utilized by high status farm units as means of reaffirming social connections.[166] Once obtained some, such as those of iron, entered into a pattern of recycling and reuse. Sites with artefact assemblages composed of worn goods holds a lower status. Those sites that were unable to devote human work hours or capital to farm maintenance were of the lowest status.

Orientation

The island location of Zone 2 has resulted in the same three primary drivers to activity in this area as in Zone 1: terrestrial, littoral and marine. As Zone 2 is a larger island than previously discussed, these drivers are to a certain extent mediated by site location, particularly on sites in interior valleys.[167] Sites to the interior might consider local wooded areas and fishing rivers to be amongst a farm's wild collection areas such as at Þórsmörk. Coastal sites, on the other hand, would have considered adjacent drift shores and birding cliffs amongst the subsistence network of the farm. Provisions for access to this material are detailed in *Grágás*.[168] These areas required little in the way of specialty equipment to exploit.

The gender-defined roles on a Zone 2 farm were dependent upon

Fig 55. Whale bone weaving sword utilized in the weaving of vaðmal from Þjóðminjasafn Íslands.

both social statuses within the farm but also in physical relation to the farm itself as was noted in Zone 1. Those tasks that were affiliated with the day-to-day functioning and maintenance of the human habitation were within the realm of women.[169] Those tasks that were more public in their relation to local and international networks were much more likely to be performed by males. Part of this is linked to scale – not all females are large enough to accomplish certain farm yard tasks while not all males know how to perform typically female tasks. The negotiation of this is included in many of the Íslendingasögur as locations framing other more active portions of the story.[170]

The presence of texts directly affiliated with Zone 2 allows for two things – rank can be attributed with them and they can carry evidence for further rank attribution within them. The first idea is tied into the amount of work that is required to create a text.[171] Not only would a text author be effectively taken out of many day-to-day farm activities in order to make good use of daylight but also they needed to be fed during that time as well. Hence unlike other farm workers under the employ of a higher ranked family unit a writer was a particularly expense to undertake within the local network at the microscale. Their presence in the microscale makes little sense, however, when considered in relation to the wider macroscale elements of the North Atlantic network. By maintaining an onsite text author a farm unit was able to maintain their version of history and ideas for later generations in a very physical sense.[172] This was something established as being important concurrent to the widespread adoption of Christianity – one of the first things which occurs when writing enters a system is documentation of local oral histories and beliefs. Certain valleys and farms in Iceland are more closely tied to written sources than others – this is not only due to the fact that only some farm networks were able to carry the burden of maintaining a writer but also due to conditions of preservation of the manuscripts themselves.

Conclusions

The analysis of case study evidence for Zone 2 has highlighted two concepts. The first are the microscale elements of identity that are seemingly unique to each region. An example of this is the use of straw as roofing material on Southern Quarter sites.[173] This was an environmentally linked construction resource, as evidence for other long grasses such as lyme being utilized does not occur in samples from Hofstaðir.[174] Unlike Zone 1, Zone 2 was largely unsettled at the *landnám* event that presented a new situation upon the incoming populations. This territory lacks many of the anthropogenic landscape signals developed during the settlement of the first Zone. This forced a greater reliance upon the natural environment partially evidenced by the natural elements found in place names such as the walrus related names on the Reykjanes coastline.[175]

The second concept is the large amount of gaps that continue to exist at present due to low numbers of modern excavations. In regions such as Mývatnssveit, the amount of detail is much improved as areas outside of building interiors have been excavated utilizing microscreening and intensive environmental sampling.[176] These gaps appear to be distinct – in relation to other north Atlantic assemblages. However, as these gaps are due to either antiquarian excavation practice or simply lack of excavation, the response of the learned public has been incredibly influential on the development of the modern state of knowledge concerning medieval Zone 2 and Scandinavia. They have liberally utilized all cultural evidence as representing a pan-Icelandic/ Scandinavian identity at both microscale and macroscale levels.

Chapter 5

Settlement, Economy and Lifestyles in Zone 3
c. AD 1000–1250

Introduction

The Zone 3 case study region includes the Eastern Settlement of Greenland as well as the few known North American sites. The entirety of Zone 3 including the Western Settlement of Greenland is considered in later chapters. The most socially and physically marginal farm sites of the North Atlantic are located in this Zone, which ultimately contributed to the decline of the medieval settlements.[1] Due to the remote nature of Zone 3, supplies and trade-goods were unable to make direct voyages from Continental networks of exchange and as a result, Zone 2 became an integral stop in the exchange voyage.

The climate of Zone 3 is heavily influenced by the close proximity of the Inland Ice – the icecap covering the majority of the interior of Greenland itself; see Fig 56.[2] This not only cools the ground and air making the agricultural practices utilized in Europe, Zone 1 and Zone 2 a gesture in futility but also calves icebergs on a regular basis throughout the year.[3] This causes the Davis Strait between Greenland and the eastern coast of modern Canada to be a much riskier voyage for marine travel than much of the medieval North Atlantic.[4] The recognized economic resources of Greenland were closely tied to the available amounts of marine derived goods including walrus products and driftwood.[5] Other sources of subsistence and international economy included the keeping of European domesticates such as cattle and sheep.[6] As experienced in Zone 1 and Zone 2 modern satellite imagery covers the coasts of Greenland with inconsistent detail and resolution. Evidence for the Zone 3 case study has been subjected to collation and consideration within the data tables previously described. Selections from this are included in the text when appropriate.

Biases Associated with Zone 3

There are a range of biases associated with Zone 3, some of which are shared in common with Zone 2. Several of the best known and preserved sites of Zone 3 were surveyed and excavated during the early twentieth century, in keeping with other medieval north Atlantic Zones and Scandinavian kingdoms. Many of the same surveyors and excavators who conducted research in sites such as Jarlshof

Fig 56. Map of Norse Greenland.

and Kvívík in Zone 1 and in Þjórsádalur in Zone 2 excavated at the major early excavations in Zone 3, in particular Roussell, Bruun and Norlund. Zone 3 sites are more likely to have been subject to post-depositional human scavenging for raw materials by subsequent sub-Arctic inhabitants such as the Thule.[7] They are also subject to extreme erosion from glacial runoff in a similar fashion to Zone 2.[8]

The Western Settlement of Greenland contains some of the more modern full archaeological excavations, such as Garðr, that was conducted to collect

Fig 57. Glacial runoff leading to the Eirikssfjord, as seen from Signal Hill, Narsarsuaq.

the site before total erosion occurred.[9] Zone 3 archaeological sites and regions gained heavy antiquarian influence via connection to Zone 2 written evidence, in particular *Graenlendinga Saga* and *Eirikssaga Rauða*.[10] These in turn became utilized as evidence of national claims by Norway and Denmark, and continue as accepted links to history. The most famous example of this is the farm sites associated with Qassiarsuk on the Eirikssfjord that may or may not be the site of Brattahlíð – the farm of Eirik the Red.[11] Another is the New World site at L'Anse aux Meadows, Newfoundland, which is potentially the site of Leifsbuðr, the initial camp of Leifr Eiriksson.[12] Written evidence concerning Zone 3 is contained in written texts from Zone 2 and Zone 1. As a result, there is no direct written material aside from isolated finds and thus no direct voice from internal to this population. Ecclesiastical material is contained within the *Diplomaticum Islandicae*.[13] Fig 59 illustrates textual sources by type.

Fig 58. The Inland Ice of Greenland, as viewed from an airplane.

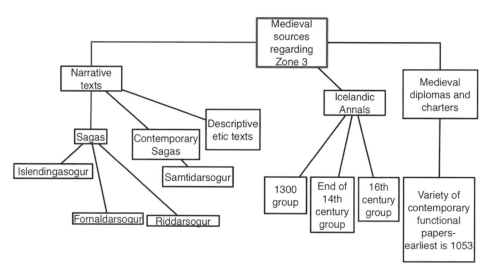

Fig 59. Zone 3 textual sources by type.

Site access in Zone 3 can be incredibly remote hence increasing the cost of excavations themselves without consideration of the logistics of publication.[14] Due to this archaeological survey dominates the available evidence.[15] In spite of these limitations, some excavation of new sites and re-excavation of older excavated sites such as at Qassiarsuk has occurred with the assistance of international research groups such as NABO in recent decades. The sites themselves utilize turf construction, which is likely to deteriorate and become overgrown by dwarf Arctic willow that prefer the richer anthropogenically derived soil deposits. Arctic fox, hare, polar bear or even the action of ice weathering may disturb sites.

A final set of biases is concerned with the divorce of consideration concerning Norse and Indigenous population migration. This has resulted in the native voice of modern Zone 3 inhabitants being largely unacknowledged, thus continuing practices begun during the height of racial hierarchy utilization during the nineteenth and early twentieth century. Views promoted in Mathiasson's 1927 works in association with the Danish Fifth Thule Expedition became unquestioningly accepted during the mid-twentieth century and have continued with some researchers in the region to this day when questioned at conferences. Unfortunately, the traditional divide of exotic indigenous prehistory and familiar European history does not accommodate the spectrum of cultural and environmental evidence.

Eastern Settlement

In general, there is a divorce of known names from active memory in the North Atlantic and Scandinavia due to the abandonment of the region during the late medieval period. Due to this, the association of physical sites to medieval literary reference dominated research and publication well into the twentieth century.[16] Sometimes these efforts have been successful – the best example being the medieval tithing barns associated with the literary descriptions of Garðr.[17] The modern village of Igaliku has since developed in and round this site and indeed is partially constructed from it. Some sites have been influential to research but the modern association of place name and site have been contested such as Brattahlíð/ Qassiarsuk.[18]

Eastern Settlement sites occur in the interior fjords of Greenland where they are protected from the variable maritime weather patterns of the North Atlantic. In general, climatic conditions during the initial *landnám* period were quite good. Although agriculture on a large scale was unable to support the incoming Norse populations and associated domesticates, managed natural areas did contribute to the maintenance of the economic system.[19] Unlike Zones 1 and 2 there are no surviving law codes for Greenland due to the Norse population not having established a settlement that survived into the modern era – or at least to a historical period. There is a growing belief as yet to be confirmed by excavation that assembly sites where laws were negotiated in the public sphere.[20]

The Eastern Settlement of Greenland contains the full range of North Atlantic building types. There has been some reconsideration over recent

Fig 60. Narsarsuaq house site overgrown with dwarf Arctic willow.

years concerning building typology and name designations.[21] This shows a progression of skali-style longhouses at the onset of settlement to row houses to conglomerate houses. This process is comparable to that found on urban Norwegian sites such as Trondheim and Bergen.[22] This was largely unrecognized until recently, however because earlier excavators had continued to hold firmly to the idea that the skali-style longhouse was the main human habitation for medieval Norse sites. The major problem – and one which occurs over much of Greenland – is that archaeological excavations are less common than archaeological survey.[23] Hence, much of the discussion is based largely on the mapping of surface features rather than commenting on the entire stratigraphic sequence throughout the site. Soil sampling features prominently.[24] This is a much more cost effective means of getting basic information about more sites in the area.[25] As with Zone 1 and Zone 2 there are a small collection of early excavations such as at Herjolfsnes and Igaliku where work was funded by national bodies in Denmark and Greenland[26]. These sites came to influence the study of medieval Scandinavian/European identities like few others in the North Atlantic due to the surprising location and the incredible preservation the permafrost of Greenland had provided.

Relatively few modern excavations have been conducted in the Eastern Settlement. Vatnahverfi and Hvalsey are two of these. The vast majority of sites have only been surface surveyed to determine location. Several of the early excavations, however, have had just as much impact as Stöng of Zone 2. This includes the Episcopal farm complex at Igaliku, the farms of Qassiarsuk and the southern-most farm at Ikigiat. These are closely affiliated with Zone 3 textual sources. The early excavations of the twentieth century were excavated by the same group of Scandinavian excavators who worked in Þjórsádalur in Zone 2 – Bruun, Norlund and the architect Roussell amongst others. They uncovered some of the best preserved aspects of the Norse North Atlantic. However, these sites are consistently large enough that it is hard to comment upon the microscale elements of a normal farm. These sites were specifically chosen

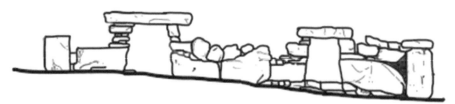

Fig 61. Igaliku tithe barn front, after Roussell.[27]

because the initial survey hinted at stone buildings and a greater potential for diverse material assemblages. In more recent years these sites are being subjected to modern survey with only a small amount being excavated, at times only soil sampling.[28] This is allowing a much more nuanced view of microscale and macroscale landscape utilization to be made. This is closely linked to the fact that the more recent survey work has been conducted by researchers who are more aware of what details can be derived by the natural environment and microscale response to it.[29] Efforts to properly sequence and date these older excavations also occur during more recent survey. It is possible to see a local economy based upon domestic animals housed in a system of saeters extending from coastal farms into the more mountainous interior. Several saeter types have been designated and described by Albrethsen and Keller.[30] Wild animals were exploited when available, however, spaces that were more likely to be frequented by desired species were noted and utilized. The common hunting fields of Norðsetr are located far to the north of the Eastern Settlement however a collection of walrus mandibles are known from Igaliku. Other wild species, particularly seasonal migratory birds, have also been found at Vatnahverfi.[31] Closer to the main farm unit were located dairy saeter to accommodate the need for fresh dairy.[32] The home fields of the farm provided a nearby source of winter fodder and were maintained by providing irrigation and fertilization when needed.[33] Outbuildings provided sheltered location for activities such as textile production and storage. These were built largely of turf with driftwood providing the timber for roof construction.

The Eastern Settlement farms excavated to date are also affiliated with ecclesiastical settings. The presence of these macroscale drivers that are exotic to this Zonal system effected site utilization by adding a public element that was potentially otherwise seasonal – assembly.[34] The presence of a church on a particularly productive location such as Igaliku was a macroscale power statement for both local power magnate and the church. This area was prosperous enough to support medieval conventions to the point where a European international power – the Church – was attempting to lay claim to both souls and the rich land they worked. At the microscale Igaliku is a well appointed farm – one powerful enough to control an Episcopal tithe barn. This implies it was at the top of an extended network of regional affiliation as the lands of Greenland are too marginal to produce the number of animals Igaliku would have been able to house. Smaller farms in the area appear from survey to be saeters for the larger Igaliku farm.

The interior region of Vatnahverfi provides greater detail on a local network composed of several farms representing the microscale. There is a church

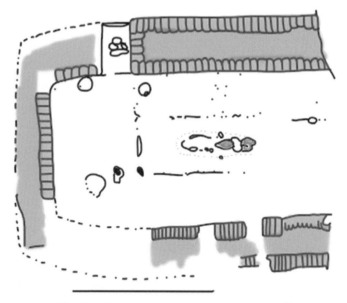

Fig 62. The Farm Under the Sand longhouse.[35]

affiliated with this effort as well with a medieval cemetery affiliated with it.[36] This network appears in survey to be similar to other north Atlantic regional networks such as the Brough of Birsay in Zone 1 or Mývatnssveit and Þjórsádalur in Zone 2. Unfortunately until the re-excavation of the region is complete little more can be said aside from survey has highlighted several series of buildings with affiliated outbuildings. Soil sampling during recent excavation efforts has highlighted the presence of middens in association implying long-term settlement in the area.

Some of the best-preserved evidence of medieval Norse material culture comes from the Eastern Settlement of Zone 3. This is due to the presence of permafrost in Greenland that allowed organic goods such as textiles to survive.[37] This allows a more complete picture to be presented on elements missing from microscale considerations. The organic material variety has been preserved at some of these sites. Wooden objects ranging from carved trenchers, to scoops and dishes, were discovered most often during the larger excavations of the twentieth century.[38] Iron goods were acknowledged at the time as being relatively low in number but ranged from small knives to a small spearhead to a small axe-head. Pottery finds were low and largely from identifiable Continental imports. Steatite finds, however, were relatively common. Items ranged from cooking vessels, to lamps, spindle whorls and loom weights. The forms of these are quite similar to those known from other north Atlantic Zones and indeed steatite exportation appears to have contributed to the general economy of Zone 3. At this time the full extent of this macroscale economic network, particularly the microscale elements of production such as quarries and ship's cargo is unknown due to the lack of material and known location. However, Greenlandic soapstone was associated with the medieval construction of Trondheim Cathedral until the seventeenth century.[39]

Microsediment analysis has proven the presence of multiple insect species of European origin. Several are linked to the keeping of sheep for wool production.[40] Spectacular examples of liturgical equipment have been removed from the Norse burials of Igaliku. Burials have produced the other best-known artefact type from Zone 3 as well – clothing constructed from the famous vaðmal. This was the end product of a microscale economic process for many of the Zone 3 farms evidenced by loom weights, saeters and textual reference within contemporary records.[41] The best known is the collection assembled from the early excavation of the medieval cemetery at Ikigiat. From this collection maintenance of European fashions can be directly seen in the pattern the garments were cut. The garments of a small population were uncovered, which allows certain comments to be made regarding the orientation of daily tasks. Male clothes were designed to provide warmth for active bodies – bodies requiring extended amounts of movement. This is affiliated with the need for work outside of the farmhouse and outbuildings, at both terrestrial and marine activities. Female clothes, on the other hand, were designed to provide terrestrial warmth while performing tasks that required less bodily movement. These clothes are tied to microscale tasks internal to the farmhouse and yard.

North America

There are small selections of surviving Norse place names which are associated with Norse activities in the New World. These have been studied intensively since the 1850s. *Helluland* [Flat-Rock Land] being modern Baffin Island while *Markland* [Forest Land] was the name given to the extensive forests along Canada's eastern coast.[42] Others are much more debated in no small part to a clever hoax whose exposure created a jaded attitude amongst the research community and wider public alike concerning Norse North American material – the infamous Vinland Map.[43] Of these other sites, the two most influential upon archaeological evidence are *Vínland* [Vine/Wine land] and *Leifsbuðr* [Leif's booths {camp}].[44] These are central to two of the major textual sources for medieval Norse in the New World – *Graenlendinga Saga* and *Eirikssaga Rauða*.[45]

Norse North American sites and texts are distinct from other Zonal evidence in that there is evidence for both indigenous inhabitants in the New World, who were not of European origin, and Norse contact with them.[46] This was a driving vector unique to Zone 3, particularly after Thule Inuit began to arrive in the Davis Strait region circa AD 1100–1200.[47] This is incredibly important as the culture contact evidence can be utilized as another anthropological means of commenting on identity construction and maintenance as illustrated by Silliman at La Purisma, Kirch and Sahlins at Anahulu and Lightfoot and Martinez at Fort Ross.[48] Unfortunately, it is unknown what law applied to the New World sites, if any. This is linked to the external nature of the textual evidence. It may be that family law and blood feud ruled due to the apparent dispersed nature of the sites as is hinted in the textual sources.[49] Due to this, it is difficult to comment upon certain aspects of site utilization and orientation that is achieved in both Zone 1 and Zone 2. Like Greenland, this has led to the law codes of these earlier established regions being linked to the region in publication merely on the fact that physically the sites are recognized a being established by medieval Norse.

New World evidence for Norse archaeological sites has recently expanded. Historically evidence from this region has been much contested due to the

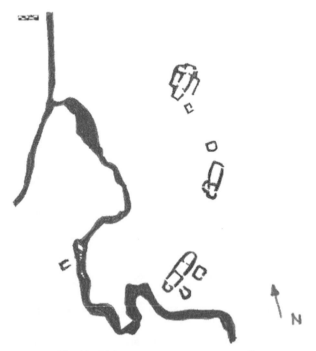

Fig 63. L'Anse aux Meadows site map.[50]

difficulties of corroborating place names from medieval sources and the physical reality of the rugged Canadian coast. There is another huge problem with as well – the indigenous Dorset peoples also utilized a form of longhouse that can be mistaken for Norse concurrent to the Norse presence.[51] However, when these sites were excavated by Maxwell during the 1960–70s they were designated as Late Phase Dorset.[52] Due to this excavation, techniques, theories and conclusions are all reflective of a Pre-Contact – and hence prehistoric – indigenous site rather than leaving room for interpretation. This has been highlighted by the recent confirmation by re-excavation and re-analysis of a further 4 sites which contain strata affiliated with both cultures.[53] However, even these are contested at the time of writing as the professional lives of the site directors over shadow the strength of the evidence, which is mysteriously poorly published.

New World settlement sites follow a pattern that appears to be closely linked to water-borne communication. The classic example for this is L'Anse aux Meadows [LAM] the Norse site up until recently to be the only medieval outpost on Newfoundland prior to the Frobisher expeditions of the sixteenth century. Since the re-analysis of Tanefield, Nunguvik, Willows Island and the Avayalik Islands aspects of LAM can be considered within a wider context with more reliability than previously possible.[54] This was a conscious decision as even more so than Greenland the regions explored to maintain a means of quick and economic retreat back east into the European Atlantic long distance networks of trade and exchange.

Once again, there is evidence for self-sufficiency of the site. Adjacent to the site is a source of flowing fresh water.[55] This helped to drain the rest of the site. Thick grasses with substantial root mats provided insulative turf for construction were located in nearby or even adjacent meadows. Unfortunately, for the state of clarity concerning Norse and Native archaeological sequences in eastern Canada Late Phase Dorset also utilize these to make seasonal use of nearby littoral areas for food collection.[56] At LAM and at Tanefield excavations exposed constructions of turf blocks laid on shaped stone foundations with long walls more than 12 m.[57] Previously, Dorset sites averaged buildings much smaller with both sub-rectangular and sub-circular formats.[58] Re-excavation of Tanefield showed provisions for drainage and a recognizable latrine – both architectural inclusions unknown from indigenous arctic and sub-arctic sites.[59]

Space utilization on New World sites other than LAM is very difficult to discuss currently, as although Tanefield, Nunguvik, Willows Island and the Avayalik Islands sites have been re-excavated and analyzed they have not yet been fully published at the time of this writing. LAM is illustrated in Fig 63.

As can be seen there is a fresh water source through the site. An outbuilding for iron extraction using a forge lined in kaolinite clay was constructed to the north beyond the water source – perhaps even the original outfield for a site which seems to have had no need for one.[60] This building may have been located closer to sources of bog iron that had collected around root nodules of marshy plants.[61] There are larger constructions with the infield with long sides and internal walls that were substantially constructed of turf blocks.[62] Entrances to these buildings are located to the east and south in order to maximize upon available natural sunlight and heat.[63] There are two exceptions to this, Hall A and Hall B, which open upon Epaves Bay and Black Duck Brook.[64] Each of these larger constructions has affiliated outbuildings. These larger buildings have well defined walls that directed the overall flow of rooms.[65] The excavation of LAM expanded beyond the walls of the structures to consider the wider landing area of the site, including across the water feature of Black Duck Brook. Due to this and much more rigorous excavation practices over the course of the site applied by the Ingestads and Wallace, usage of the site as a unit can be discussed. Excavators suggest three foci of human effort – one for each of the hall buildings, but notably no provisions for animal accommodation and maintenance within the landscape.[66] There are large concentrations of iron slag and rivets, and even more of worked wood.[67] These are concentrations known from other sites in Zone 1 and Zone 2 where boats and ships underwent servicing and repairs. The biggest concentration of clipped rivets and boat nails occurred in Hall F.[68]

Unlike Zone 1 and 2 sites, LAM in particular has a lack of accumulated evidence signifying long-term occupation – middens are small and no cemetery is known.[69] In general, the evidence of cultural deposits is quite slight. There is evidence for both male and female work areas on site. Although halls and outbuildings exist, other aspects of Zone 3 farms are not present, such as field delineations, *saeters* and byre. In short, instead of a terrestrially oriented farm there is a marine oriented terrestrial base that enabled exploration and potentially exploitation of the local area by water.[70] The open location on a small peninsula made a visible statement in the landscape. For those travelling over land a boundary separating the non-affiliated lands from the Norse site existed in Black Duck Brook. For a short time, at least LAM appears to be the Norse outpost of the New World serving as a base of Norse maritime functionality and identity via practice. LAM later was definitively abandoned and two halls subsequently set on fire.[71] In this case, it is possible to say that the burning fully ended the Norse phase of the site.

Material culture has been heavily relied upon by Zone 3 researchers to determine excavated Norse assemblages from indigenous peoples both prior and subsequent to the medieval period. Unfortunately, New World sites only give a limited sample of what is affiliated with others in the North Atlantic. This is largely due to two things: 1) very low number of excavations published and 2) sites which were closed, rather than a disaster occurring or continuance of site habitation. Zone 3 artefact decisions are illustrated in Fig 63.

Once again, LAM provides the best-detailed published evidence for the New World. Famously a Hiberno–Norse hexagonal pin was discovered on site.[72] This is the only item of personal adornment known from the time currently at this location. Other famous finds include butternut shells which were exotic to the site and the buildings themselves.[73] Discussed less often are the scatters of iron rivets, clipped rovings and wood scrap found between the long house structures themselves.[74] The presence of the rivets and rovings has been linked to terrestrial based ship maintenance.[75] This would have been incredibly important as for a short time at least the vessels that carried the settlers and maintained the North Atlantic networks were serviced from the western periphery. This required a source of iron – either local or brought in – and subsequently shaped on site. LAM was placed near a local source of bog iron, which was collected and processed in the outbuildings across Black Duck Brook.[76] It is suspected that an unknown amount of iron robbing has taken place on Norse and indigenous sites alike which effects the amount of iron within Canadian assemblages dated to this period.[77] This took place in the form of iron recycling by Norse populations when tools and iron fastenings wore out but also robbing by subsequent site occupants. There is little evidence for the accumulation of midden material implying that at LAM at least medieval European occupation was actually quite short.[78] Soapstone vessels were discovered within the turf tumble.

Turf shovels were used to help cut the turf blocks used in construction. There are other types of material evidence that provides insight into life in the Norse New World but also have been recently used to help acknowledge a further four sites on Baffin Island from a selection of sites previously assumed to be solely Late Phase Dorset which had exotic anomalies. The first of these is the presence of twisted arctic hare fibres – evidence of at least indirect contact with Europeans as neither the Dorset who were present upon Norse arrival nor the Thule Inuit how arrived subsequently utilized animal fibre textiles during this time.[79] Re-excavation of Tanefield/Nanook in particular was linked to realization of this fact and what it might imply. Whetstones from these sites – some thirty from Tanefield alone – as well as from LAM are comparable to whetstones throughout the Norse North Atlantic.[80] Unfortunately, in shape they are also similar to those utilized by both Dorset and Thule Inuit that contributed to the attribution of Tanefield, Avayalik, Nunguvik and Willows Island as being solely indigenous.[81] These whetstones bore wear grooves from sharpening metal blades. They were subjected to energy dispersive spectroscopy and it was discovered that copper alloys unknown to the North American arctic were present.[82] This corroborated the arctic hare fibre yarn evidence. Re-excavation of the newly acknowledged sites also has wood above the arctic tree line.[83] These have only been described as being potential tally sticks or perhaps spindles used in fibre processing. Also found was wood scrap with iron staining around square holes. This was radiocarbon dated to the fourteenth century, although at this time only the results from this.

Biological evidence of lifestyle is remarkably detailed in the New World primarily for two reasons. The first is that the excavations are reasonably modern and have been subjected to more rigorous modern archaeological procedure.[84] The second is the conditions of preservation are remarkably good due to consistently cool, moist conditions.[85] Due to this sediment samples recently analyzed from Tanefield contained evidence for pelt remains of rat species originating in the Old World. A latrine was also discovered.[86]

Perhaps what is the most diagnostic form of evidence for medieval Norse, however, is what is not present on New World Norse sites: skeletal evidence for domesticated animal exploitation such as known from other Zones of the North Atlantic.[87] What is found instead is a greater reliance on local wild species for exploitation. This includes terrestrial, marine and littoral species.[88] Other forms of subsistence such as ships provisions may have also contributed to the diet of Norse settlers, however, left little evidence within archaeological assemblages due to their organic nature.

The Farm Under the Sand

Given the very low number of full modern site excavations the well known modern excavation near Nipiatsoq in Norse Greenland's Western Settlement has been included to provide comparative evidence to the Zone 3 case study sample. This site, first located in 1990, was given the name of Gård Under Sandet [GUS] due to the conditions of excavation which was heavily impacted by glacial runoff from the nearby Inland Ice.[89] Rescue excavation efforts of an international group of specialists by the Greenland National Museum and Archive located in nearby Nuuk worked to salvage the turf and earth construction from the permafrost.[90]

Due to the rescue nature of the excavation, GUS was fully excavated.[91] This showed the presence of a partial longhouse and large farm complex that was actively being affected by erosion.[92] A three-aisled longhouse that was occupied over the course of eight phases had internal dimensions of 12 x 5 m.[93] The eastern long wall of the house was quite thick at 1.8 m.[94] This is illustrated in Fig 62. Conditions of preservation were so good under the meter of frozen river sands that the process of laying out the hall with sticks into the well-drained soil of the region.[95] Walls were then constructed of turf blocks while the turf was stripped from the interior. A paved entrance brought the inhabitants into an entrance area that protected the dwelling room with central hearth from direct drafts. Here there was also evidence of a small cooking pit as well as a storage vessel.[96] The hall also contained a room for work activities and storage.[97] Floors were prepared using insulative peat, wood chip and twigs.[98] This created a layer between daily microscale use of the house and the permafrost associated with the Western Settlement's sub-arctic location.[99]

The rescue efforts of the 1990s at GUS uncovered a small Norse farm with approximately thirty rooms under threat.[100] The first phase of utilization established a three-aisled longhouse with living area, storage and a protected entryway.[101] Blocks were laid out in a format designated by sticks inserted into the ground before hand.[102] Within the center aisle was a long hearth that would later degrade into multiple hearths in a line prior to the secondary function of the longhouse began.[103] The internal walls of this initial phase of human utilization were constructed from thinner pieces of wood however; the external load bearing walls were thickly constructed from local turf.[104] Although the interior walls are not completely marked it is possible to see the accommodations made into the turf walls to fit them. GUS proved to be an excellent site to sample for palaeoecological and paleoentomological analysis and the results from this work has highlighted some of daily practices undertaken by the original inhabitants and the local environment they undertaken in.[105] There are very few Norse excavations in Greenland that actually conducted environmental sampling in conjunction with the archaeological excavation itself. GUS is one of these.[106] Areas that were kept warmer such as the dwelling room allowed colonies of houseflies to be maintained.[107] Human lice were found in areas where people seem to have slept, or at least spent a lot of time de-lousing. Sheep lice and keds were found in areas where wool was stored and animals were kept respectively.[108]

The early phases of the farm site had affiliated outbuildings that helped to contribute to the total number of rooms discovered. Within one of these was discovered evidence for textile creation – a vertical loom known from other North Atlantic Zones.[109] A small corner hearth was included in the turf building to provide warmth for the weaver. Small scraps of textiles were found throughout the site due to the waterlogged and permafrost conditions.[110]

Later phases of the longhouse occupation highlight a shift of human habitation away from the longhouse. The entranceway and barrel storage was removed and animals were housed in the longhouse.[111] The house was abandoned subsequent to the thirteenth century.[112] Feral sheep and goats used the derelict buildings as shelter until their final collapse.[113] Later Thule Inuit hunters would use the area to camp and their fires caused part of the constructions to burn.[114]

Evidence for microscale identity practice from the initial period of human occupation largely comes from the protective floor layer. These were largely items lost at the sides of the hall.[115] Carved wooden bowls and trenchers made from imported wood rather than driftwood were perfectly preserved by the permafrost and glacial sands.[116] Textile remains of homespun cloth highlight the presence of a local wool economy.[117] This is also evidenced by a wooden vertical loom that had been part of the initial site discovery.[118] This was housed in one of the few rooms to be assigned a function. Other finds included horn spoons, wooden devotional crosses and even a shoe last.[119] Rooms with barrel holes once provided storage for the farm. Those with small corner hearths, such as the textile room, provided sheltered places to undertake crafts.[120] To this extent, GUS has produced a variety of tools for working in soapstone, wood, iron, bone and horn.

The farm was later abandoned by the medieval Norse although there is evidence for continued use of the centralized farm complex by feral sheep until the collapse of the turf walls.[121]

Discussion

Until recently, the tale of the medieval Norse in North America is one that was hinted at in literature in typical medieval form and one attached to more extreme political views. There are associated hoaxes such as the Kensington Rune Stone and the Vinland Map.[122] Increasingly at the base of this is a growing corpus of recognized Norse archaeological characteristics. There is a single fully recognized and reliably published site – L'Anse aux Meadows, Newfoundland, which is sometimes associated with Leifsbuðr of the sagas.[123] In October of 2012, however, it was publicized to the archaeological community that a further four sites on Baffin Island previously considered to be Late Dorset contained within them layers of Norse occupation.[124] The newly recognized sites, such as Tanefield, are within sheltered valleys with fresh water, nearby being coastal access. There are longhouse layers with affiliated Norse materials and longhouses with solely indigenous Dorset material.[125]

The sites of Greenland and the Canadian eastern coast have been closely affiliated in texts since the medieval period. This is corroborated by archaeological evidence from both sides of the Davis Strait. Many of these similarities are due to shared physical characteristics. Although marginal in terms of crop-based agriculture parts of Zone 3 had abundant natural resources available for exploitation that were less dependent upon short growing seasons. As with previous case studies evidence quality for Zone 3 has been rated in accordance to overall quality. This quality rating has been taken into consideration in the following analysis of microscale aspects of identity construction and maintenance in Zone 3. Intercontinental cultural contact occurred in Zone 3: initially between incoming Norse populations and indigenous Dorset but later on between Norse and incoming Thule populations from Alaska.[126]

House and Settlement

As with other North Atlantic Zones, the early excavations of the late nineteenth and early twentieth century have heavily influenced the views of subsequent excavators and the public. There are several aspects to this that have been particularly influential as Zone 3 does not have the number of full excavations that other Zones of the North Atlantic. The first is an early focus on building interiors in Greenland. This means that the recognizable human habitations were considered without benefit of their wider farm context. The second was designation of ruin groups as being longhouse types when in fact the actual floor plans reflect other building types. In Zone 3 this has resulted in reanalysis in recent years of not only the Greenlandic building evidence but also reanalysis of indigenous Dorset longhouses on New World sites.[127] In Table I a summary of the house styles and characteristics found in Zone 3 are presented.

House Type	Description	Dimensions	Date	Examples
Skali longhouse	Early examples have curved long walls, later have straight long walls, central hearth, benches, potentially end room portioned with light wall	12 x 5 m internally	10–11th century	Ø17a Narsaq early phase, Ø29 Qassiarsuk, V51 GUS earliest phase
Row-house	Row of rooms with substantial interior walls that has one room or more located to the back	c. 23 m long	12–13th century (onset is unclear)	Ø20, Ø47, Ø71, Ø17 Narsaq last phase, V51 last phase
Conglomerate house	House with rooms that has one room or more connected by passages	c. 20 m	Late 12th-14th century (onset is unclear)	Ø2, Ø29 ruin 18, Ø83, Ø52a, Ø16, V53c and d

Fig 64. House styles and characteristics in Zone 3.

Zone 3 is the most marginal of the North Atlantic settlement regions due to latitude and location. As a result, the combination of agriculture, animal husbandry and wild resource exploitation that was developed in Northern Europe is adapted to accommodate.[128] This is reflected in the format which settlement farms take in Zone 3.

This generalized farm unit strategy was utilized to translate incoming European cultural practices to the new environments of Zone 3. Microscale elements are expressed in these strategies visible within the current corpus of excavated sites. This includes the choices in building material made from available resources during initial construction, to those made to maintain the farm system physically within the landscape.[129]

Identity was initially expressed in Zone 3 in the accommodations settling populations made in terms of co-existence with indigenous populations, reduction of timber availability and those affiliated with climatic conditions. Zone 3 was inhabited prior to Norse arrival by descendents of the Maritime Archaic Tool Tradition – the Dorset. Although southern Greenland appears to have been abandoned by the Dorset prior to the Norse arrival the episode of discovery described in *GS* and *ESR* may allude to an initial sighting in the New World.[130] As the Dorset exploited the more exposed coastal portions of fjords and Norse preference for settlement areas was for the more sheltered interior areas actual competition and site reutilization expressed by Norse populations is low in Greenland. It is unknown whether this will hold true for Canadian sub-Arctic and Arctic sites at this time.

Changes over time to the styles of human habitations can be linked to wider North Atlantic trends.[131] The early *skali* longhouse gains distinct rooms, losing the centralized hearth and aisle while gaining greater heating efficiency and floor space. This became more similar to the row-houses of urban Norwegian towns.[132] These maintained the presence of straight long walls found in the later *skali* sites but added room divisions in the interior that were made from thick walls of earth and turf. This resulted in a drastic change in how the roofs of turf constructions were supported. Previously a system of crossbeams and a floor mounted parallel posts which lent *skali* the familiar tri-aisled format was utilized – this is what is known from the earliest phases of Zones 1 and 2. This required a certain amount of timber of a usable size. By converting to a row-house format, the need for longer timber was reduced. The internal turf walls were able to carry the weight of the roof without the internal aisle because timbers of shorter lengths could be utilized. Roof timbers were supplied both by driftwood and by short voyages across the Davis Strait to the rich old growth forests of the eastern Canadian coast.[133]

Another way identity was expressed environmental pressures on choices made is by heavy reliance upon wild resources to make up for the calories, protein and prestige normally derived from agriculture. This is well evidenced on recent excavations that employ modern bioarchaeological sampling and processing techniques such as at V51 the Farm under Sand. This required a more nuanced utilization of wild species by season.

Family and Gender Relations

Evidence for family and gender relations in Zone 3 is actually fairly slim. This is due to several factors which have resulted in several biases for this evidence. Although early excavations of settlement sites focused largely on the internal features of assumed longhouses many details were lost via a lack of sieving and other practical elements of archaeological practice during the late nineteenth and early twentieth century. As a result modern excavations have subsequently focused heavily on the environment present within the structure and commented upon features present more in passing. In spite of this full excavations such as at V51 and at L'Anse aux Meadows have provided a small amount of insight into microscale elements of family and gender relations in Zone 3. Another factor heavily influencing this evidence is linked to the divorce between the Greenlandic past and the later North Atlantic populations. Because Zone 3 did not establish a population which continued into the modern period medieval textual sources that concern the Zone have not been internally maintained. This is important as such practical elements of cohabitation provide valuable information on family and gender relations. In the case of Zone 3 textual sources, with the exception of short runic texts and legal papers, which were originally made in multiple copies, are all actually Zone 2 in origin and maintenance. This presents a serious problem in terms of analysis of evidence for family and gender relations as the physical evidence is restricted to only a few sites. In fact, without use of textual sources from Zone 2 it is difficult to comment which members of a farm unit are accomplishing tasks. It is easier to comment upon mariners who were primarily male. Not only does this reflect the wider European tradition but it also evidenced in the masculine verb tenses utilized in provisions in law codes from Norway and Iceland.

Social Rank and Status

Evidence for social status and rank at the local microscale of Zone 3 has been based on three areas. The first is the overall quality of the archaeological material. This is closely tied to the practical requirements of Norse settlements that both fulfills needs with the environment and culture and create more needs of their own. The location of home farms in relation to their affiliated outbuildings and resource exploitation areas contain commonalities. Some of these are linked to location in the wider landscape – mountain farms sacrifice ease of travel and communication to make greater use of secluded *saeter* sites. Commonalities throughout Zone 3 include utilization of a variety of resources and land management strategies to maintain themselves as a social unit in the more marginal farm while those of higher rank would have access to the more favorable conditions or at least more sites in general – both quantity and quality of site being desired. This would allow for greater self-sufficiency and quicker accumulation of capital in the form of secondary animal products.

A high status farm in Zone 3 during the *landnám* phase was located on the well drained sloped of inner fjords where they were protected to a degree from the full effects of the North Atlantic.[134] They were set back from shore in Greenland – perhaps an adaptation to accommodate the development of pack ice during the winter. Early on humans were housed in *skali* longhouses that internally were 12–15 m long and around 5 m wide such as at Ø17a in modern Narsaq, Ø29 at Qassiarsuk, the early phases of V51, at L'Anse aux Meadows and at Tanefield.[135] This style was utilized during the tenth and eleventh centuries. During the twelfth and thirteenth centuries row-house buildings are found on some sites. Concurrent to this on other sites conglomerate style buildings are found. This tradition was utilized until the complete collapse of the medieval European Zone 3 settlements.[136] Farmhouses were accompanied by outbuildings that served as storage and as locations for specialized activities such as iron-working.[137] Domesticated animals were housed both separate from humans over winter and within human habitation. If they were not housed with humans over winter, they were housed within an outbuilding. The presence of domesticated animals necessitated the establishment of outfields distinct in the landscape to provide some fodder for the stock during the year. These fields were well managed – evidence for irrigation has occurred at sites such as Garðr.[138] Another form of evidence is the palynological record as managed fields such as at Vatnahverfi have elevated levels of meadow grasses during the period of Norse occupation.[139] Similar levels were associated with all areas managed as grass-hay fields for fodder.

High status farms had access to landing places early on, however, once deeper drafted ships became adopted control over a harbor was another element of a high status site. This allowed high status sites to more directly control trade and exchange with the wider North Atlantic network. Away from the farm sites further managed domesticate stock in areas which were provisioned with water, meadow areas and turf outbuildings.[140] Other areas that were accessed by Norse for wild resource exploitation may have been commonly shared. A good example of this is driftwood exploitation. It is difficult to comment on the general progression of buildings in Zone 3 due to the low number of full modern excavations in relation to a high number of surveyed sites. This is a topic that has been recently approached by Hoegsberg who highlighted the fact that Roussell's designations may have been false.[141]

High status sites can also be signaled by the presence of public accommodations. Potential assembly sites have been suggested for the well-known sites of Igaliku and Qassiarsuk.[142] Another microscale on-site accommodation for the wider public also includes churches.[143] The inclusion of these local ties to a macroscale vector were another way for higher status farm units to exert power over the local system by providing religious service.[144] This requires the upkeep of a priest. Only the very largest sites might have had the capital to support a full-time priest, or even multiple such as at the Episcopal seat of Garðr at modern Igaliku.[145] Although it is a process which appears to have occurred within a Christian population this is a microscale element of religious provision which is also implied at pagan sites in Zones 1 and 2.[146]

Another way to determine a high status site is by literary affiliation where sites have been described and only rarely named. Two of the major sources that discuss Zone 3 discovery and settlement – *GS* and *ESR* – mention sites such as Garðr and Herjolfsnes. These sources are also affiliated with an extended kin group that later returned to the Borgarfjord region of northwestern Iceland who were attempting to manufacture a creation myth explaining their social/economic control over Zone 3 and the western extension to the North Atlantic network.[147] Whether this was the actual reality of the situation is unknown as the extent sources are related to one another in terms of content.[148] Unlike Zones 1 and 2 high status site affiliation with public space appears to be linked only with church sites in Greenland, some of which also have affiliated assembly sites, and potentially not at all in the New World in the European sense.[149]

Lower status farms are difficult to determine from the extent corpus of Zone 3 excavations. However, in general lower status farms can be assumed to have less of the available resources and space which high status sites might have control over. They may have commonly shared some of the wild resource exploitation areas of even *saeter* areas in an effort to pool economic and social capital.[150] It may have also alleviated some of the demand for human working hours that a farm network might generate. This demand is also linked to microscale farm social hierarchy. Farms in Zone 3 were associated with extended family units and auxiliary farm members as demonstrated in *GS*, *ESR* and *Íslendingabók*. Unlike Zone 1 and Zone 2, slaves for the most part do not appear as a regular

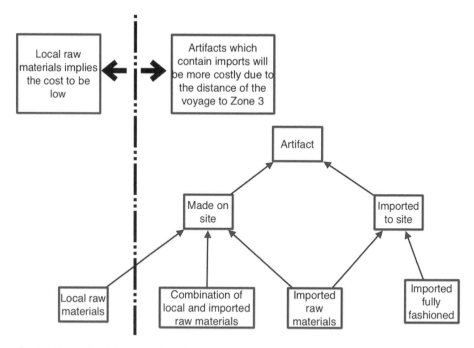

Fig 65. Zone 3 artefact decision diagram.

part of archaeological assemblages and literary sources.[151] An exception to this may be the Southerner Tyrkir who accompanies Leif Eiriksson. Within *ESR* he is referred ambiguously as either a long term servant or slave.[152] This lack of conclusive evidence for slavery is relative proof it was not a constituent of Zone 3 Norse society.[153] Had law codes and other textual evidence survived for direct transmission to subsequent populations this would be more conclusive. Slavery was not practical in Zone 3 as there was no agriculture to quickly provide bulk stores from which to feed slaves from. Changing the state of evidence in Zone 3 will require full excavations of farm sites. The actions of the lower elements of society are present in the form of physical tasks completed on site.

Orientation
As with Zone 1 and 2 micro-scale evidence for the orientation of identity in Zone 3 expresses seasonally dictated fluctuation between terrestrial and marine loci. A balance between these loci is affected by available light, available technology for resource exploitation, and economic drivers in the form of available markets for exports. The amount of available light was particularly limiting given the high latitude location of Zone 3 as the sun is simply not present in the sky

for months on end. This effect is reduced on the southern sites of Zone 3, producing similar practical activities as evidenced in Zone 2. In spite of this, the warmer period from late April to early September, when the sun makes an appearance, are those which are packed with the greatest amount of outdoor activities. These activities are determined by need for action in combination with driving conditions. Terrestrial activities on coastal sites are chosen when the tide and weather makes littoral and marine activities to be high-risk ventures. Marine activities are most dependent upon favorable weather and tide conditions. When conditions are not favorable, marine activities become high risk and are less likely to be chosen to be accomplished. Littoral activities are the highest risk during high tide although poor weather and light can also influence choice in performance of activities.

Another vector to choice in microscale identity is closely tied into economics. This is a concept this is a concept that is based upon economic fitness of individuals and groups. At the microscale of analysis these are tied into the choices affiliated with local trade and exchange and are assumed to be largely selfish in nature. These vectors also form the local extension of trans-Atlantic networks.

Consideration of gender in Zone 3 is a similar situation to that of Zone 1 due to the heavy influence of Iceland upon the medieval textual sources that contain ethnographic evidence.[154] Also similar to Zone 1 is the heavy influence of early archaeological excavations of Danish longhouses upon the corpus of evidence in the past.[155] Perhaps the greatest change occurs with the levels of farm hierarchy. Greenland was settled immediately prior to the formal Conversion of Iceland that occurred circa AD 1000.[156] This is important for local hierarchical breakdown as there is little evidence for the hierarchies being linked with slavery.[157] Slavery was simply too expensive to maintain throughout the population. It was increasingly socially unacceptable due to the adoption of Christian belief. There is no archaeological evidence from Zone 3 that can solely be attributed to the presence of slaves.[158] An exception to this in terms of textual sources comes from *ESR* – Tyrkir the German and the Hebridean slaves brought on the voyages of Leif and Eirik within Zone 3. This source appears to make use of slaves as a literary trope for later Icelandic generations who fully recognized that slavery was only possible if the owner(s) were wealthy enough to offset their cost of upkeep. Zone 3 appears to utilize hierarchies based upon levels of economic dependence. Daily activities were determined by a negotiation of physical capability and skill, social propriety, subsistence, and social obligation. As the region, furthest west the working population of Zone 3 was proportionately reduced leaving a potential hole in a farm's subsistence strategy. There was a choice available – either call in more labor locally or from other Zones, the tasks needed go unperformed or else those not normally affiliated with such activities become more proficient in them. Due to this it is more difficult to affiliate task and social status.

Conclusion

As with Zone 1 and Zone 2 analysis of Zone 3 case study evidence has shown a dominance of practicality in the microscale elements of identity construction and maintenance present on Norse archaeological excavations. Local construction materials were utilized from Sandnaes to the Farm under Sand in the patterns developed in Europe and Zone 1. The marginal climate of Zone 3 resulted in a need for greater reliance on local wild resources and resources external to the Zone to provide subsistence than attempting true agriculture. Hierarchies based upon levels of indebtedness maintained this local system. These hierarchies also expressed and influenced macroscale elements of identity construction and maintenance.

Chapter 6

Trade and Economics

Introduction

The daily domestic elements of North Atlantic island identities during the medieval period did not exist within a static social environment internally or externally. This chapter considers an important central common vector and driver of identity construction and maintenance externally linked at this time – trade and exchange. It shall first consider the prerequisites for this early trade, moving on to the changes that occurred as early trade networks expanded across the North Atlantic. Finally, the networks are discussed in relation to trade's circumnavigation of the globe – when the Old World met the New and maintained contact for economic reasons. The impact that trade and exchange had on North Atlantic identity must not be underestimated in more marginal periphery where externally imposed vectors of cultural change were reduced in number due to location. Trade provided an influx of new cultural trends such as religion and fashions – contextual stimuli from European markets of the continent[1]. It subconsciously replicated cultural practices via the choice in vessel, crew and cargo constituents. Trade offered an economic productivity. It also blended elements of marine and terrestrial exploitation in the form of goods but also indirect elements such as trading place location and transportation type.[2] The littoral zone was where the marine transportation met terrestrial places and a ship was laid ashore to off load cargo.

North Atlantic trade during the AD 800–1250 period undoubtedly has its basis in the late Iron Age trade networks of north-western Europe, in some cases these networks were even older than that dating back to inter-island networks of the Neolithic.[4] They consist of the North Sea Zone, the Irish Sea Zone and to a lesser extent the Baltic Sea Zone. Prior to the consolidation of socio-political power from chieftainships which were unlinked and maintained via individual prowess and largess into early-medieval monarchies tied into geographic locations and control of economic outlets trade and exchange occurred between locations on familial and affine networks.[5] Much of this is dependent upon the lack of available natural resources of Continental Europe – control over what was available had long ago been established. New sources of materials were increasingly needed

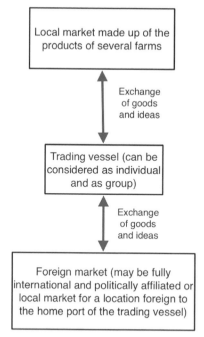

Fig 66. Trade and exchange via merchant intermediaries.[3]

as the population of Europe increased.[6] Nucleated settlements increased in size and diversity, in some instances outstripping the ability of the local hinterland to support the human and animal populations.[7] Island groups located along the maritime trade routes, which existed in the North Sea, Irish Sea and the Baltic, were excellent locations from which integration and exploitation of these trade networks took place.[8] By the ninth century, several island groups within Zone 1 functioned in this capacity including Orkney, Shetland, and the Hebrides and later in the century the Faroe Islands as well.

Context of Early North Atlantic Trade

This system functioned both economically and socially.[9] Economically this allowed local demand for external supply to be met by the exchange of demanded goods for those materials in locally abundant supply – trade and barter. Depending on how well equipped for a trade journey someone was the round trip voyage between localized trading areas such as coastal *wics* would be quite large. Trade over land and water was dependent on transport to carry items in bulk. Transport options for trade during this period are illustrated in Fig 67.

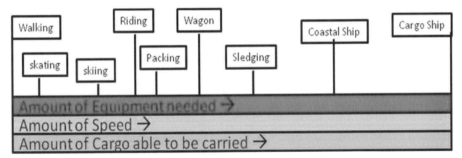

Fig 67. Diagram relating transportation to equipment, speed and cargo capacity.

Water transport was the most relevant form of cargo movement across the North Atlantic. This allows low value bulk trade goods as well as smaller high value luxury goods to be considered viable options for trade within the wider European economic system.[10] The modern versions of these vessels continue to be utilized throughout the North Atlantic. This is described in Fig 68. The most valuable form of open water transport from the initial period of settlement until the fourteenth century was the *knórr*. This vessel is best known archaeologically from Denmark.[11] An example of a *knórr* is illustrated in Fig 7. Like other Norse vessels *knórr* are clinker-built, however, the open water utilization of these vessels is shown via the deeper draft these vessels had in comparison to the glorified *langskip* that certainly was coastally utilized. *Knórr* were primarily driven by sail power as opposed to oars that freed up space for cargo.[12] This is evidenced via the presence of substantial mast fittings on these vessels.

The boat type most heavily associated with both Viking Age Scandinavian trade as well as the North Atlantic colonies was the stoutly built *knórr*.[13] The deeper draft of this vessel type allowed for not only a greater cargo capacity than its more recognized 'cousin' but also the deeper draft allowed the ship to ride the rough waters of open North Atlantic with a higher degree of safety.[14]

An archaeological example of this includes Skuledev 1 – the finely preserved eleventh century large cargo vessel scuttled long ago in defense of a Viking Age settlement on the Roskilde fjord.[15] This vessel was primarily sail-powered, rather than being oar-driven like the vessels used in coastal and river waters, as the overall design of the ship left few areas for rowers.[16] Other evidence for this comes in the form of the 'tree-knee', the engineering feat that allowed the force of the mind to travel from the mast to the body of the ship through the keel. This is a feature not found in clinker-built ships prior to the ninth century[17]. The stouter *knórr* would also have had at least one ship's boat known as a *færing* or four-oared boat. This smaller vessel would have been used to approach those

Method of Transport	Capability	Greatest Profit	Seasonality
Coastal Vessel	Greater cargo amounts with range only limited by shore access and boat, boat is required but crew is minimal	Luxury and bulk goods in combination	Less restricted by seasons due to the protection provided by location
Ocean Vessel	Greatest cargo amounts with range limited only by the stores, boat required but a larger crew needed	Bulk goods with a smaller amount of luxury goods	Spring to mid-autumn
Walking	Low cargo, limited range but with low overhead cost	Luxury goods	No restriction
Riding/ pack animals	More cargo transported with a greater range and speed but upkeep is required for the animal(s)	Luxury goods	No restriction
Wagon	Greater cargo and range at higher speed but requires wagon, animals, roads/ smoother land to roll upon and either peace or protection to travel with	Bulk and luxury goods	Summer
Skiing	Low cargo, greater range and speed, skill and skis required	Luxury goods	Winter
Skating	Low cargo carried at a greater range potentially, requires frozen rivers or waterways and so may have been used in combination with other methods	Luxury goods	Winter
Sledging	Greater amount of cargo carried with greater range at higher speed, requires a sledge or sleigh and at least one animal to pull it, smoother travel conditions provided by snow	Bulk and luxury goods	Winter

Fig 68. Transport descriptions relevant to this period.

parts of the coast which a *knórr*'s deeper draft would prevent a closer advance. When not in use it would have been towed behind the larger vessel or brought up onto the larger knórr deck and stored overturned. This also would provide an element of protection for the goods stowed under the ship's boat.[18]

Norse Vessel	Dimensions	Example		Notes
Ship's boat	7.25 x 2 m	Scar burial vessel	Coastal usage; funerary usage in certain north Atlantic sites	Ship's boats are primarily coastal, short distance vessels used for a variety of jobs that other vessels were too large to do
Small cargo vessels	14 x 3.6 m; 4.5 tons of cargo	Skuludev 3; *c.* 10th–11th century	Quite a versatile ship size which would have been able to carry a substantial cargo while still being able to be easily beached	Smaller trade vessels would have formed at least part of the north Atlantic trade network between the island archipelagos
Large cargo vessels (early)	14.3 x 4.5 m; 24 tons of cargo	Skuludev 1; *c.* 10th–11th century	More efficient than coastal vessels taking less crew to maintain and hence being able carry more cargo	The deeper draft of cargo vessels in general allowed goods to be brought more efficiently and safely across increasingly longer distances
Large cargo vessels (later)	25 x 5.7 m; 45 tons of cargo	Hedeby 3; c. late 11th century	These long distance vessels made the movement of bulk goods and settlement much easier across open oceans	Utilization is reflected by changes in docking practices, movements away from shallow landing beaches and towards deeper harbors; these vessels were later replaced by cogs

Fig 69. Norse vessel types.[19] All of these vessels would have been constructed using the clinker-building techniques.

The deeper draft and overall design of *knórr*-type ships allowed for a greater amount of space to be devoted to cargo drayage with less actual human-power being required to man the rigging.[20] The *knórr* vessel type was quite strongly associated with trade in medieval Scandinavian and Icelandic sources.[21]

Given the size of the vessels in question their utilization with the medieval Scandinavian trading system in the North Atlantic most likely would at both the local regional market economy and the international market economy levels.[22] The local regional market is considered here to have consisted of the trade conducted between those settlements sharing a common coastline. This would have equated to short trading voyages of up to several days.[23] The stouter hull and deeper draft of the *knórr* made it ideal for the more exposed rugged coastlines of the North Atlantic archipelagos just as the more slender and streamlined *langskip* was much better suited to the more sheltered coastline of the Scandinavian fjords.[24] A Norse landing area from the Isles of Lewis illustrates a preferred location of the medieval period, see Fig 70.

Within the wider picture of the international market system, the *knórr* functioned as the workhorse of the North Atlantic. They served to bring the goods of contemporary European life to the western-most reaches of the Norse world, such as fine cloth, raw materials for everyday domestic goods like iron blooms and food items which were otherwise unavailable, such as grain.[25] The *knórr* would have taken luxury goods such as polar bear pelts, sealskins and oil, and, perhaps most famously, walrus ivory.[26] Live animals would also have been included, particularly fine hunting falcons that fetched exorbitant prices in the markets of medieval Europe.[27]

In the contemporary literary sources, mentions of *knórr* vessels are normally found in reference to two topics. Greenland, where the stout sides and deeper draft combined with the flexibility of the clinker-built ships proved an excellent combination in the rough iceberg-laden waters on the western Greenlandic

Fig 70. Norse landing area and medieval pier, Isle of Lewis. Photo taken by Dr R Lenfert.

coasts.[28] The other topics are merchant vessels, which would have been able to afford long voyages through the wide North Atlantic to various ports in the known world. Sometimes the references include aspects of both. It is important to remember that the views on ships express a view both contemporary to its time of translation into written text during the twelfth through thirteenth centuries but also one that expresses the view held in the earlier Viking Age past that was verbally transmitted down through time.[29] The following quote comes from Kapituli 2 of *Graenlendinga Saga*.[30]

> Herjólf farmed first at Drepstokk. Þorgerð was his woman called, and Bjarni their son, who was a very promising man. He had been eager while young to sail abroad; he got himself both wealth and good standing amongst men, and spent his winters alternately in other lands and with his father. Bjarni soon had a ship for himself.

Like many peoples of the late Migration Era through to the Medieval Period, trade and exchange formed a method of wealth accumulation available to much of the population, even those who were lower status. What limits the range of this system's impact into the amount of capital the individual can put into this system. The cargo carrying ability of the *knórr*-type vessels here was utilized for a variety of goods of varying size along their voyages, thus breaking down the voyage into shorter sections as well as maximizing the amount of product turnover.[31] Hence, a greater amount of accumulated personal wealth in the form of material goods and renewed mercantile contacts would have been accumulated. This is the capital necessary to extend influence further into the international long-distance trade networks.

Travel to and beyond the Faroe Islands required a certain size of ship, although the majority of Zone 1 could be served by smaller vessels discussed below. Not only does open water require a deeper draft to ride out the ocean swells but also the longer voyages necessitated room for the supply of the crew amongst the cargo.[32] In light of this, ships such as the *knórr* were designed to require less crew to operate in relation to the amount of cargo volume able to be carried. These vessels required a substantial amount of social and economic capital to construct and maintain, let alone outfit for a trading voyage.[33] Due to this, only a certain economic level of society would have been able to express their identity in this way. Lower status levels simply would not have the economic capital necessary to do this. Construction of vessels were expressions of local microscale just as much as a longhouse on land, but with a distinctive marine orientation and often much more active acknowledgement

Fig 71. Modern rowing vessels from Torshavn, Faroe Islands.

of use in practice. However, as lower status men were able to be employed as crew on these voyages they also not only maintained this bulk exchange system but also were provided the opportunity for trade and exchange themselves on a much smaller scale[34].

In coastal water voyages of short duration, smaller vessels similar to the *faering* in format and construction were utilized. The amount of cargo able to be carried by a smaller vessel would limit the amount of exchange able to be undertaken per voyage. This may have been utilized in conjunction with a local base of operations to more fully integrate the long distance voyages undertaken via *knórr* into local networks of trade and exchange while contributing to local economy by the facilitation of local resource exploitation. These smaller vessels have modern survivals because of their extreme utility in the North Atlantic marine environment. A sample of these from the modern Faroe Islands are shown in Fig 71. These were utilized around the island archipelago but were too small to be economically viable for longer open ocean voyages. These vessels allowed a more complete translation of human maritime needs and aspirations to the changeable maritime environment. The further from the centralized Continental markets a trading voyage began, the greater the risks were in

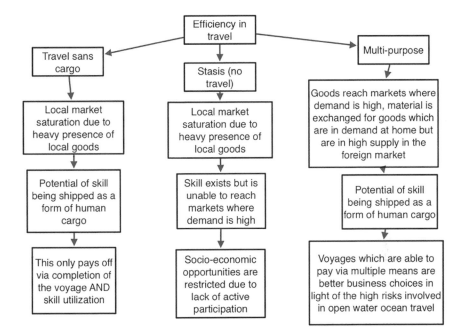

Fig 72. Efficiency in long distance travel.

association for the voyage. Due to this, the likelihood that economic travel was utilized was correspondingly greater. The cost of this is indirectly reflected in later medieval Norwegian law regarding a guaranteed yearly ship.[35] This was to guarantee an economic influx and outlet for the area.

The faering, on the other hand, would have been utilized on a more local scale, not only the internal trade played out in gift exchange and reciprocity but also the collection of marine derived goods and the drayage of victuals. This is the role that ships' boats and other small coastal vessels have played since it was discovered that coastal water travel could be less time consuming than travel over land with much less effort.[36]

Networks of trade and exchange provided the physical means of maintaining social ties across an ocean. Whether these networks also initialized these social ties by making settlement of islands beyond northwest Europe is difficult to ascertain from the surviving evidence. Whether or not these networks were initialized and utilized by Papar, or other hermetic Christians, is also unknown. Early-medieval sources allude to the presence of earlier inhabitants and their nautical practices, however, the only archaeological evidence for this group occurs on various Zone 1 islands.[37]

Establishment of the North Atlantic Trade Network

The establishment of trade networks across the North Atlantic settlement Zones was a multistage process rather than the result of a singular planning event. This has been broken into six separate phases for ease in consideration, however, it is important to remember that this was not adopted at the same pace across the region. As this system grew with the settlement of the area it supplied the goods, people and skills that were necessary to not only maintain the existing network but to expand it as well.

Phase 1 corresponds with trade occurring concurrently to the settlement voyage and conducted via exchange of goods and services to meet demand with supply. The presence of some of these goods is contingent upon the intended destination market – i.e. in Zone 1 islands such as Orkney, Shetland and the Hebrides foundation domesticated farm stock was not as necessary due to the established presence of domesticated farm animals prior to the Norse arrival. From the Faroe Islands west, however, farm stock and seed would have been amongst initial cargos of those who could afford the risk. This allowed the practices of animal husbandry known from sites to be developed and refined once breeding populations were established. The associated risks of the shipping of livestock are somewhat alleviated by species and breed choice. The open water voyage in unenclosed vessels potentially would have resulted in seasick livestock. With the exception of horses, all farm stock evidenced within the archaeological records of the north Atlantic Zones are from species with the ability to vomit. This is not normally a concern when shipping stock long distances in modern conditions.[38] The fact that horses would have been more difficult to safely ship is something which may have contributed to the overall value of the species within each Zone. The greater risk is actually from shipping sickness. This is an umbrella term for primarily respiratory infections such as bovine pneumonia that continue to effect modern stock populations when transported long distances.[39] Another concern for the shipping of stock is the effect on joints of uneven standing surfaces during transport. The stress of shipping was reduced by off-loading the livestock during re-supply/trade stops at islands along the way. This process allowed joints to relax from the changeable positions and any weight being lost to be supplemented by fresh fodder that would also raise the corresponding amounts of fresh vitamins maintaining animal health. This bears implications for how the cargo was actually loaded onto the ship – it would be impractical to unload the entire ship for a few days to let the stock relax from shipping stresses. However, loading the ship so that only a partial unloading is required – which potentially may have been done anyways during the course of trade and exchange – would make this concession feasible. At this early phase, this may have occurred at locations affiliated with the voyage sponsor and crewmembers including kin and extended affine relations. This is similar to the process occurring in Continental Europe.[40] If individuals and groups sponsored Phase 1 voyages based in the Scandinavian core, then the cost of returning the profits of the voyage must be considered due to the lack of initial exports at the peripheral settlements.[41]

There are differing priorities in accordance to the choices being made in import cargo constituents. At a basic microscale level there is a practical priority – the material needed to make a profitable voyage with the least amount of risk and then potentially establish a farm quickly. This priority considers practical aspects of settlement cargos in the order that it is needed. A priority of settlement is also expressed in Phase 1. This priority is the material necessary to make a trip to establish a settlement in a location foreign to the core region. This is a terrestrial view of a farm package exported from Europe. A maritime priority included the material needed to make the trip safely over open ocean. It might include local knowledge of weather and shores as well as how to weather storms at seas. This is a self-contained and self-maintained maritime view of a ship voyage the amount of risk experienced was reduced by greater numbers of ships undertaking the voyage. The following quotation comes from the *Konungs Skuggsjá* [The King's Mirror] and is concerned with the proper provisioning of a merchant's ship. This mid-thirteenth century source is written in a didactic format that reflects the growing impact of Continental influences in the Scandinavian homelands.[42] It also heavily reflects the influence of the patron's social status and thus literary needs, upon the text's author.

> Always buy shares in good vessels or in none at all. Keep your ship attractive, for then capable men will join you and it will be well manned. Be sure to have your ship ready when summer begins and do your travelling while the season is best. Keep reliable tackle on shipboard at all times, and never remain out at sea in late autumn, if you can avoid it.[43]

Another priority is economic in nature. This is the material necessary to make the trip to a guaranteed market. This priority is considered to be economic precisely because it exploits the needs generated by other priorities while simulating the choices associated with those priorities. Certain risks, if undertaken, would have proven very lucrative, however. An example of this is the transoceanic transportation of domesticated farm stock. There is no existent evidence promoting the establishment of new identity aside from making the decision to settle a foreign area. However, a subconscious priority of the preservation of previous identity is expressed during Phase 1. Identity was practiced in the choices of what to include in the cargo. *Habitus* would have made much of this common – the 'obvious' choice. This process was mediated by the availability of supply when loading cargo as well as the practicality of the material on the open voyage. This included the material needed to make the voyage while maintaining the culture known to the crew and passengers. This considers those elements that were practices earliest in the voyage.

What distinguishes Phase 1 from Phase 2 of this process is the delay to exports from the newly settled areas. Some collection time would have been necessary to have enough exports to be a full cargo. If this were done at several points on the voyage the amount necessary from each spot would have been much less and hence faster to accumulate. Another reason for this delay may have been linked to the length of the voyage. If a ship under sail left Scandinavia at the beginning of the sailing season in spring, by the time it arrived at Zone 2 or even Zone 3 the safe sailing period was well underway.[44] This does not count any layovers experienced at island archipelagos on the way. Due to the distance and the time necessary to make the trip if a ship were to make a return voyage that year cargo would have needed to be waiting to be loaded when the ship arrived at its landing location.

Phase 2 farms are in the earliest phases of establishment although in the period before reliable returns on the animal stock. The trade goods that were transported in the North Atlantic trade network are the same as with Phase 1. The transition from Phase 1 to Phase 2 was not even across the region. In some areas Phase 1 is ongoing and people continued to be a substantial addition to cargo. Priorities exhibited in the choices made in import cargo are illustrated in Fig 72. There is little change to the ordering of priorities with changes to settlement priorities, economic priorities and the preservation of identity that is subconsciously expressed. As the North Atlantic network extended information and heirlooms from kin networks was added as a ship transported import in settlement priority as well as the preservation of previous identity. Information such as ideas, fashions and current European events would have also held a place within the economic priority. The shipping of livestock was increasingly a high risk venture which was not met by the high return needed animals once brought. The established farm animals of Phase 2 farms meant the need for animals would have been lessened. The delay in export collection experienced during Phase 1 is no longer evident – there has been time to collect wild resources for some amount of export cargo to be stockpiled. Exports during Phase 2 are primarily derived from food collection already developed in an incipient fashion during Phase 1. Onsite production of domesticated animal products is not great enough at this time for it to be a major contribution aside from basic farm subsistence. Hence a return voyage or the continuation of a multistep trade voyage into the safe sailing season. Any stop on an open water voyage is potentially a period to re-supply and repair the vessel as well.

By Phase 3 farms are established and experiencing returns from animal stock within an expanding network of land exploitation. In some areas Phase 2 was still in effect, while in Zone 3 Phase 1 had begun. There is some change associated with imports linked to the North Atlantic import network. There is no longer any need for animals or seed to be sent from Scandinavia as intra-network sources are available for settlements farther west to make use of.[45] Priorities are unchanged with the exception of stock and seed being removed as an import cargo option. Trade goods are beginning to be driven by other vectors at both the microscale and the macroscale.[46] Exports are surplus derived from food collection in a system that is well developed and increasingly managed because of an ongoing presence in the region. On site, production of material with a surplus had begun while in certain areas there is local extinction as wild resources of species such as walrus and auk are over-exploited.[47] Trade voyages are beginning to be initialized by Zone inhabitants who have both capital and contacts in Europe.[48] Voyages sponsored from Europe also continue to occur. Although no conscious priority of previous identity maintenance being practiced as farms begin to be able to exert more control over the system the opportunity for change begins as more choices become available.

By the onset of Phase 4 farms are established and all productive land is claimed. Social stratification of the population of this terrestrial system is also established. Phase 3 continues in some areas while in Zone 3 Phase 2 is still found. Differing priorities are little changed from Phase 3. Trade goods are demanded and supplied by markets within Zone and within markets in northwest Europe.[49] Trips are initialized by both core and Zone inhabitants as a means to gain wealth and prestige locally and in international courts in a similar fashion to the earlier motivations of warriors during the Late Antique period.[50] A priority to establish unique island and North Atlantic identities is being exerted via the influence on local and international markets. This is evidenced by the presence of trade goods being supplied by foreign markets on sites in the North Atlantic and in Europe. There are choices being exerted for this to occur. Walrus ivory in European collections is the most famous example but much of this would have been organic and less durable in nature such as textiles, skin rope and preserved foods.[51] Written material also begins to outline designated Zone identities as well.

Phase 5 is differentiated from Phase 4 by the power consolidation of elites being at its height there is little other change. In the western reaches of Zone 3 Phase 4 is underway. Across the north Atlantic Zones, European influential power bases such as churches were being established.[52] These collected the goods of the wider local region on the microscale and acted as both facilitator and intermediary to transfer the collected capital into the long-distance trade network maintained. Trips were initialized by both core and Zone inhabitants as a means to gain wealth and prestige locally and international courts. This system is much larger by Phase 5 as the greater amount of capitol offered by Crown-backed voyages an eventual takeover of the North Atlantic system was inevitable as the climatic downturn began to influence the Zones more heavily.[53]

By Phase 6 North Atlantic Zone farms are being directly impacted by the Little Ice Age resulting in reduced production and in some places reduced physical access to open water trade routes.[54] As with Phase 5, there is little change to import choice prioritizing. Trips are being instigated by continental political vectors in Europe – a change in economic context.[55] Not only is there an identity priority being actively pursued by North Atlantic Zone inhabitants but it is increasingly important to differentiate island populations in these Zones as being distinct in comparison to the imposed demands and influences of European courts and markets. This is linked to the flourishing of writing concerned with the Settlement Period – a medieval example of nationalistic manipulation of the past.[56]

Regional Markets

The economics of the North Atlantic during this time was not only tied into the existing market economy of northwest Europe but also utilized the wide variety of natural resources available in coastal environments. Within this network the local market economy is that which is the immediate region to the farm unit. In Zone 2, for instance, this would correspond with the commerce network of localized farms but also might occur in relation to þing gatherings.[57] This is expressed in practice as both economic exchanges fulfilling demand with supply but also in networks of local gift exchange as well. Local gift exchange networks were reinforcements of social stratification and hierarchy via the exchange of goods as gifts that held associated obligations of reciprocity of labour or goods later.[58] This might have occurred between the farm holder and a local chieftain. The regional market economy occurs across an entire archipelago or Zone. This involves inter-island, or inter-Quarter, transport of goods economically exchanged fulfilling demand with supply but also in networks of local gift exchange.

Zone 1 is dominated by an anthropogenetically derived landscape that is treeless in nature.[59] The Northern and Western Isles in particular are far enough south in latitude that grain agriculture was considered a viable means of farm subsistence.[60] This contributed to the rise of Orkney with the medieval balance of power of North and Irish Sea trade networks. Shetland, on the other hand, was exploited for steatite at sites such as Clibberswick and Hesta Ness.[61] Animals such as sheep and the products that they are raised to produce contribute to not only farm economy but also wider exchange.[62] This allowed a textile driven economy to develop in relation to Zone 1 farms. The islands in this region are located within the North and Irish Sea networks of exchange. Shetland and the Faroe Islands were also increasingly involved in north Atlantic trade and exchange networks following the settlement of Zones 2 and 3 because of their locations between these Zones and the European continent.[63]

Zone 2 is the most geologically recent of the archipelagos considered during this study. At the time of initial settlement of a forest of trees, primarily *Betula spp* covered the Zone. Since this time, over-utilization of marginal lands by both humans and human introduced sheep has resulted in a landscape that is ovigenic in nature.[64] The location of Zone 2 between the confluence of the warm Irminger Current and the cold East Greenlandic and East Icelandic Currents has resulted in a rich supply of fish in the Zone 2 waters.[65] This rich fish and mollusc source attracted both marine mammal and marine bird populations. The presence and migrations of such species from Zone 1 to Zone 2 would have provided a natural route to other remote islands in the north Atlantic for open water sailors. The exploitation of this type of knowledge was a constituent of a European marine *habitus*.[66]

Zone 3 was composed of sites located along interior fjords such as Qassiarsuk and Narsarsuaq along the Eirikssfjord as well as the northern hunting fields of Norðsetr. With the exception of L'Anse aux Meadows, this strategy reduces some of the climatic and environmental effects associated with the nearby confluence of West Greenlandic and Labrador Currents. Interior locations subjected settlements to the effects of Greenland's inland ice, however. Due to this, grain agriculture was largely impossible and increasingly so as the effects of the Little Ice Age became more apparent.[67] Animal husbandry became the primary form of economy present in Zone 3 as transhumance remained the most efficient means of exploiting the marginal lands of Zone 3 domestically. Domestic sheep were managed to provide the wool necessary for textiles.[68] Wild species increasingly satisfied much of the dietary needs for protein by the inhabitants of the Zone while also providing the material for long distance exchange.[69]

Walrus and seal hunting, at least for the Norse of the North Atlantic, occurred on a primarily opportunistic basis if the prey was around it would most likely be hunted.[70] Within Norðsetr, walrus exploitation would have occurred during the spring, when walruses would move in closer to shore for breeding and birthing purposes. The literary sources concerning this species' exploitation are not at all clear, however. Much of this is this may be attributed to medieval source material. The fairly reliable post-medieval Olavus Magnus gives a very fanciful description of walrus exploitation off the Norwegian coast.[71] The walrus in question scaled some of the steep fjord walls and was subsequently brought down by skinning the walrus as it was pulled down from the rocks. This action was supposed to have caused the walrus to bleed to death and was thus easier to dispatch.[72] Seals, on the other hand, were exploited both on shore as well as while they surfaced through the pack ice. As seal exploitation was quite well known to the Norse North Atlantic settlers, the father figure didactically narrating the *Konungs Skuggsjá* has a number of things to say about Greenlandic seal resources which implies that the author's sources were quite familiar with the variety of species found in the region.[73]

Temporary settlements were probably constructed for usage during the procurement period, unlike the experienced Thule ice-walkers these settlements were probably not on the ice itself.[74] For both walrus and seals, attempts at clubbing females on the pupping beaches may have provided a somewhat safer opportunity for procurement. This is especially important with reference to walruses as hunting beasts like that is a good way to sink a smaller boat and crew. Other walrus and seals were taken from the waters of Norðsetr by harpooning from ice flows as portrayed by Olavus Magnus in the mid-sixteenth century.[75]

For the Norse, seals and walrus represented two different types of utility – seals being taken for their subsistence value and walruses being exploited for their economic/social utility. They could be exploited using much smaller hunting groups due to their smaller size. Seals from the cold waters of Norðsetr provided the Norse settlers of Greenland with not only meat for eating and blubber for oil rendering.[76] Their water repellent skins were turned into boots and shoes while softer-tanned were turned into clothing for some.

Other sealskins were turned into twisted skin rope, an occurrence also known from the earlier travels of Ohthere when discussing what he received from the *Finnas*.[77] Walrus, as stated previously, represented a valuable economic resource, primarily because of their ivory tusks, for the Norse of Greenland as well as those of the North Atlantic back to the Scandinavian homelands, and had been for some time.[78] This is one of the more famous of the Greenlandic commodities as for a time the ivory of Europe was supplied not by elephant ivory, but rather by walrus.[79]

Walrus skin, perhaps twisted into stout, utilitarian rope also formed part of Greenland's economic basis within the world market.[80] Unfortunately the organic nature of twisted skin rope leaves physical proof somewhat lacking. In spite of this, however, sources such as thirteenth century ecclesiastical tithing lists, telling of goods received by the Archbishopric of Niðaros from the Greenlandic settlements, hint at the amount of economic worth to be found in a walrus's hide.[81]

Trade and Exchange within the North Atlantic System

Trade in the Viking Age is traditionally associated with the exchange of luxury items rather than in bulk goods. This practice was linked to the associated prestige an item potentially carried when it came to be considered a luxury good. This could be linked to local scarcity, high artisanship, or even the resource material itself. This type of small bulk/ high social exchange facilitated the gift exchange networks upon which northwestern European chieftainships established and maintained themselves.[82] Within early Norse poetic references the men who did this were known as 'ring-givers' who gifted their affiliates with riches or weaponry.[83] This practice is indirectly reflected in the shape of pre-Viking Age and early Viking Age vessels. These vessels were shallow-drafted allowing them to be drawn up on shores easily with a sizeable crew.[84] There was no enclosed hold location to keep commodities safely on these vessels in bulk – smaller, higher value goods were preferred. As time passed the chieftainships of the north consolidated into medieval kingdoms. This began first in Denmark due to affiliations with Merovingian and Carolingian Frankia as well as the growing influence of the medieval church.[85] Trade derived revenue gained via power over public trading areas in combination with growing dependent populations resulted in a shift in trading practice patterns. Although luxury goods still had a place within this system of economically driven exchange, bulk commodities that supplied a population began to be desired more. By having sufficient surplus of stores, a population was then able to free laborers from tasks associated with subsistence for those associated with artisanal activity. Political power consolidated socially via the maintenance and control of the spaces where public trading occurred. This practice was exerted via economic interactions and taxation/rent. As this process occurred within the North Sea Zone drafts began to increase in clinker ship design and sail power became the dominate means of propulsion. A large vessel was able to be manned by a smaller crew thus increasing the amount of cargo to be carried via technological efficiency.

Trading voyages became recognized by power magnates local to Zone 1, 2 and 3 as a viable means of maintaining not only local power but also to maintain an international presence within Scandinavian political networks. Simply put the trading voyages and the associated wealth of holding on in combination with the potential wealth to be gained began to supersede the earlier raiding voyages and military efforts present during the consolidation of the Scandinavian kingdoms. By utilizing the practice of gift exchange based on social obligation and reciprocity, Scandinavian political powers were able to integrate themselves into this system and so directly benefits from the wealth generated.[86]

Trading voyages were multileveled events that carried with them physical and intangible elements. Early on, this would have occurred concurrently to settlement voyages – tradable items brought along with the goods necessary to establish a new farm on wild land. There may have been a surplus of the same goods, preserved food, or even textiles traded for re-supply access to fresh foods on extended ocean voyages. If the sagas are to be believed, slaves might also be considered with this lot.[87] Aside from physical goods, however, trading voyages provided an influx of news, ideas, technology and new people into the north Atlantic networks, thus making them incredibly powerful drivers of identity construction and maintenance in their own right at the macroscale. The actual practice of seafaring by each crew can be considered as microscale aspects of this marine oriented system.[88] Each crew had their own distinct habitus based upon their own context, which in effect makes them as individual and unique as each of the farm unit constituents.

Socially the concept of a trader was changing during this period – taking on socio-political aspects held by warrior supporters of Scandinavian chieftains. The trading vessel itself was equated with a farm in terms of sailors' rights within *Gulatingslog*, *Grágás* and even the later *Seyðabrævið* and Norwegian *Jónsbok* adopted during the later thirteenth century.[89] These provisions prevented sailors being outside the local law when they landed. These voyages existed at the juxtaposition of local and international networks of exchange.

The demand for commodities change over time as does the nature of the trading unit itself. Although trading voyages continue and are mediated via traders and crew of the vessel the cost of long distance shipping bulk goods of lower value per individual unit over high value, low bulk goods becomes prohibitive for all but the wealthiest of society or those groups whose pooled capital allow them to function at that level economically. In Zones 2 and 3 textual references, it is possible to see this association in contemporary practice.[90]

It was in this economic environment that the settlement of the north Atlantic Zones took place. The deeper-drafted *knórr* was much better suited to the open water journeys required for the establishment of farm units in distant lands than the shallow-drafted coastal vessels of earlier centuries. These ships also were able to carry enough supplies on board to provide time for the construction of shelter – in smaller vessels this space had been utilized for carrying crew and their provisions. The new established populations provided new locations with which to trade and initially in Zone 1. At least the choice of expansion into the indigenously settled areas such as the Northern and Western Isles occurs in economically strategic locations in the landscape. Not only was this a statement of social power being exerted over previous inhabitants such as the Picts inhabiting the Birsay Bay local area but it was also a wider statement of local change in power to the regional trade networks.[91] This process was particularly successful in Orkney where strategic archipelago location as well as a comparatively rich agricultural economy developed the local power magnates into the powerful Orcadian Jarls who established themselves over Shetland and Fair Isle as well.[92]

As this consolidation of capital by regional elites occurred in the wider north Atlantic Zone, a change began to occur within trading patterns. As land resources became the legal property of fewer and fewer land owners more sites became affiliates via rent paid in farm product or animals and social obligation practiced in trade and exchange. An extended kin group of such a landowner would result own considerably more farm product than could be produced on a single farm unit.[93] This is a pre-condition for sustainable international trade as an economic practice: there must be a surplus in supply of goods with which to exchange. Local exchange increasingly would have been informal and incorporated as part of the seasonal practice of these wider farm conglomerates consisting of several farm unit networks under the legal ownership of one kin group. These groups collected bulk items as land rents.[94] Luxury goods and raw materials were collected this way. Once enough goods were collected that a sizeable profit would be made from the sale of the ship's cargo a voyage east to the markets of Zone 1, Scandinavia and the Continent was made once the time of year was favorable for the journey.[95]

Landowners intent on establishing themselves on a level greater than their own zone needed to be able to make their presence known beyond the Zone. Location alone made a ship and crew a vital aspect of this. In this time before the ease of mass communication, a voyage undertaken just to get from point A to point B was incredibly impractical in terms of economics, labor and personal risk. Voyages conducted for a wider variety of reasons, such as trade, communication and to maintain a personal presence in foreign courts and markets, resulted in enough prestige and potential economic gain to outweigh the risk inherent to medieval ocean travel.

Between Zone 2 and Zone 3 trade networks had to be established in areas which had not previously had large-scale trade and exchange with medieval

Europe. Initial trade was carried via family networks and affiliation networks of settlement. This provided a guaranteed market as well as a tailored supply for expanding north Atlantic trade networks. Within this context, those farms that were established early in the settlement period and developed a connection to the wider North Atlantic trade and exchange early became very powerful by the twelfth and thirteenth century. Particularly in Zone 3 these more powerful areas became affiliated with Church and cathedrals. Examples include Qassiarsuk and Igaliku where the cathedrals at both of these are dedicated to St Nicholas, rather than St Olaf of Norway or St Magnus of Orkney who were contemporaneous and popular in Scandinavia.

As governments became intermediaries in this system via levies and personal representatives this begins to change. The demand for luxury resource is more directly tied into international economic networks. Resources included walrus ivory, arctic furs, and live animals such as polar bears and hunting falcons. When African networks with less associated risk than long distance open water meet the demand for ivory voyages the change is swift. By this time, there is no ritual reason to maintain the amount of prestige associated with goods made from walrus ivory and the aesthetics were affiliated more with choice and overall cost. The demand for exotic arctic live animals such as polar bears may have continued – this is evidenced not only by direct literacy practice such as the tale of Auðun Vestfiska and within copies of the *Grágás* law code.[96]

Furs and skins may have also been a continued resource with some market value. Continued exploitation of fur bearing species is difficult to date as hunting traps are not often recognized in ruinous conditions and as a result are rarely excavated.[97] Osteological material of fur bearing species showing evidence of skinning is another way to determine this, however, evidence of this practice in Zone 2 and Zone 3 is slights. This lack of evidence may hint at skinning activities away from the home farm unit, differential preservation or even as of yet undiscovered sites. Walrus skin prepared as twisted skin rope also may have continued as a community within the north Atlantic sailing routes until cheaper forms of stout rope material such as hemp or jute was widely available.

This provides a view of a very changeable point in north Atlantic identity construction – the social rise of the merchant as the social decline of warriors less necessary for daily defense in the wider medieval Scandinavian world. In a way, these are similar function of macroscale male identity in the north Atlantic. The ability of a chieftain to maintain and arm skilled warriors also precluded enough capital for weaponry; travel to and from battle, room and board but also luxury gifts to maintain social obligations. The ability to conduct ship-scale trade over open ocean precluded enough capital for ship, crew, cargo, steersman and foreign duty fees.

Chapter 7

Religion

Religion and the Church

An important cultural vector external to the North Atlantic settlement population that heavily influenced subsequent regional society was religion. This was initially carried via the trade networks discussed in Chapter 7 as parts of the *habitus* of included human passengers and potentially crews, of these voyages. This chapter considers the external macroscale vector of religion. It begins with the pagan religious context of the North Atlantic settling populations. It then moves on to the initial Christian religious context of the settling populations and the developing Christian network of North Atlantic Zone sites. Finally, the social aspects of religion are discussed. The impact which religion had on identity is difficult to quantify because of its nature – belief is part of *habitus* and as a result is directly evidenced in practice and indirectly evidenced by the physical remains of social and economic interactions. Religion provides a worldview that places the local familial reality within a universal context. It provides a context for cultural values, norms and morals – it assists with the spiritual contemplations of life and death as well as right and wrong. Religion can potentially provide a longer held view of familial *habitus* provided conversion has not interrupted this familial link. The initial context of religion in the north Atlantic is obscured by biased sources in combination with unknown influences of religious syncretism. Religion indirectly influenced the social interactions of inhabitants providing potential links to the social hierarchy. Later this would be most evident as the medieval Christian Church became a powerful social, economic and political force. Religion was another element of wider commonality for populations and a way to express a similar identity on the macroscale.

Pagan Religious Context of the North Atlantic

Although the exact nature of Norse pagan religion is unknown, particularly via archaeological evidence, a medieval mythological base which was linked to practices of oral history present in not only the Norse settlements of the north Atlantic but in the Scandinavian homelands as well. The later medieval writers in Iceland heavily impacted the modern concept of early-medieval

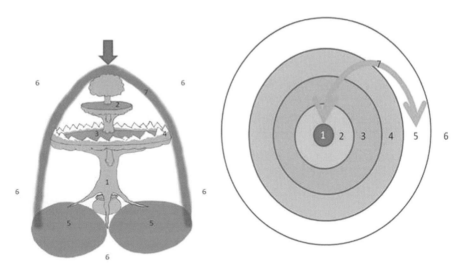

Number	Name	Definition	Comments
1	World Tree	Center of the universe	This motif is normally portrayed with associated animals that are active on the tree itself.
2	Asgard	Home of the Gods	This is where roles are most defined by the extent mythological evidence.
3	Midgard	Home of Men	The affiliated areas of the everyday world. The closer to the center this is the more defined it is.
4	Jotunheim	Home of the Giants	The unaffiliated chaotic areas of the everyday world which may be beneficial at a cost.
5	Underworld	Exists in two extremes – ice and fire	These are the same two environmental extremes as known from Zone 2.
6	Undefined nothing	Essentially chaos	This must exist in order to define where there are defined places.
7	Bifrost Bridge	The Rainbow Bridge which is the road between worlds	This element exists to provide a transition between the levels.

Fig 73. (Top Left) Traditional portrayal of the World Tree remembered in Norse pagan mythology. The arrow indicates the view point from which the image at top right is seen. (Top Right) Generalized view of the construction of the Norse pagan universe.

Norse pagan religion.[1] During the pagan period, the structure of family present on the farm replicated the centrally focused universe structure noted from mythological references found primarily in medieval Norse poetry. In this view the longhouse central long hearth and its range of activities corresponds with Yggdrasil the world tree that forms the centre of the universe and upholds the levels of existence within its boughs. This format considers the fact that physical domestic rituals that occurred within the longhouse – the center of this social space utilization – would be incorporated within domestic deposits. This results in physical evidence of religion being indistinguishable from material of purely domestic activities. The location contributes to their effectiveness as a practice of non-Christian religion. This view is based upon a reorientation of the traditional format of the construction of the Norse pagan universe.

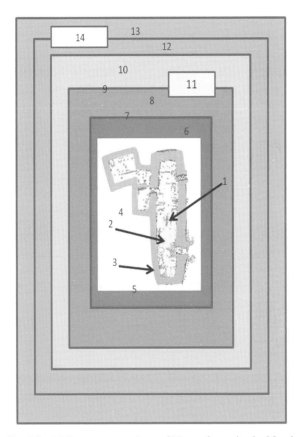

Fig 74. Generalized Social Space conceptions of Norse farms in the North Atlantic. Table explaining is on the following page. Also includes following page.

Number	Detail	Function	Comments
1	Central hearth	Heat, light.	
2	Domestic area (shaded)	Low light activities which may or may not require heat to accomplish. Includes but is not limited to food preparation, handicrafts and sleeping.	Familial and auxiliary interactions occur here.
3	Turf wall	Domestic boundary as well as structural wall.	
4	Home farmyard	Potentially high skill activities and the site of most physical of human and animal interactions within animal husbandry cycle.	Smithy, byre, barn, weaving-house, midden, kitchen garden may all be located within this region.
5	Homefield farmyard boundary		
6	Infield area	Tended managed crops maintained on intentionally improved lands.	An example here is barley.
7	Infield/outfield transition	Potentially a boundary is used to delineate this otherwise field use practice is the best indication of use.	This practice is mentioned in Grágas.
8	Outfield area	Tended crops requiring less maintenance.	An example of crops here would be oats.
9	Outer farm boundaries of the home farm unit	Delineated by walls in areas where multiple home farm units were abutting, according to Grágas.	To the interior of this boundary is where the defined gender roles of male, female and age-defined neutral apply. To the exterior of this boundary is where the roles are more ambiguous.
10	Area of farm held lands	Farm affiliated lands with the wider world which are separate from the home farm unit.	Examples include shielings, birding cliffs, fishing rivers, lakes and coasts, littoral zones, woods.
11	Familial burial area	Located in the furthest extent of home farm near the boundary of the outside world.	The family members are still nearby yet are not being obtrusive into everyday existence.
12	Common access areas	Areas where there is common access to the resources of the wider world which is unmediated by direct farm affiliation.	Examples include open water fishing and ocean travel. There is a chaotic element to this due to lack of mediation.
13	Natural world without human influence	Area where survival dominates over cultural roles and practices	
14	Interactions with other family farm units are here	This assumes the units are separate, not related by blood or marriage nor do they have any social affiliation beyond being a local neighbor.	

Fig 75. Social space terms with relation to Norse North Atlantic sites.

This is illustrated in the top left portion of Fig 73. This view attempts to maintain the figure of the World Tree in relation to the worlds described in its branches and roots rather than viewing it as a central figure shown in the top portion of the same diagram. This is known because of the common poetic corpus referenced by medieval writers in not only Zone 2 but also from Zone 1 and Norway as well. The complex cross-referencing nature of medieval Norse poetics required an intense knowledge of the mythological corpus. Sources such as *Skaldskarpismal* written by Snorri Sturlusson detail this in brief – possibly because such knowledge was no longer as common following the Conversion of Zone 2 to Christianity *c.* AD 1000.[2] Hence, Sturlusson references not only the forms of verse via examples of earlier poetry but also lists names and mythological cross-references. Based on this apparent mythological base of the practice of oral history and poetry a few elements of a remembered religion can be discussed. This is utilized in the construction of not only the traditional view of Norse universe format but also the proposed view as well. The use of this remembered religion shall be discussed in Chapter 8.

The modern concept of early-medieval Norse pagan religion is heavily impacted by the later medieval writers in Iceland.[3] During the pagan period, the structure of family present on the farm replicated the centrally focused universe structure noted from mythological references found primarily in medieval Norse poetry.[4] In this view the longhouse central long hearth and its range of activities corresponds with Yggdrasil the world tree that forms the centre of the universe and upholds the levels of existence within its boughs. This format considers the fact that physical domestic rituals that occurred within the longhouse – the center of this social space utilization – would be incorporated within domestic deposits. This results in physical evidence of religion being indistinguishable from material of purely domestic activities. The location contributes to their effectiveness as a practice of non-Christian religion. This view is based upon a reorientation of the traditional format of the construction of the Norse pagan universe.

According to these remembered sources the male head of family functioned as the male representative in rituals with designated females as priestesses. This format is alluded to with some saga references as well as *Heimskringla* and *Voluspä*. It is important to question whether or not this is oral tradition contributing to the portrayal of pagan ritual reality or if this is the view of the authors. The medieval authors were most often Christian trained clerics, highlighting female involvement as being perverse in relation to religious *vitae* that contributed to the knowledge base utilized in saga creation or if this is actually another set of evidence from which a spectrum of possibilities is available and dependent upon the context of each text.

Aside from rarely found votive gods and Þórr's hammer amulets there is no range of artefacts on sites which can be attributed to a purely pagan religious function.[5] Organic materials such as wood may have been used for this purpose so an absence of evidence in this case may not actually indicate that no pagan ritual equipment was associated with Norse north Atlantic settlements.[6] Contemporary Continental histories regarding Scandinavian home lands refer to sacrifices such as the references of Adam of Bremen related to the pagan practices at the Uppsala Temple.[7] This links into an early practice of sacrifice in association with ritual known from Germanic tribes of North-west Europe prior to the Viking Age. This practice is corroborated by accompanying burial goods and animals known from excavated burials found within Zone 1 and particularly in Zone 2.[8]

Of animals included within burial assemblages horses are the most common.[9] The evidence is numerically dominant in Zone 2 in particular where

Fig 76. Bishop from the Lewis Chessmen on display at the National Museum of Scotland. Photo by Dr R. Lenfert.

horses are the most common recognized followed by dog. It is unknown from the available evidence whether these animals were included for religious or non-religious reasons. However, in mythological writings these are both animals associated with transition over boundaries.[10] In mythological references written down as orally transmitted folklore following the Conversion to Christianity the most famous mythological horse was Slepnir, the eight-legged steed of Oðinn.[11] This horse had the ability to cross between the realms of the dead, the living, the gods and the chaotic lands of the giants. Horses also allude to another macroscale element of pagan religious practice: the importance of travel. Dogs, on the other hand, signal a transitional period within the extent texts. One of the most famous of these is Garm, the hound of Hel who swallows the moon at the onset of Ragnarök.[12] The practice of making transitional areas distinct is one known elsewhere archaeologically at places such as Jarlabanka's Bridge in Sweden, which mark the public gift of a bridge/walkway as well within the mythology.[13]

Ships are another form of sacrifice known from pagan North Atlantic that are associated both with travel and the transition of boundaries. Boat burials involving the interment of water conveyance as well as votive boats outlined by stones around interments are known from Zone 1, Zone 2 as well as much more famously from the Scandinavian sites of Oseberg, Gokstad and Tune.[14] It appears to be a practice that was not brought to Norse Greenland by the initial settlers. Boat burials that involve actual boats are known from Scar, Pierowall and at Breckon Sands.[15] These burials are always accompanied with other goods. They are located in prominent locations that have subsequently been damaged by erosion – a statement within the microscale landscape no longer immediately recognized. Within textual references boats and ships are often mentioned practically however episodes such as Þórr fishing for the Midgaard Serpent with the head of an ox show ships to be a viable means to transverse the chaos of the waves. In this view, ships represent enclaves of human order over the chaos. Men were preferred crew because of this as women would not be able to control their inherently chaotic nature that would be potentially deadly in the environment. Order was required to undertake the long distance open water voyage necessary to maintain inter-Zonal networks. The best evidence for the necessity of order on board ship is known from the source *Konungskuggsjá*, from the thirteenth century.[16] This source is quite explicit in what to take on board, routes to take and even what to expect from each of the stops along the way. According to this, a single steersman was the leader and his choices held control over life and death of those on-board. Female gender roles are obscure concerning the religious concept of the ship and function primarily as a literary trope within texts that may be related to the biases of male Christian clerics involved in ethnohistorical data transmission.

Christian Religious Context of the North Atlantic

The religious men recognized by incoming Norse populations to the west were known as '*Papar*'. Toponyms, or place names, related to the *Papar* are found throughout Zones 1 and 2 in the North Atlantic Zone.[17] This is best evidenced by *Pap*-names and the presence of other certain name elements in place names that have been included into a table for consideration, please refer to Fig 77. For instance in the Northern and Western Isles, as well as other sites around the British Isles, quite often have associated chapel sites or carved stones near sometimes quite good agricultural land.[18] It is very important to remember in Zone 1 there was previous habitation prior to the Norse arrival. This consisted of not only the *Papar* but also Pictish populations who formed part of the Kingdom of Pictland based in Scotland.[19] Realistically this is the area of overlap between not only the 'Atlantic Zone' of cultural influence and the 'Scandinavian Zone'[20] but also the proposed 'North Atlantic Zone' as well. By the location of the British Isles alone within this historical confluence, it is apparent that this would have been a quite dynamic region.

In the Faroe Islands, on the other hand, there are only two place names that have been associated with the *Papar* which are much more remotely located near the shear basalt cliffs that also hold the steep 'Celtic fields '.[21] The pre-Norse occupation of the Faroe Islands has been contested over time however, so these sites have formed a point of contention for many researchers in the past.[22] Iceland has a handful of *Pap*-related names, although some of the exact locations have been lost over time.[23] The majority of these are located on the northwestern and southeastern coast where some sagas cite land taking by Hiberno-Norse settlers.[24] Like the Faroe Island sites the *Pap*-names in Iceland are somewhat contested due to the heavy reliance upon saga literature and references as historical fact.[25] Zone 3 has no known *Pap*-related names, although it may have during the initial Norse occupation for which evidence has since been lost.

The extent archaeological evidence for the *Papar* in the North Atlantic represents a differential distribution much in the manner of the toponymic evidence discussed above. Around the British Isles, in particular we find evidence for contemporary existence of the *Papar* with both the Pictish and the Irish indigenous population that can cause some difficulty in differentiating the cultural groups.[26] In the Northern and Western Isles *Pap*-named sites often have associated chapels or carved stones but there remains little else on the ground.[27] There is little in the remains of physical evidence that can be undeniably attributed to the *Papar* as a cultural group, especially in an area that has another more widely known and better-attested contemporary occupation – the Picts.[28] At sites in the Irish Sea region such as on Iona, on Church Island in Co. Kerry and on the Dingle Peninsula of Ireland are located beehive cells known as *clochán*. These sites further point to the presence of an ascetic hermit population in the region.[29]

In the Faroe Islands, there are no confirmed excavated constructions for the *Papar* unless the 'Celtic Field Theory' holds true. There are long standing debates in the history of Faroese archaeological research that are associated not only with proving, or disproving, the pre-Norse presence of Celtic ascetic priests but also in terms of the validity of the *Færeyinga Saga* as a historical resource.[31] The modern form of the saga has undeniably been subject to the work of later

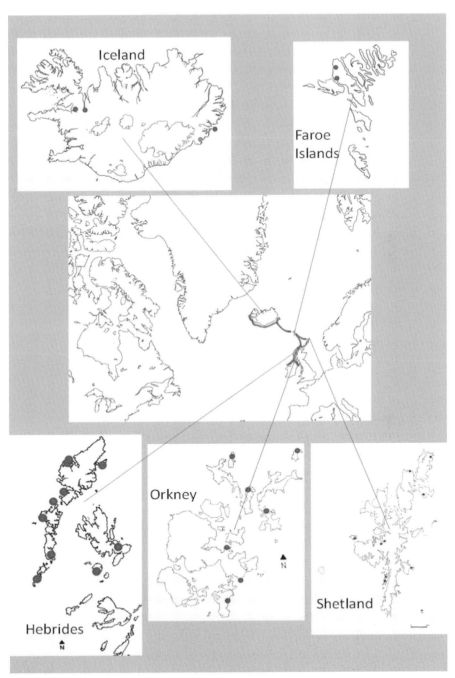

Fig 77. Papar place name locations and movement map.[30]

editors as it did not exist in a collected work until the publication of Rafn's work in 1832.[32] Prior to this time the chapters of *Færeyinga Saga* existed as side stories and details found in several Icelandic sagas, including *Heimskringla*. In spite of this there are several sites which local tradition have associated with the Irish Sea priests in the past, although few have been confirmed with full excavation. The site of Bónhústoftin is considered by some to be the proof necessary, although Sandøy has been suspected in the past.[33]

In Iceland, there have been some crosses found in cave sites in the south, however, and sagas directly mention *Papar* leaving behind the tripartite trope of bells, books and crosiers.[34] As in the Faroe Islands, these cave sites have spawned much debate over their validity, particularly as several of the Icelandic Sagas mention direct interaction between the *landnám* population and the *Papar*. This is, however, merely another aspect of the history of archaeological research in Iceland, where a heavy reliance upon saga-evidence existed well into the 1990s.[35] With particular regard to the *Papar* related cave sites Ahrónson cites the crosses which were found within some of the sandstone caves as being proof positive of an early Christian ascetic presence on primarily stylistic considerations.[36]

Fig 78. Bónhústoftin chapel site, taken within the site enclosure.

Sveinbjarnardóttir, on the other hand, highlights the location of the sites and their subsequent re-usage following the initial site occupation.[37] Aside from the cave sites found in Iceland the only other potential physical evidence for *Papar* presence in Zone 2 would have to reside in the material assemblages found during proper archaeological excavation. There is in certain cases an undeniable British influence to the ecclesiastical elements of the assemblages in publication, however, this is far more likely to be in relation to the Hiberno-Norse portion of the *landnám* population than the influence of hermitic monks.[38] Zone 3 of the North Atlantic, Greenland and the New World, to date has no known *Pap*-name sites.[39] In spite of this, some researchers link the *Papar* to Greenland at least, via chapel sites, in particular the contested chapel-site of Bónhústoftin in the Faroe Islands.[40] In this case, these sub-circular chapel sites are cited as being non-Norse, and hence by default *Papar* related, due to the format of the site itself.[41] Not often highlighted in such comparisons are the local geological and drainage features or the effect of degrading turf block which degrading turf blocks might have.[42]

The Norse written evidence of the Papar, on the other hand, captures a view on place name origins and site relations that has been impacted by the

Fig 79. Hogback from St Boniface chapel, Papa Westray, Orkney.

context and location of each unique text. In general, as the majority of the sagas date from the twelfth or thirteenth century, they are subject to anachronistic inclusions concerning the past. There are three references to *Papar* that are particularly relevant for this consideration. The two earlier references can be directly attributed to Ari Þorgilsson, noted early Icelandic historian.

The later reference comes from a Norwegian source of the thirteenth century the *Historia Norwegiae*. MacDonald highlights the fact that there is a common source for all three sources.[43] This source is quite fantastic in its inclusion and so can only confirm a presence in the Scandinavian North Atlantic. For instance, the Northern and Western Isles needed explanations for the ruins of obvious chapel sites. In this region, there is also an added element of indigenous cultural memories concerning certain physical features of the landscape. Due to this are there is mention not only of the *Papar* but also the small-statured ground inhabiting Picts, referred to by *Peti*-related names in the landscape.[44] In the Faroe Islands and Iceland, however, the settlers themselves were not only from the Scandinavian homelands but also from the more recently settled lands in and around the British Isles and so as a result there may be added elements

Fig 80. Chapel dedicated to St Boniface on Papa Westray, Orkney.

of cultural memories being applied to the landscape features of a *Papar*-linked world.[45] Fig 80 illustrates a medieval Norse chapel dedicated to St Boniface which was founded on Papa Westray in Orkney. Fig 79 illustrates a hogback from the same site, implying a local statement of affiliation to a macroscale practice from further to the south.

The conversion from a naturally oriented kin-linked religion whose universal structure was replicated in the traditional longhouse to the medieval Christian Church resulted in a corresponding change within space utilization in the island landscapes of the North Atlantic. This process took place concurrently to the settlement of the north Atlantic Zones, the diversification and intensification of the northern European marine trade networks and the consolidation of political power into medieval Kingdoms in Scandinavia. Although there is commonality in this import of Christian religion, how the conversion process occurred in practice was dependent upon the context of Zone identity and physical environment.[46] The conversion was also important in terms of textual sources as well as the adoption of the Latin alphabet in Norse vernacular resulted in a script with which it was much easier to write complex ideas in the medium of books.[47]

By AD 800 Norse settlement of Zone 1 had already begun to occur as part of the wider 'Viking' expansion during the early-medieval period which resulted in male Scandinavians west, east and south of the their homelands. During this period not only were Christian missionaries being sent to the North to convert pagan populations but also those Scandinavians who ventured beyond their homelands came into contact with Christian populations. Zone 1 archipelagos in particular held indigenous Christians as well as a previously established system of religious architecture and cult foci such as the Brough of Birsay.[48]

Many North Atlantic ecclesiastical sites are of turf wall construction, sometimes with a footing of stone and inner walls and roof architecture of wood, as were the contemporary secular buildings.[49] This is a reflection of the available building materials. When compared to sites such as St Columcille's Chapel at Beefan in County Donegal we do find some similarity of form with that of Bónhústoftin and Inoqquassaq.[50] This presents two levels of hierarchy concerning Christian burial placement – for the family who sponsored the construction and maintenance there would be little change in the location of burials from the more marginal areas of the farm. For the farm families who were members of this church, however, burials were removed from prominent yet marginal areas in the landscape that were associated with the farm.[51]

As the inter-farm Christian network was established Christian burial practices of unaccompanied interments in a consecrated cemetery, a religious focus was adopted. This process involved not only the newly dead following the AD 1000 conversion to Christianity but also the translation and re-internment of familial ancestors to maintain familial continuity in place of burial.[52] Zone 2 textual evidence provides several levels of insight into the local impact of the conversion to Christianity. These later medieval sources highlight that many settlers and slaves who were included in such works arrived in unsettled Iceland as Christians already, particularly those from Zone 1 archipelagos.[53] The sources also detail a conversion that was only secondarily religious in strategy to establish Iceland were firmly within the international networks of trade-based economics and power of contemporary Europe.[54]

Christianity in the North Atlantic

Christianity became both assimilated and acculturated in the north Atlantic over a relatively rapid period in relation to the Late Antique conversion of southern Europe. By the time that Christianity began to make a serious impact at the political macroscale in northwestern Europe it was already well established in Southern Europe and the Mediterranean region. The build-up of capital and human resources had already occurred at this point in these regions. In the Scandinavian medieval kingdoms, the upper echelons of macroscale society have adopted Christianity partially due to the inherent reinforcement of the divine right of Christian kings such as developed in medieval England and France.[55] This process allowed a missionary element to be developed and maintained. In this view pagan Scandinavia represented the closest pagan 'wild' in relation to the relative Christian safety of the southern European Continent in the late ninth and tenth centuries.[56] This is the process of the establishment of Church rights as Continental archbishoprics were able to establish spiritual affiliation over wider areas via the conversion efforts of their missionaries.[57] There are only a few directly associated with early Conversion efforts in the north Atlantic. During the ninth through eleventh centuries, conversion efforts began to occur internally within Scandinavia, centering on converted elites and their familial and client affiliates.[58] A series of homegrown saints became recognized not only by the Roman Church but also by the lucrative medieval pilgrim network.[59]

Archaeologically the onset of this process is difficult to determine, highlighting several aspects of this macroscale identity vector. The first, and perhaps most important Conversion in religious outlook was a change in theological philosophy – religious thought including the shape of the Universe and humanity's place within it. The method of transmission from learned Christians to heathen populations was initially verbal and created no physical evidence. These events are sometimes remembered as episodes retained within regional oral histories and later remembered strategically within written texts. An example of this is *Krístní saga*, which documents the Conversion process in Zone 2.[60] Wide-spread literacy follows Conversion in the North-Atlantic.[61] The people who provided the means of transmission of these incoming microscale concepts were transported via open water ships. Whether this is the only job which these idea-bearers performed on board or is they were performing other tasks as well is a question unable to be answered by the existent evidence. Performing tasks on board would be more efficient than being a passenger. Physical evidence for Conversion does not become visible of population levels until the adoption of Christianity as part of a wider north Atlantic community statement of identity linked status as well as a statement of personal piety. This is linked with a strengthening of pagan burial traditions in comparison to earlier periods which is eventually superseded by unaccompanied oriented burials.[62]

Shortly after the conversion to Christianity by Zone 2, the Norse discovery and settlement of Greenland began. Both *Graenlendinga Saga* and *Eirikssaga Rauða* to Eirik's Christian wife with holding her sexual favors from her pagan husband until he had a chapel constructed on the new farm site.[63] There is

1.   Above are the ruins of turf church.
Below is a reconstruction of this turf church.

2. Cathedral ruins.

3. Ruins assumed to be Brattahlíð.

4. Ruins of two farms at this site, shown by arrows.

Fig 81. Qassiarsuk, Greenland.

some debate as to the exact location of this well-documented chapel, although it is accepted that it was on the Eirikssfjord of southern modern Greenland.[64] Qassiarsuk has long been seen as the site of the Brattahlíð home farm begun by Eirik the Red. Indeed this is the location of not only an early-medieval turf chapel, two Norse farms, a late Norse cathedral dedicated to St Nicholas and the modern reconstruction of a Norse longhouse and chapel but also a series of seventeenth and eighteenth century Thule winter houses.[65]

The second proposed site is less well known at Qinngua. This site corresponds with textual descriptions to a higher degree.[66] This same group of surveyors promote the presence of a distinct round form of turf built chapels attributed to Irish ascetic priests across the north Atlantic – examples being from Bónhústoftin, and an as of yet undisclosed southern Greenlandic location[67]. No full modern excavation has been conducted on any of these sites to either confirm or deny this association.[68] Another location which is unexcavated in spite of several indication of continued utilization is Kirkjubøur, in the Faroe Islands.

The physical evidence provided by chapel locations in Greenland illustrates that chapels were integrated within the inter-farm networks present on the

1. From harbour head. Ruins shown by arrow.

2. From the mountains behind the valley. Ruins shown by arrow.

3. Farther pasture lands. Site located just beyond the ridge in the mid-ground of the shot.

4. Local stone and grass resources.

5. Tithe barn ruins.

Fig 82. Igaliku, Greenland.

marginal Zone 3 landscape.[69] The majority of these localized chapels were constructed of turf with a front wall of wood – the same materials utilized within a Zone 3 longhouse and outbuilding construction. The front wall of wood made for a distinct building in relation to its secular neighbors. Chapels were surrounded by a round or sub-rectangular wall of turf and earthworks.[70]

Burials have been traditionally seen as the most immediately recognizable evidence for this transitional period however, there are many difficulties in utilizing this material due to unanswerable questions concerning the reasoning of body placement, following certain funerary rites and respecting the dead. In zone I, earliest Norse burials were affiliated with farm mounds and prominent rises in the landscape. As the pagan population converted, we begin to find evidence for interments placed within the boundaries of medieval church cemeteries such as at Yviri I Troð in the Faroes. Unlike the earlier pagan familial cemeteries as known from Pierowall in Orkney and Breckon Sands in Shetland, these interments contain only those goods attached to clothing while the bodies themselves are oriented around a church yard focus.

1. Wall of the early stone church in the foreground.

2. Later medieval church.

5. Later farmhouse constructed on Bishop's Palace foundations.

3. Múrúrin

4. Panoramic view of farming area. Church is shown by arrow.

Fig 83. Kirkjubøur, Faroe Islands.

Social Aspects of Religion

Conversion to Christianity began the process of removing familial immediacy present in the pagan religious practice as the Church via local representatives became integrated into the north Atlantic settlements. These representatives mediated contact with spiritual maintenance via use of local liturgical equipment and the local mass. This provided standardization concerning incoming ritual practice as Christianity, in essence, had a far wider reaching 'familial' network to draw upon than the numerically smaller kin oriented practices which were replaced.

The shift to an externally focused Christian network is facilitated by the Christian 'family 'of the medieval Church.[71] This pyramid of power became reflected in the structure of political power in the secular kingdoms of northwest Europe[72]. In the more environmentally marginal north Atlantic region the majority of local islandscapes were not conducive to the development of kingdoms in the European sense due to a lack of supply to support a larger population including those who did not work the land or tend animals directly to earn their way within the local economic networks.

Christianity became the means to connect to the wider known European world on a spiritual macroscale level. This adoption was an effort to reduce the insular nature island life induces and was conducted in terms of becoming part of a larger family. This transcended worldly constraints and borders. It also suggests that religion – the act of having it – was included within the medieval north Atlantic populations' familial *habitus* during the Conversion period. By adopting the Christian concept of patriarchal power on Earth and in Heaven, an already culturally familiar internal network of extended kin was maintained and potentially extended. The European kingdoms paid for the initial missionary efforts officially

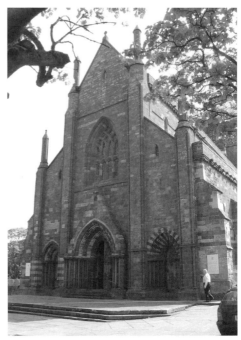

Fig 84. St Magnus's Cathedral, Kirkwall, Orkney.

as a part of a proto-colonization effort in which there was no initial official sanction to the onset of settlement in order to assist in the collection of church dues and payment in kind of raw materials.[73] This was an economic choice on the parts of the political powers of Norway and Denmark, one concerning the economics of the spirit.

Christianity supported the consolidation of power that mediated access to God via control of the sacrament. This provided a widespread and increasingly international system of legitimacy that is closely linked to inheritance not only in the north Atlantic settlements but in Continental Europe as well. In this new system, God, via His representatives, made births, deaths and marriages legitimate and thus subject to the benefits of the local law. This replaced the earlier process of public acknowledgement via family heads and the local community. The Conversion allowed the North Atlantic populations to be able to prove their legal identity to the wider world while simultaneously belonging to a much larger extended kin group.

The widespread Conversion to Christianity reflected the consolidation of local socio-political power occurring during the early-medieval period across the North Atlantic Zones.[74] The personal power of the family head became one more firmly socio-economic in nature although physical expression of this was not restricted from ecclesiastical constructions and foundations. These were social obligation gifts to the wider public.[75] A family which was able to afford to maintain a priest to say the Mass and perform sacraments for a community, the liturgical equipment and a devoted location is one who's farm(s) and economic choices are sound or at least is well connected by socio-political networks, for instance the medieval Scandinavian kingdoms. As in North-West Europe, the North Atlantic Church became co-dependent upon existent social hierarchy in this fashion. As time passed, Church representatives were gifted with lands both by parishioners and by their own extended kin. This allowed the Church to be established not only physically and functionally as well when Church farms became established. These farms were top farms – social obligation gifts to God via the mediation of the Church. An example from Zone 1 is Kirkjubøur on Streymoy, shown in Fig 83. Examples from Zone 2 include the Episcopal seats of Skáholt and Holar. Examples from Zone 3 include the Episcopal farm at modern Igaliku, and modern Qassiarsuk, shown in Figs 82 and 81 respectively.

Discussion

The relatively brief period was incredibly changeable on a variety of levels thus creating the preconditions not only for the reinforcement of traditional and new practices of identity. This is most evident from burial evidence that is numerically abundant in Zone 2 as well as a similar process in literature production, which is also best represented in Zone 2. Due to this only Zone 2 is truly able to be considered and as a result has been heavily relied upon as source material regarding the Conversion process across not only the north Atlantic region but Scandinavia as well.[76] Burial evidence becomes more distinctly pagan or Christian in nature during the period immediately preceding and following the official Conversion of Iceland.[77]

The process as evidenced by literary material is linked to the oral history and folklore of a society first being written down when the new medium arrives.[78] This process was first seen locally as a means of continuing memory of events and practices that were being lost via the transition from traditional pagan practices such as accompanied interments to the incoming ideas and practices of the medieval Christian Church.[79] At least in Zone 2 this evidence highlights the presence of populations who were aware of this process of change and importantly were active participants within this exchange of ideas. These populations utilized the Conversion process being officially offered from Episcopal seats in Continental European kingdoms to reinforce macroscale concepts of identities within this medieval international milieu. As texts were created within the newly converted North Atlantic Zones heirlooms of local oral history and remembered 'traditional' pagan practice were embedded within.[80] This fusion of traditional and Christian elements was desirable to medieval Scandinavian kingdoms in particular and it is unsurprising that North Atlantic poets were desired at Court.[81] This luxury export of Zone 1 and Zone 2 was externally recognized and utilized as a tie to the period prior to kingdom consolidation when practices of gift exchange and adoration of leaders via battle prowess and generosity as a means of establishing and maintaining power with the chieftainship network of the Late Antique and Early Viking Age circa AD 1–1000.[82]

Chapter 8

Building and Maintaining Identities in the North Atlantic – A Material Perspective

Introduction

This chapter attempts to bring together the thoughts on North Atlantic identity development and maintenance during the Norse medieval period. It begins with consideration of the contexts present at onset of settlement. It then moves on to consider the potential drivers that may have contributed to the migration and how that influenced identity practice via the prioritization of cargos sent from Scandinavia westwards. It compares the domestic practice evidence of microscale identity from all Atlantic Zones and subsequently comments upon the overarching networks of trade and common religion in light of the impact this wider context has upon macroscale identity construction and maintenance. It goes on to critique the use of comparative identity methodology and its capability to clarify homogeneous archaeological assemblages in the north Atlantic.

Identity and the Preconditions for Norse Expansion West

Unless fleeing persecution and bodily harm no major move such as that undertaken by North Atlantic settling populations is undertaken by humans unless some degree of success is guaranteed at both microscale – survival – and macroscale – network – success. This is evidenced via the variety of priorities evidenced in settling, and subsequent trade, voyages. There is no singular cause of settlement in the North Atlantic but rather a collection of preconditions that are evidenced by their subsequent responses. This includes climatic optimal which occurred during the Medieval period resulted in calmer seas with less dangerous sea ice being present on the ocean currents providing much of the trade routes across the North Atlantic.[1] Due to this, more socially peripheral and climatically marginal regions such as Zone 3 and northern Zone 2 were able to be accessed directly by sailing vessels and land on sandy beaches. Another impact of the Medieval Optimal is the effect upon the long distance migration routes of sub-arctic and Arctic species such as the North Atlantic walrus.[2]

Socio-political pressures linked to the contemporary consolidation of north-western European chieftainships into medieval kingdoms such as Denmark and

Internal	External	In between area
On ship	Those not undertaking the voyage	Affiliated contacts which directly impact success of voyage
Settlement Farm	Those not part of the farm unit – essentially kin	Those hired to work, traders, extended kin
Free State Farm	Within farm networks [locally, socially etc]	Those hired to work, traders, extended kin, priests
	Within local commune network [economically etic]	Those hired to work, traders, extended kin, priests
	Within Zone, as occurred during Assembly meetings [legally, wider social implications]	Those hired to work, traders, extended kin, priests
	Within the Christian world [religiously]	Those hired to work, traders, extended kin, priests
Medieval Farm	Within farm networks [locally, socially etc]	Those hired to work, traders, extended kin, priests
	Within local commune network [economically etic]	Those hired to work, traders, extended kin, priests
	Within Zone, as occurred during Assembly meetings [legally, wider social implications]	Those hired to work, traders, extended kin, priests
	Within the Christian world [religiously]	Those hired to work, traders, extended kin, priests

Fig 85. Designation of internal and external group elements.

Norway as well as principalities such as Orkney.[3] This is anachronistically cited in later medieval textual sources, however, the increasing social and political intrigue may have provided some driver towards migration.[4] Population pressures have been casually linked in the past; however, there is little evidence for this archaeologically in the North Atlantic. Was there a desire for freedom of a group from the context of the Scandinavian world? The reality of this situation is difficult to discuss. Again – this is anachronistically alluded to in thirteenth century Icelandic sources. Internal and external group elements found in this system are illustrated in Fig 85.

The concurrent Conversion process is also important to consider as a majority vector. This process began due to efforts from the South with missionary efforts being staged from England and Germany. Economics became tied in as well as acceptance of the Sign of the Cross became a prerequisite for medieval trade in north-western Europe. The power structures of medieval European kingdoms

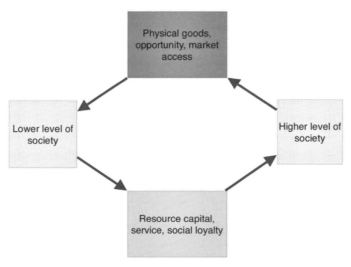

Fig 86. Hierarchal interaction applicable to both microscale and macroscale levels of identity.

were supported by ideas found within Christian doctrine and Church practice. Christianity applied the kin-based format known to the North on an international scale – hence it was acceptable to most of the population. Those people who were unable to cope with the change were able to retreat west becoming effectively beyond the law of the wider population and maintained their preferred pagan practices. For these groups individuals rather than national bodies dictated local religious practice. Pagan religion was kin-linked with the locus of activity being local and reinforcing social hierarchy. Kin-units ran farms and only consolidated power after some negotiation. The same kin-units established the networks of exchange and maintained them as long as it was convenient to the wider family unit. Once the local power at the periphery of the North Atlantic consolidated it began to exert power over access to the kin-originated international trade networks. This process in turn reinforced the power of the core over the network. Hence the maintenance of medieval Scandinavian kingdoms was possible in part due to this process. The local networks became associated with maintaining their part in the international bulk trade.

North Atlantic Identity Development
Early in the period identity can be visualized as having these key components which are used to answer specific needs identification inside. All of these components are impacted by spatial and temporal element of the contextual

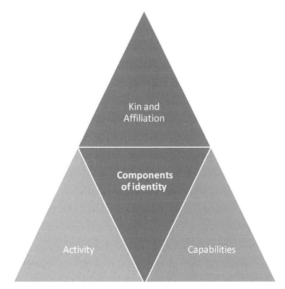

Fig 87. Identity expression vectors in the ninth and tenth centuries.

environment. When considered together this results in the fluidity and spectrum of identities present on site and the wider network.

Distinct preservation of previous identity is made initially in regions with prior inhabitants. This is best evidenced by the placement of Norse farms and burials in relation to older settlements and prominent places in Shetland and Orkney. In these areas not only were soils more suitable for agriculture present but also networks of exploitation were already established including wild species collection, social hierarchy and trade. This does not occur in the Faroe Islands or Zone 2 until the eleventh and twelfth centuries due to increased North Atlantic presence politically, socially and economically within Scandinavian networks and vice versa. The settlers trying to establish themselves are promoting no new identity. The importance of maintaining common family connections and practices is maintained – good examples of this exist as burial evidence from throughout the region. In Zone 2 in particular the amount of available burials shows practices present in both Scandinavia as well as in Zone 1. This hints at some attempts to maintain a family identity that was emic in nature. This does not necessarily imply a strictly Scandinavian identity, however. This is expressed by farm inheritance. These farm sites were being chosen because they were seemingly familiar to areas known elsewhere in the settler's life experience. These were areas where the methods of construction, land exploitation and the diversity of farm economic scheme would be more likely to work. Hence, this would be a reduction of the risk inherent to moving to foreign areas. Oral histories later recorded rely on use of these connections as the means of information referencing in medievally collected sources.[5]

At the beginning of the settlement process trading in northwestern Europe was dominated by exotic luxuries which were low in bulk. This allowed traders to integrate themselves as middlemen within sociopolitical networks of power and prestige on a scale that was larger than that of their immediate locale. Settlement may have been initiated to find new resource areas for markets in medieval Europe. The best-known example of this is walrus ivory.[6] Following the twilight and fall of the Western Roman Empire the trade networks that had brought elephant ivory to northern European artisans failed, creating a void and unfulfilled need.[7] This supply was met from the sixth through the eleventh centuries by another source of ivory – walrus tusk. Walrus are found in sub-arctic and arctic areas where they spend much of their existence feeding on molluscs and sunning on pack ice. They have not existed in Continental European waters for millennia. However, the northern most coasts of Norway, the White Sea and Svalbard all maintained walrus breeding populations. The hunting techniques that procured the animals were parts of a male habitus due to the inherent risk. The exploitation of populations in the White Sea region is known from contemporary text sources as well such as the account of Ohthere made in the court of Alfred the Great.[8] Walrus evidence has been found amongst early Zone 2 assemblages such as at Aðalstræti.[9] Walrus evidence is also known from several Zone 3 sites, most spectacularly arranged at Igaliku.[10] This was able to be collected as a by-product of subsistence hunting as well as via intensified specialized hunting to supply ivory needs at a higher profit. Once reliable trade was re-established with Africa elephant ivory returned to the European market. As elephant ivory is more desirable to carve than walrus tusk due to size and the thickness of the enamel layer to the tooth, the demand for walrus ivory declined.[11] Associated with this economically driven need to expand resource networks may have been one driven by human curiosity and fuelled by knowledge of earlier voyages later remembered as being affiliated with early-medieval priests from the Irish Sea and North Sea Region.[12] By exploring lands further west, new resource regions could be claimed and existing trade networks could be infiltrated.

Archaeologically the North Atlantic can be placed economically and to a certain extent even ideologically in the medieval world. This is not without some difficulty however as site assemblages across the region are notoriously homogenous in nature. This is due to a variety of reasons. The geologic basement rocks of these island archipelagos have created some diversification to what types of economy supported the farms. There are also influences on the types of plants available as well. This includes latitude-linked temperatures, the maritime effects of salinity and the types of trees and woody-stemmed plants.

Another influence of homogenous site assemblages in the North Atlantic is long distance economic exchange. The presence of trade goods both mediated and heavily skewed the availability of regional specialization evidence concerning identity. Trade goods in this period were chosen due to market need and demand. They ranged from food stuffs – grain, spices and animal stock – to woollen textiles to animal by-products such as walrus-skin rope. Trade goods may have also included information as well. The evidence of exchange comes from the presence of exotic material within both north Atlantic and Continental medieval archaeological assemblages. For this region domesticated animals, grain and current fashions of culture and thought would have been exotic imports. Exports appear as desired exotics but also as incredibly practical textiles. The amount of available evidence is linked to preservation – the inorganic elements of trade cargos exchanged into farm unit networks over time are what survived. Market demand may have also later suppressed a variety of organic material production. Organic goods such as textiles may well have been an example of regional specialization linked to the visual expression of identity in the North Atlantic. The process of diversification is prolonged with the physical evidence because of the distances that had to be travelled between the archipelagos. In spite of this maintenance of identity via trade became a specialized maritime assisted activity due to the environmental pressures in a similar fashion to the Thule Inuit populations which began to migrate into Zone 3 during the eleventh century.

Socially only Zone 2 is able to be discussed both in terms of what was practiced internally in conjunction with external presentations of practice, and even then only in an detail subsequent to the Settlement period. This is due to the wealth of literary evidence that survives in Iceland and in Scandinavian libraries.[13] Sources such as these were utilized to provide a historically linked social context for several excavated sites in Zone 2, in a nationalistic writing or archaeological history.[14] By utilizing Zone 2 material this expression of identity can be compared in relation to the rest of medieval European identities being concurrently expressed.

The international trade in the Early Middle Ages focused on portable luxury goods which were exotic in origin. This type of good is easily utilized within networks of gift exchange. By exchanging such items an individual's trader and middle-man identity in both the local and the international network was maintained and potentially built higher. This network integrated several drivers of North Atlantic life and identity – economic, political and social – and allowed physical goods to effect the non-physical medieval social hierarchy.

However, this begins to change during the 11th century with kin and affiliation in particular changing overtime as national groups established themselves over the network. This process can be viewed in Fig 88.This process is best known and discussed relationship consolidation of the continent kingdoms. It begins early with proto-emporia establishing in the North Sea region. Power was exerted by local magnates who control over trading locations. It was negotiated to trade in social gift exchange. The international trade of the later Medieval Period focused on high bulk goods where a trader's money was made by the sale of a full cargo. Ships were larger and more costly to run, however, the potential economic gain was much higher. Market demand shifted from small luxuries for use within gift exchange networks to being more dominated by bulk goods such as grain. This was possible due to changes in ship technology which were costly in terms of enacting. For the north Atlantic settlements, particularly that furthest west, extended networks based on siblings and cousins formed a means of entering the increasingly nationally dominated networks. Instead of fleets, ships were able to set sail on a much smaller scale while still interacting with the wider international medieval market of continental Europe. This type of voyage was costly but has a high potential gain for the financial backer of the

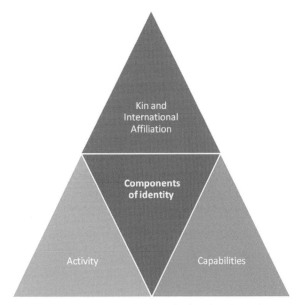

Fig 88. Identity expression vectors during the eleventh century.

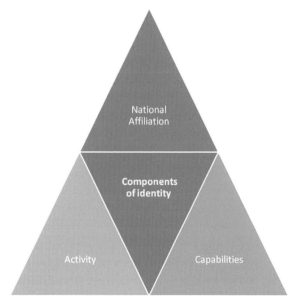

Fig 89. Identity expression vectors in the twelfth and thirteenth centuries.

voyage. Due to this, this type of shipping is increasingly associated with national sized bank rolls, international trading groups and the Church. Later networks became associated with maintaining their part in the international bulk trade.

The final stage of the effect this process had on north Atlantic identity is illustrated in Fig 89. By this point national influences are exerted on the extended network taking dominance over kin and affine networks. This is maintained by economic service experience. Once the national bodies make policy decisions over international trade the heavy kin influence which maintained the earlier network is obsolete.

There are broad generalities in domestic site interactions. Common sites were initially chosen which reflect the practical elements of living on an island. Certain jobs are affiliated with a farm unit and the basic necessities of human and beast – everyone needs to eat and shelter is necessary in the North Atlantic region much of the year. Feed for both needed to be collected and prepared. Fuel needed to be collected. Building construction and maintenance had to occur and fencing where needed. Animals needed access to food and water via seasonal movement through the local landscape. In harsh winters, animals would need to be over-wintered in shelter. Assistance or intervention is necessary during some births.[15] These are distinctly terrestrially oriented aspects of social practice for the North Atlantic populations. Finally, any over abundance of product that could be spared from the long-term stores required for subsistence was exchanged for goods not locally available.

The impact of considering material at this level is linked to the fact that most often internal local evidence is displayed on site and hence has no context for modern study. This is dominated by practicalities because of the marginal environment. The annual cycle of diurnal extremes somewhat mediates this. Also important to consider is the fact amongst a local population overt expression of identity may not have been necessary as their family on the farm units knew individuals and the animals did not care.

The case study of Zone 1 represented by Shetland and the Faroe Islands shows several commonalities to site usage in comparison to Orkney and the Hebrides. This is expressed in the format of longhouses as well as similarities in an animal and land exploitation scheme.[16] Similar trajectory and placement in economic networks occurred concerning Scandinavia and North Atlantic interactions. The major difference comes in the presence of inhabitants, their religion and

Fig 90. The Lewis Chessmen King on display at the National Museum of Scotland. Photo by Dr R. Lenfert.

the continued utilization of sites. In the Faroe Islands, the populations were establishing themselves in a less known and exploited environment. Shetland, on the other hand, had previously established networks and regional affiliations. There has been a skewing of physical evidence concerning the overt expression of identity that is linked to the nature of preservation, as discussed in Chapters 4 and 5. The Later Norse constructions utilized more durable stone in their constructions that is linked to practical adaptations to the local environment as well as the height of island prosperity. Intensive modern archaeological survey has been undertaken on Unst has shown that a variety of constructions and a social hierarchy of sites constructed of turf exist.[17] Some of this is linked to the subsequent history of the region from the medieval period – some areas were abandoned prior to the adaptation of modern farming techniques such as deep ploughing. The subconscious practice of a *habitus* in the form of farm networks occur which is evidenced along Scandinavian coasts and affiliated islands.

The case study of Zone 2, Iceland, shows broad regional generalities in site utilization. Iceland is by far the most intensively studied of the North Atlantic archipelagos due to the quality of its oral traditions and literature. In fact this skill became a viable export to Europe for a time. The Western Quarter of Iceland, in contrast to the Southern Quarter, is both more extensively settled and more extensively studied than other parts of Zone 2. This is linked to both geologic structure of the landscape as well as the presence of sheltered bays that were rich in littoral species like walrus and auk. These species exploited the same oceanic currents the medieval North Atlantic populations travelled on.

As with Zone 1, overt expression of identity is difficult to ascertain due to the practicalities of life in a largely unsettled region. Upon death the deceased's family, or affiliates, had the option of presenting elements of identity via funerary activities and burial deposits. Affiliations present accompanied burials sometimes allude to a previous family identity via the inclusion of heirlooms. As time passed and the Zone became firmly established within North Atlantic economic networks identity display became more important. This was done not only to express placement within local hierarchy displayed at gatherings such as at assemblies and the Alþing. As familial ties back to Scandinavia were stretched by time while concurrently economic ties were maintained it became more important to establish an outwardly recognized identity. This was linked to the change in the orientation of the population.

The case study of Zone 3, the Eastern Settlement of Greenland and L'Anse aux Meadows, shows generalities in domestic site utilization as well in comparison to the Western Settlement. In the marginal environment of Zone 3, a working farm was a farm that continued to exist – to feed its humans and livestock and to survive winter.[18] The format of the sites highlights the need of insulation in the thickness of the turf walls. Animals were brought into houses to both protect them and to provide a source of heat that did not require a separate source of fuel. They also highlight the greater need to manage stock in these areas in extended saeter networks.[19] Zone 3 more than other Zones was subject to the effect of timing in the most marginal of areas – in terms of religion, economy, and identity.

Macroscale External Vectors

The basis of the kin-linked farm unit is tied to the previous identity and familial *habitus* expressed prior to settlement. External vectors to this domestic system include trade and economics – the means of maintaining ties between Scandinavia and the North Atlantic. Another vector that was internally replicated yet externally derived in relation to this region was religion. Pagan religion formed a portion of the original *habitus* of settlers to Zone 1 and Zone 2. Christianity, on the other hand, was not only part of Zone 2 and Zone 3 *habitus* but was also part of the wider conversion process of Europe.

Each of the three vectors correspondingly answers identifying questions for the individual and wider group. The early settlers of the North Atlantic experienced a shift in how they were able to establish the credibility and hence identity in the Western European system. North Atlantic populations described their claims over their new lands by expressing the local establishment history in contemporary accepted terms in relation to the Continental European network. At this time activity and capability established individuals as well as groups with affiliation being less important and more directly related to bloodlines. As time passed affiliation became the important catalyst in this extended system providing opportunity to apply capabilities and directed activity. An example of this is the increasing amount of pressure placed on Iceland and Greenland by the medieval kingdom of Norway and the Archbishopric of Trondheim/Niðaros.

Marine technology became well adapted to exploration voyages during the seventh and eighth centuries.[20] Its use became further integrated into the coastal northern European habitus in practice. There are several which are relevant to the North Atlantic. Clinker construction created a hull that was flexible, strong and shallow drafted in comparison to the amount and cargo potential.[21] This was ideal for extended open water voyages that ended by laying the ship over on land to off load cargo. Another development in marine technology important to the settlement of the North Atlantic during the medieval period was the adoption of the sail as a means of propulsion.[22] A rowing crew and their provisions had previously taken this freed space onboard. Efficiency in travel choice is diagrammed in Fig 72. The final important development was the utilization of the *knórr* format that has been discussed previously. This vessel represented long distance travel but not always to foreign lands.

The medieval kingdom of Norway was ultimately able to use the familial ties of high status families to take control of the north Atlantic network. With Zone 1 in particular the line of the Jarls of More in the more prosperous lands of southern Norway became linked by descent to the Isle lords of Orkney and the Inner Hebrides. This connection was also stressed in Zone 2 textual sources via a collateral line as a reason for contemporary medieval success within the north Atlantic economic network. The spiritual care over the western-most portions

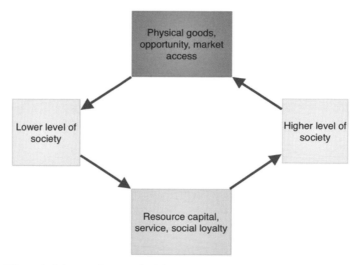

Fig 91. Hierarchal interaction applicable to both microscale and macroscale levels of identity.

of the network were also maintained by Norwegian bodies – the Archbishopric of Niðaros/Trondheim.

Medieval identity is expressed as negotiations and choices existing between localized individuals who function in extended networks of exchange. At its earliest stages identity was still incredibly fluid responding to the context of social needs of the individual and group in accordance Practice Theory. In the North Atlantic this is reflected by a lack of identity specific evidence within the first generation population of immigrants. Choices to reduce risk here were those associated with subsistence. This prioritizes an identity based upon life and its maintenance. The methods utilized to exploit the environment are reflections of the more commonly held North Atlantic habitus of the medieval period. This is expressed in settlement locations and species excluded which are considered viable as well as who was considered to belong in the extended family network.

Another reason why North Atlantic networks developed may be linked to the desire to gain social prestige in relation to Scandinavian and European socio-political hierarchies. Evidence from Zone 1 shows that these hierarchies did not necessarily have to be previously affiliated Scandinavian networks themselves. Hierarchical interaction is illustrated in Fig 91. There were changing social priorities as early on movements that were sometimes violent expanded into already inhabited areas brought an influx of luxury wealth to Scandinavian

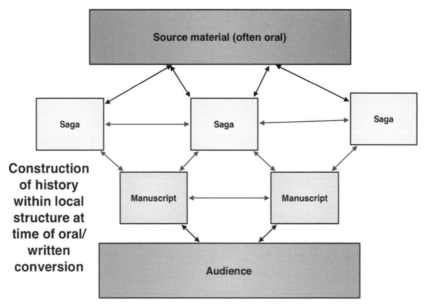

Fig 92. Initial construction of history.

social networks. Once available these goods were utilized in gift exchange interactions that established and maintained relationships dependent upon social obligation. Concurrent to this process raiding and harrying was also increasingly not acceptable for long term economic interactions with a largely Christian Europe, although it too had its merits in a similar fashion to collecting coup. If long-term economic stability and potential prosperity were to occur for northern populations, it would have to be via another route, both literally and figuratively. The social merit once associated with more violent acquisition of high value goods – a risky venture – become associated with long distance trade – another risky venture.

Socially only Zone 2 is able to be discussed both in terms of what was practiced internally in conjunction with external presentations of practice, and even then only in an detail subsequent to the Settlement period. This is due to the wealth of literary evidence that survives in Iceland and in Scandinavian libraries.[23] Sources such as these were utilized to provide a historically linked social context for several excavated sites in Zone 2, in a nationalistic writing or archaeological history.[24] By utilizing Zone 2 material this expression of identity can be compared in relation to the rest of medieval European identities being concurrently expressed.

This status quo maintained until the wider economic and social context of North Atlantic began to change with consolidation of the Scandinavian kingdoms and further development of medieval European economic markets. This process began to occur prior to the onset of the Viking Age. This shift parallels the adoption of Christianity by the Northern European population. Trade, as discussed previously, takes the place of the more violent warrior elite concept. This process is facilitated by the contemporary European context – socially warring factions increasingly had no place. The position of the medieval Catholic Church which strengthened subsequent to the eleventh century also contributed to this shift. The bodily risk affiliated with long-distance maritime trade began to be acknowledged in the same manner as the bodily risk associated with the earlier violence.

Any one, or a combination, of these drivers may have provided impetus to leave Scandinavia for the more sparsely settled resource-rich west. This is an internal view from the perspective of a prioritization of choices. A maritime priority is evident because of the location – islands are affected by the medium surrounding it. The priority is indirectly expressed by the vessel, route, crew and pilot. A terrestrial priority is also expressed. This is accomplished by packing cargos which facilitated the exploitation of little known areas. This

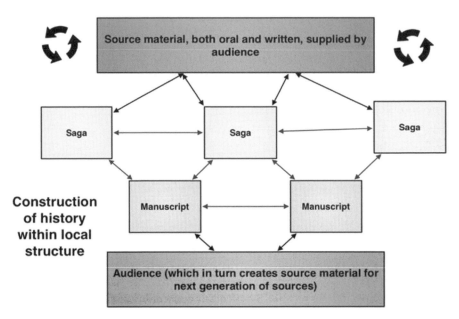

Fig 93. Maintenance of history.

includes the farm unit elements needed to fully translate a farming system, a land and animal exploitation scheme of tools, livestock, land choice, timing and ideas on how to use it all.

The process of settlement – translation of identity via population migration – can also be considered in terms of orientation of microscale voyages between the origin point and north Atlantic Zones and the terrestrial needs of the domesticated species had to be heavily considered and potentially manipulated. This necessitated the practice of terrestrial oriented aspects of identity in order to reduce the risk to stock while reducing the amount of time needed to establish stock post voyage once the farm unit began to be settled. For instance, males were potentially shipped while young so as to be easier to handle on board for the longest amount of time and were thus a reduction of risk to ship. Neutered males would not benefit the establishment of farms subsequent to arrival and hence were less likely to have been brought save as a food source. In order to be at a young age during the time of voyage the pregnancies of mothers would have needed to be timed. This ensures smaller animals that are easier to manage, requiring less feed per animal. Thus more animals or a greater amount of non-living cargo could be sent on a voyage. Less male animals would have been brought as mammalian domesticated livestock species are herd animals – monogamous male/female relations are not required in order to provide offspring.

There are two options for shipping female livestock. The first is young, as potential breeding stock with the same constraints mentioned with reference to males. More profits would have been possible if females were shipped as mothers. By shipping pregnant females who were proven to have few complications during their terms meant within the first year the number of stock on the ground could potentially greatly increase. The safest time to ship pregnant females is during the second trimester as the risks of self-abortion due to shipping stresses.[25] In order to time the second trimester with the onset of the sailing season two types of knowledge are evidenced – a terrestrially oriented demonstration of animal husbandry and a marine oriented knowledge of the season's relations to the seas. If pregnant females were shipped on board the immediate needs for fodder upon landing and during re-supply may have been greater than a cargo of non-pregnant livestock.

Another consideration that must be made is what combination of sexes would contribute to the cargo. Females of or near sexual maturity could only be sent with other females or non-sexually mature males. Pregnant females, however, could share a voyage. Cargos of only males would be less successful for establishing a farm aside from being potentially difficult to control. Once farms

Time Frame	Overt expression of identity evidenced by existing material	Orientation of local population	Why?	Continental Context	How do me know?
Settlement AD **800–950**	No. There is not much new identity although the subconscious and conscious expression of previously held group European identity, however.	Inward- kin and affine	Practicality as establishing farms in new areas	Continental kingdoms solidifying, while in Scandinavia this process occurred concurrently with conversion to Christianity. As a result random violent acts present at the beginning of the period increasingly no longer having a place in society. Hence some horror associated with initial Zone 1 movements.	Archaeology, contemporary history, oral history and poetry later textualized
Conversion AD **950–1050**	In regards to religious identity yes as burials which are accompanied are better represented for this period- the last vestiges of a familial statement of religion. Also the first statements of new familial religion as Christianity is adopted	Inward however Christianity creates the context for this to change.	Kin and affine alike struggle to establish local hierarchies.	Medieval kingdoms- diversification and development of bulk trade networks which is at times politically maintained by violence. This directly impacts trade networks.	Archaeology, contemporary history, oral history and poetry later textualized

Free State AD **1050–1150**	Yes, as influences of the continent increases this becomes more important to establish a foreign other yet when convenient economically, socially and politically claiming Continental ties.	Inward and outward as there is a diversification of place such as island groups being recognized as distinct populations.	Local hierarchies interact in power negotiations politically and socially while economically this occurs with some diversification as this is a further method of establishing a place in the world.	Increasing influence of the Continent in social and political networks of the North Atlantic. This is essentially the control of a guaranteed market.
Sturlung Period AD **1150–1264**	Yes, as the continental domination of the network is achievedithis becomes more important to establish a foreign other yet when convenient economically, socially and politically claiming Continental ties.	Outward projection of a remembered national past which is important to establish. This is increasingly important following AD1264.	The previous context results in fewer and fewer elite families who have greater power. This is done in socially acceptable ways of the Continent.	Increasing influence of the Continent in social and political networks of the North Atlantic. This is essentially the control of a guaranteed market.

(Final column) Free State: Archaeology, contemporary history, of emic and etic nature oral history and poetry later textualized

Sturlung Period: Diversification of archaeological and textual evidence

Fig 94. North Atlantic identity orientations in context.

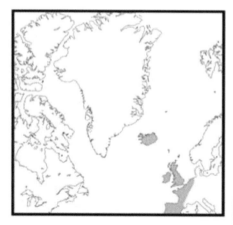

A) The European Atlantic Zone of the Sixth-Seventh Century.

B) The North Atlantic of the Ninth Century. The European Atlantic Zone and Scandinavian Zone are shown.

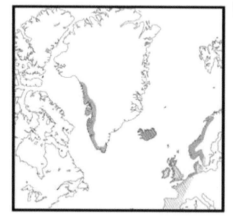

C) The North Atlantic Zone of the Twelfth Century, shown with. the Continental Atlantic Zone and the North Sea Zone.

Fig 95. The Atlantic Zone and its Changes over time.[27]

were established an influx of new blood may have been desired and more males brought. Economic priorities include sourcing new areas and maintaining long distance networks has been discussed in Chapter 10. Both sexes are potentially able to be determined as foreign within archaeological assemblages containing a variety of animal-derived osteological material by utilizing strontium isotope analysis on sampled dental enamel. This should determine the origin location of these individuals from those who were bred and born on site subsequent to the initial settlement population.

Critique of Methodology

This consideration of the north Atlantic utilized a multi-layered consideration of a variety of source material in an effort to move past the homogenous nature of many site assemblages within the study region. Certain aspects fit well with the largely archaeological nature of this study – in particular the elements of group identity. Others, such as the individual level are much more difficult to find archaeologically and hence textual sources were utilized to provide insight into the more elusive evidence. There has been an over-reliance on textual sources within the north Atlantic and Scandinavia to provide the 'truth' of the settlement process which has made archaeologists naturally hesitant, and at times even fully opposed to. This work attempted to sort the fact from fiction by considering how textual sources express the view of a group via the medium of an individual with their own needs and desires which play out in identity.

This study has been heavily impacted by the differences in evidence gathered over time and place. This has been unavoidable due to the low number of fully excavated and published sites across the North Atlantic region in combination with conditions of preservation inherent to studies of the past. Lacunae within the archaeological and textual assemblages have been unavoidable because of this. This context has necessitated an approach that considers material historiographically in relation to evidence of identity. Logistically this study has made heavy use of computer assistance in order to organize and analyze this body of material. In spite of this it is still important to undertake this type of approach as this allows the researcher to consider how identity was perceived and remembered by the past both internal to the population and in the wider European public. At the onset of early-medieval Norse expansion prior to an inclusive of AD 800 populations had no real social and political context requiring them to consider themselves in relation to a national population. As European continental national groupings tied to physical locations were still in the process of consolidation at this time migratory populations moved without a national negotiation for colonization. Identity was composed of the population, by the population and was utilized for the population's perceived benefit. For the modern researcher the overlap between the material record examined by archaeologists and the textual record exists in the generator of both are human populations. Divorce of one from the other inherently results in a much-reduced consideration of cultural context as discovered during Contact Era studies of the Pacific archipelagos including Hawai'i.[26]

Over the history of Old Norse and Viking studies in general these lacunae in the record have been utilized as opportunities to present cross-regional comparison and referencing. This resulted in a homogenous concept of medieval Norse culture existing from Scandinavia to the New World being exported en masse. As this study has shown the reality of this expansion is that island identities were fluid in nature and developed in a similar fashion to medieval identities being expressed on the Continent. These island identities were adopted by groups at will and when convenient as dictated by external contexts. A recent change to this in modern research is that these previously perceived lacunae are now being explored by modern survey and research. Modern techniques are allowing more sites to be found such as at Unst in Shetland.[28]

Fig 96. Leif Eriksson statue at Qassiarsuk, Greenland.

As mentioned previously textual evidence provided by Iceland has allowed identity to be more fully discussed in Zone 2 while simultaneously mediating textual evidence of other Zones via the context of Zone 2. Archaeologically this has been expressed in an allowance of certain sites to be named, where affiliation with sites described in saga texts in particular. The site of Qassiarsuk has been attributed as being Brattahlíð, the farm of Eirik the Red, and subject to the creation of a site monument consisting of reconstructions of the church and farm on site as well as the erection of a statue of Leif Eriksson.

The importance of named sites is tied into the ability to attribute individual and group action to a specific place. These perform a function of legitimization within a wider consideration of the world past. Named sites became site archetypes in the North Atlantic nationally and internationally funded excavations continually referenced cross-regionally to consolidate the idea of a singular unified Norse culture.

The story of the settlement of the North Atlantic has been a national identity debate since the medieval period. Local island populations present at this time began to consider themselves as distinct from Scandinavia. However, populations who belonged to neither group saw the only real difference being the physical location of origin. As time passed, it became increasingly important to North Atlantic populations to establish themselves overtly as distinct. As social and political powers based in Europe began to establish themselves within economic networks this became reflected in textual evidence as references to an anachronistically nationally sponsored colonization of the North Atlantic were imposed to strengthen an increasingly modern nationalistic view. A physical representation of this colonization of history is the Leif Eriksson statue gifted from Norway to Greenland and mounted overlooking Qassiarsuk during the 1960s. This is illustrated in Fig 96.

The settlement of the North Atlantic provides a unique situation for the modern researcher as upon initial inspection this appears to be another example of imperialistic archaeology being applied across colonial area. This is due to the major early excavations of the Norse north Atlantic being conducted under the needs of the late nineteenth and early twentieth century public. However, the colonization of this region was not initially driven by a national political body – a macroscale driver for identity and migration. This is claimed only after the initial settlement phase by Norway during the 1260s when Zone 2 is incorporated formally into the region. This occurred concurrent to the creation of the written texts as cultural artefacts, statements of prestige in and of themselves, which became another way for macroscale ideas to be presented to North Atlantic populations. This use of texts as cultural artefacts is in keeping with wider macroscale European practices. This resulted in the texts which were written within this context of social and political negotiations being taken as historical fact by subsequent generations when these North Atlantic texts and their affiliated farm sites became included in modern historical research. The role of these texts changed.

The corpus of evidence was rediscovered and added to by nineteenth century European researchers who were intent upon confirming nationalistic/ imperialistic elements of a common Scandinavian past both physically on archaeological sites and within written works perceived as history. Zone 2 microscale efforts of establishing a recognizable European identity – an inherently macroscale statement. These statements existed within larger collections enclosed in manuscripts. This process is diagrammed in Figs 87, 88 and 89. This format is quite similar to the breakdown of the system of trade and exchange which consolidated integration into the international network. In this view, manuscripts can be seen as intermediaries of ideas, identities and ideas about identities which are both emic and etic in nature. Fig 94 places North Atlantic identity orientations in context.

The settlement of the North Atlantic is one that does not appear to be initially planned by a government – one of the last to occur in Western civilization prior to the exploration efforts of the Renaissance. It is important to consider that these populations previously familiar with maritime environments may have known some resources. Certain migratory species of marine birds as well as mammals and fish may have been followed the knowledge of their migratory nature being exploited as a practice of marine oriented practice. Previous exploration occurred prior to settlement in Zone 3 and it is not unreasonable to assume that a similar process occurred in Zone 2 and in Zone 1 as well.[29] Once farms were established and making an impact upon economic networks European-based desires to control or at least profit from this lengthy network began in earnest. Once the European powers, such as the Church, were established in the region, it became more important to link identity to the official efforts of colonization – a national colonization of history. The distinct identities became the root of the modern nations known today in the North Atlantic.

Conclusions

Identity and its constituents were not solely consciously defined by those experiencing them, nor are they in modern populations. There is inherent difficulty in defining typological differences with a combination of tangible and intangible evidence. Due to this, the situational context of the identity under construction is incredibly important in order to define what contributes to identity and what existed as separate and thus distinct. Material culture, landscape utilization, physical attributes, the choices made in relation to these as well as the intangible aspects such as mores, norms, values, traditions and history interact and modify each other via humans themselves resulting in a cultural tapestry which occurs internal and external to populations. In the multivalent approach utilized by this work a singular approach is inherently unable to comment upon populations exhibiting similar cultural habitus. The cross-referencing of material properly applied is able to reduce effects of bias inherent to the evidence and its manner of collection that facilitates a more complex view of north Atlantic migration and settlement. This is a view that will benefit from greater amounts of modern excavations as they are published to help counteract the amount of early excavations that continue to be utilized as cultural references throughout the north Atlantic. Only in this way can the homogenous view of north Atlantic settlement be surpassed.

Grænlendinga Saga[1]

Translator's Note: This translation has been edited to create a slightly easier text to read. To this effect the worst of the run-on sentences have been broken up and punctuation edited to reflect more modern utilization. Where possible the medieval construction of the text has been maintained.

Kapituli 1

Þorvald was a man called, the son of Asvald, son of Úlf, son of Oxen-Þórir. Þorvald and Eirik the Red, his son, travelled from Jaðri[2] to Iceland due to a killing.[3] Then was well settled Iceland. They settled first at Drangr in Hornstrands. There died Þorvald. Eirik married then Þjóðhild,[4] daughter of Jorund Úlfsson the son of Þorbjorg the Ship-Breasted, who at that time was married to Þorbjorn of Haukadale. Travelled Eirik then north and farmed at Eiriksstaðir near Vatnshorn. The son of Eirik and Þjóðhild was named Leif. But after the killing of Eyjólf Saurs[5] and Dueller-Hrafn was Eirik sent away from Haukadale. Travelled he then west to Breiðafjord and farmed in Øxney, at Eiriksstaðir. He lent Þorgest of Breiðabólstaðir [his] bench boards and [they were] returned not when he requested them. Thence after it was quarrels and fights with Þorgest, same as is said in Eiriksaga.[6] Styrr Þorgrimson supported Eirik in his lawsuit and Eyjólf of Svíney and the sons of Þorbrand of Álptafjord and ÞorbjornVífilsson. But Þorgest was supported by the sons of Þorðr Bellower and Þorgeir of Hítardale. Eirik was outlawed at Þórness þing; prepared Eirik then his ship to sail forth from Eirik's Bay. And when he was ready, accompanied Styrr and the others with him out beyond the islands which Gunnbjorn, son of Úlf Crow, had seen, when he was driven west over sea, there where he found Gunnbjorn's Skerries.[7] He declared he would return to seek his friends, if he found this land. Eirik sailed out past Snæfell glacier.[8] He found land and came there where he called Middle glacier, but is now called Blue-shirt.[9]

He travelled thence to the south with land in sight, seeing if it was suitable for settlement. He spent the first winter at Eirik's Island,[10] near the middle of the Eastern Settlement. The following spring travelled he to Eiriksfjord and established there his farm.[11] He travelled that summer in the unsettled lands to the west [of his settlement] and extensively gave names. He was another winter on Eirik's Islets near Hvarf's Peak.[12] But in the third summer travelled he up north to Snæfell and into Hrafnsfjord[13]. Then he declared to himself that he had come in further inland than Eirikssfjord. Then he turned back and was the third winter on Eirik's Island before the mouth of Eirikssfjord. The following summer travelled he to Iceland and brought his ship into Breiðafjord.[14] He called that land which he had found Greenland because he declared that many more men should go thence if the land was named well. Eirik was in Iceland for a winter, but the summer after travelled he to the settled land. He farmed at Brattahlíð on Eirikssfjord.[15] So say learned men, that the same summer that Eirik the Red travelled to settle Greenland, then twenty-five ships sailed from Breiðafjord and Borgarfjord, but only fourteen came out thence. Some had been driven back but some had been lost. That was fifteen winters before Christianity was taken as law in Iceland. And it was also the same summer that Friðrek Bishop and Þorvald Koðránsson travelled abroad.[16]

These men named land in Greenland, who had travelled out with Eirik: Herjólf at Herjólfsfjord,[17] he farmed at Herjólfnes,[18] Ketil at Ketilsfjord,[19] Hrafn at Hrafnsfjord,[20] Solvi at Solvadale,[21] Helgi Þorbrandsson at Álptafjord,[22] Þorbjorn

Fig 97. The reconstructed Viking Age longhouse located at Qassiarsuk, Greenland.

glóra at Siglufjord,[23] Einar at Einarsfjord,[24] Hafgrímm at Hafgrimsfjord[25] and [the] Lake District, Arnlaug at Arnlaugsfjord. Some travelled on to the Western Settlement.

Kapituli 2

Herjólf was the son of Bard, son of Herjólf. He was kin of Ingólf the First Settler.[26] Herjólf's family[27] had been given by Ingólf land between Vog and Reykjaness. Herjólf farmed first at Drepstokk. Þorgerð was his woman called, and Bjarni their son, who was a very promising man. He had been eager while young to sail abroad; he got himself both wealth and good standing amongst men, and spent his winters alternately in other lands and with his father. Bjarni soon had a ship for himself. The last winter which he was in Norway then Herjólf sold his farm and moved to Greenland with Eirik. With Herjólf on ship was a Hebridean man[28], Christian, who created the 'Disturbed Waters Poem'.[29]

This is its refrain:

I bid the sinless tester of monks
To lend a hand on my journeys;
May the Lord of the High World's Halls
Hold his hand over me.

Herjólf farmed at Herjólfnes; he was a man of good standing.

Eirik the Red farmed at Brattahlíð. He was there with highest honors, and all looked to him. These were the children of Eirik: Leif, Þorvald and Þorstein, and Freydís was called his daughter. She was given to a man, who Þorvarð was called, and farmed they at Garðr, there where is now the Bishop's seat.[30] She was a greatly haughty woman but Þorvarð was little-minded, she had married mostly for money.

Fig 98. Modern Igaliku, Garðr that was, as seen from the peaks above the settlement.

Heathen were people in Greenland at this time.[31] That same summer came Bjarni's ship into Eyrar, when his father had sailed forth that spring past. About this news thought Bjarni greatly and wished nothing to be taken from his ship. Then asked his crew what he had in mind. He replied that he intended to keep his tradition and over-winter with his father, 'so I will sail my ship to Greenland, if you are willing to come with me.' All replied to him that they would follow his will.

Then replied Bjarni, 'Ignorant this journey will seem as none of us have ever travelled the Greenland Sea.' However, they set out to sea once they were readied and sailed for three days until the land was hidden by water. Then the fair wind failed and laid in northern winds and fog and knew they not where they travelled. They sailed thus for many days.[32] After that saw they the sun and got their bearings. Then sail was raised and they sailed a day after which they sighted land, and discussed amongst themselves, what land this might be, but Bjarni declared that he didn't think it could be Greenland. They [the crew] asked whether he would sail to this land or not.

Bjarni answered, 'This is my council, to sail in close to land.' They did thus and soon could see that land was without mountains and greatly wooded, and with small hills, and they lay on with land to the backboard and lay on from land once more.[33]

Following this they sailed two more days, and they then saw another land. They [the crew] asked, whether Bjarni believed this land to be Greenland. He replied that he did not think this to be Greenland anymore than the first, 'because there are said to be great glaciers in Greenland.' They brought themselves close to that land and saw that it was flat and widely wooded.[34] The wind left them then. Then the crew counseled that they thought it advisable to take to that land but Bjarni desired that not. They [the crew] claimed themselves to need both wood and water.

'You have a shortage of neither,' said Bjarni. Later though he was criticized for this action by his crew. He bid them to raise sails and so it was done and set out over sea from that land and sailed over the sea to the southwest for three days and saw then land for a third time and that land was high and mountainous and full of glaciers.[35] They [the crew] asked then if Bjarni desired to land on this particular land but he replied to desire that not, 'because it seems to me that this land is without worth.'

Now they did not lower their sails, following the land around and saw that it was an island. Once more the stern was set to land and held themselves before the same good wind. But the weather became an ox in the hand[36] and bade Bjarni then to shorten sail and not press the ship and the rigging. They sailed now for four days. Then saw they land a fourth time. They [the crew] asked Bjarni whether he believed this [land] to be Greenland or not.

Bjarni replied, 'This is like most what has been said to me of Greenland, and here we shall land. 'So they did thus and took to land on a particular promontory[37] at the end of the day, was there a boat on the shore. And there farmed Herjólf, the father of Bjarni, on that promontory, and because of this the promontory was ever after called Herjólfnes. Existed Bjarni now with his father and halted sailing and stayed with his father, while Herjólf lived, and afterwards farmed he there after his father.

Kapituli 3

Sometime later Bjarni Herjólfsson came east from Greenland to visit Eirik Jarls,[38] and the Jarl was well taken with him. Said Bjarni the tale of his journeys and the lands he had seen, but thought people that he was lacking in curious spirit because he had no knowledge of those lands and he was criticized for this. Bjarni was made hirð man of the Jarl and travelled back to Greenland for the summer after.

There was now great discussion of land looking. Leif, the son of Eirik the Red of Brattahlíð, travelled to visit Bjarni Herjólfsson and bought the ship from him and raised a crew, so that there were 35 men on board. Leif asked his father Eirik to be the first to be on these journeys.[39] Eirik was reluctant, declaring to be too old and said he could endure less than he once did. Leif declared he should still command more luck than his other kin. And this caused Eirik to let Leif have his way and rode home there where they were prepared as the way was short to travel to the ship. The horse stumbled, that which Eirik rode, and fell he from the back, and injured his leg. Then swore Eirik, 'It seems to me I am not intended to find lands other than this, which we now inhabit. We shall no longer travel together.' Travelled Eirik home to Brattahlíð but Leif readied his ship and his crew with him, the thirty-five men. There was a single Southern[40] man in the group, who was called Tyrkir.

Now prepared they the ship and sailed out to sea and left when they were ready and visited then that land first where Bjarni had visited. There sailed they to that land and cast anchor and shot the boat[41] and travelled the land and saw there was no grass. Great glaciers were all over but between all seemed to be one great stone all with glaciers from the sea, and it appeared to them that land to be worthless. Then declared Leif, 'Now we have that which Bjarni has not as far this land is concerned, we have actually landed on it. Now must I give a name to this land and call it Helluland.'[42]

Fig 99. Location map for the site of L'Anse aux Meadows, shown on the island of Newfoundland.[43]

Afterwards they went back to the ship. After this they sailed over sea and found another land, sailed into land and cast anchor, after that they shot the boat and walked on the land. That land was flat and greatly wooded, and wide white sands where they travelled, and gentle slopes down the beaches. Then declared Leif, 'This land shall be named after its gifts and called Markland.'[44] They travelled quickly back to the ship then.

Now sailed they thence over sea on a north-eastern wind and were out for two days until they saw land, and sailed towards the land coming to an island[45] which lay to the north of the land. They walked there out and saw about themselves good weather and found that there was dew on the grass. The thing they did first was they took in their hands some of the dew and brought it to their mouths and they knew it to be the sweetest thing that there was. Then they went back to their ship and sailed into that sound which lay between the island and the promontory which was north from the land. They steered to the west of the promontory. There were extensive shallows so that at low tide their ship was left up out of the water. But they were so greatly impatient to go to land that they could not wait for the tide to re-raise their ship and ran to land there where a river fell from a lake. Once the tide came back under their ship then took they the boat and rowed to the ship and sailed that up a river and after a lake and cast there the anchor and bore from the ships their skin bedding and put up booths. They then decided that they would over winter there and built in that place houses great.[46]

There was no lack of salmon in the rivers or the lakes, and bigger salmon than they before had seen.[47] There was such good land gifts that it seemed to them there should be no stock fodder needed for over winter. To there comes no frost in the winter, and little withering to the grass. Here there were more even days than in Greenland or Iceland; the sun was up by 9am and set after 3pm.[48]

Once they had finished their house building then declared Leif to his crew: 'Now will I split our group into two, as I wish to know the lay of this land, and shall one group be with our homes, but the other group shall explore the land and go out no longer than they are able to come home at night and separate not.' So it went thus with them for a time. Leif took turns himself, that he should travel with them or was home at the halls. Leif was a tall man and strong, and very impressive to view, a shrewd man and moderate in all his behavior.

Kapituli 4

One particular night there came news, that one man was missing from their group and was that Tyrkir the Southern man.[49] Leif took this knowledge poorly because Tyrkir had long been with his family and devoted great was Leif as a child.[50] Leif told his family and devoted great was Leif as a child. Leif told his men off greatly and made ready to search himself and 12 men with him. But when they were shortly come from the halls then came Tyrkir towards them and was he well acknowledged. Leif realized quickly that his foster-father[51] was in very good humor. He was broad-headed and shifty-eyed but not much to look at little-statured and puny-looking but a clever man in all his hands produced. Then spoke Leif to him: 'Why are you so late, foster-father mine, and how did you break from your group?'

He spoke at first for a time in German and shot his eyes all around and made faces but they understood not what he had said.[52] He spoke then in Norse and told the group, 'I was not much farther than you. I have some news to tell you, I found vines and grapes.'

'Is that true, foster-father mine? 'said Leif.

'Of course is that true,' said he, 'because there where I was born there are lots of vines and grapes.' Now slept they then that night, but in the morning spoke Leif with his crew, 'Now shall there be two tasks before us and shall we on alternate days gather grapes and cut vines as well as fell trees so that there will be cargo for my ship.[53] 'And this was the council taken. So it is said that their boat was full of grapes. Now was the cut wood cargo on board ship. And in the spring then prepared themselves to sail forth and gave Leif a name to the land after its gifts and called it Vínland. Sailed they at this point over sea, and got good winds, there until they saw Greenland and the mountains under glaciers.

Then spoke one man of the crew with Leif: 'Why steer you our ship so close to the wind?'

Leif replied, 'I am watching my steering, but even though still watch something else. Don't you see something?'

They [the crew] replied to see nothing there where something should be.

'I am not sure' said Leif, 'whether I see a ship or a skerry.'[54] Now saw they [the crew] and declared it to be a skerry. His sight was better than theirs, so that he saw men on the skerry.

'Now will I take the boat close under the wind' said Leif, 'so that we can reach them if the men are in need of us we are bound to give it, but if they are hostile then the advantage is with our men there shall not be cost to us but none on theirs. 'Now they approached the skerry and lowered their sail, cast the anchor and shot a little boat, which they had brought with them.

Then asked Tyrkir, who there led the group. A man declared himself to be called Þórir and was a Norwegian man by birth, 'But what is your name?'

Leif replied this in return.

'Are you the son of Eirik the Red of Brattahlíð? 'said he.

Leif declared to be so. 'Now will I 'said Leif, 'bid you all onto my ship and their goods with them which my ship will take. 'They accepted this and sailed then to Eirikssfjord with the goods there until they came to Brattahlíð and emptied the goods from the ship. Afterwards bade Leif Þórir to visit with him and Guðríð, his woman, and three other men and found lodgings for the crew, both Þórir's and his own group. Leif took 15 men from the skerry. He was there after called Leif the Lucky. Leif gained now both in wealth and in worth of men. That winter came a great illness in Þórir's crew and Þórir himself died from it and many of his men as well. That winter died Eirik the Red as well.

Now there was discussion great about the Vínland journey of Leif and thought Þorvald, his brother, that this land was not known enough. Then spoke Leif with Þorvald, 'You shall journey with my ship, brother, if you will to Vinland, and so wish I, though the ship must first go after that wood, which Þórir had left on the skerry. 'And thus it went.

Kapituli 5

Now prepared Þorvald for voyage with a crew of thirty men as well as the council of Leif, his brother. Once the ship was prepared they set off over sea, and there were no tales of their journey until they came to Vínland, to Leif's Booths. They prepared there their ship, and sat it for the winter and caught fish to feed themselves. But the following spring spoke Þorvald, that they should prepare their ship and the ship's boat [as well] and a group of men with would travel west before the land[55] and explore there during the summer.

They found the land to be attractive and wooded nearly to the shore with white sands. There were islands many and shallows great. They found no evidence of men's lodgings or animals but on one western island where found they a *kórnhjalmr* of wood. That they found was the only work of men and travelled [they] after until they came to Leif's Booths in autumn. But the summer after travelled Þorvald first east with his trade ship and then north before the land. Then a great storm came before them from a headland and were driven then there up, and broke the keel and [they] were held there long and repaired their ship. Then spoke Þorvald with his crew men, 'Now will I raise here up the keel on the headland and name it '*Kjarlarnes*'[56]. And so they did this.

Afterwards sailed they thence away east before the land and then between fjord mouths where there was a headland and onto that head they there went forth. It was all wooded greatly. Then lay their ship alongside and shot the gangway onto land, and walked Þorvald there up the shore with all of his crewmen. He spoke then: 'Here it is beautiful and here will I raise my farm.'

After that they walked back to the ship and saw before them three humps and travelled further and saw there skin boats three and three men were under each.[57] Then split they[58] their force and took them all in hand, except for one who got himself away with his boat. They killed the other eight and walked then back to the headland and viewed there around and saw in the fjord other humps and believed they this to be settlements. Following that came a great sleepiness so that they could not remain awake and slept they all. Then came a call over at that point so that they all woke up. Thus spoke the voice, 'Wake you, Þorvald, and all your journey-crew, if you will have life and get you to your ship, and all thine men, and travel from the land like a shot.'[59] Then travelled out of the fjord and uncounted number of hide boats and lay at them.[60]

Þorvald spoke then, 'We shall construct defenses on the boards[61] and defend ourselves as seems best but fight back as little as possible. 'So went they but the Skrælings[62] shot out then for a time and then flew away as hard as they could, who could go as fast.

Then asked Þorvald his men if they had been wounded. They declared themselves wounded not to be.

'I have gotten a wound under my arm' said he. 'Flew an arrow between the ship-boards and shields under my arm, and is here the arrow, but for me will this to my death lead. Now council I, that you should prepare your group to fly back that way, but you should take me to that headland, where it seemed to me to be home-worthy. True that to be, that I should there settle for a time there and set a cross at my head and feet, and call that *Krossanes*[63] ever after.'

Greenland was then Christian, even though died Eirik the Red before Christianity was accepted.

Now died Þorvald and they did all that had been explained same as he had spoken of and travelled after and rejoined there their expedition.[64] They told there all of their tidings that was known, and prepared there that winter and collected [themselves] grapes and vines for the ship. Now they prepared themselves for the spring after to [go to] Greenland and came their ship into Eirikssfjord and knew many tidings to tell Leif.

Kapituli 6

Those tidings were occurring while in Greenland, Þorstein of Eiriksfjord had married and obtained Guðrið daughter of Þorbjorn, who had had[65] Þórir the Eastman[66] who before was told of.

Now desired Þorstein Eirikson to journey back to Vínland after the form of Þorvald, his brother, and prepared the same ship and chose he a crew strong and in shape. He had with himself twenty-five men and Guðríð, his woman, and sailed over sea once they were ready and were out of sight of land. It went for them thus all summer that they were at the whim of the weather and knew not where they travelled. And one week was it before winter when they took to land in Lysufjord in Greenland in the Western Settlement. Þorstein searched for lodgings for them and got lodgings for all of his crew but he and his woman were without lodgings. Now were they back on the ship for another two nights. Then was Christianity young in Greenland.

That was one day, that men came to their tent early and they asked who before them was and how many in the tent?

'Two men,' said he, 'but who asks that?'

'Þorstein called am I and am I called Þorstein the black. I have come to bid both you and your wife to lodge at mine.'

Þorstein declared himself to desire the counsel of his woman but she bade him to decide and now accepted he this.

'Then shall I come after you in the morning with a cart. There is no shortage of goods to provide for your lodgings but you will find it boring with me because there are only two, me and my wife, and I am greatly of single thought. Another faith have I from that of you have although believe I yours the better which you have.'[67] Now came he after them in the morning with the cart and travelled they with Þorstein the black to lodge and entertained he them well.

Guðríð was an imposing woman to view and a knowledgeable woman and knew well how to be with unknown men.

That was early winter, that illness came to the people of Þorstein Eiriksson, and died there many of his crew.[68] Þorstein bade be built coffins for their bodies of those who had died and put them on the ship and bear them back, 'because I will lay all of their forms at Eiriksfjord in the summer.'

Now shortly after this was bidden that illness came into the home of Þorstein and took his woman ill first, who was called Grímhild. She was great in size and strong as a man but the illness brought her under. And quickly after that took ill Þorstein Eiriksson and lay then both for a bit but died Grímhild, woman of Þorstein the black. But when she was dead then went Þorstein from the house after a board to lay the body on.

Guðríð spoke then, 'Be away a short time, Þorstein my [friend],' said she.

He declared to be back shortly.

Then spoke Þorstein Eiriksson, 'Strangely acting is now the housewife, because she just now raised herself up with an elbow and is sticking her feet from the bench[69] and is searching for her shoes.' At that point came Þorstein her husband Grimhíld's in and quickly laid Grímhild down so that creaked every wooden beam in the room. Now built Þorstein a coffin for the body of Grímhild and placed her out on it and bore it all away. He was both a big man and strong and he needed this all so he could bear her from the house.

Now worsened the illness of Þorstein Eiriksson and he died. Guðríð, his woman, was grieved at this. Then were they all in the room. Guðríð had been sitting on a stool before the bench where he had lay, Þorstein her husband. Then took Þorstein the farmer from the stool into his arms and set himself on the bench opposite with her before the body of Þorstein and he attempted to console and comfort her and he promised thus that he should travel with her to Eirikssfjord with the body of Þorstein, her husband, and his crew.

'And also shall I take on more servants,' said he, 'for your comfort and pleasure.'

She thanked him.

Þorstein Eiriksson sat then up and spoke: 'Where is Guðríð?' Three times spoke he this but she was silent.

Then spoke she with Þorstein the farmer, 'What shall I do answer his words or not?'

He bade her to swear nothing. Then went Þorstein the farmer across the un-boarded middle floor and sat on the stool but Guðríð sat on his knee. Then spoke Þorstein the farmer, 'What is your will, namesake?' said he.

He answered after a time, 'Anxious am I to do this, to tell Guðríð her fortune so that she know then it is better my death because I have come to a place of good rest. But I have this to tell you, Guðríð, it is your grace to be married to an Icelandic man and long shall you be together. Many men shall from you come, shall you be together, and many men shall from you come, vigorous, bright and excellent, sweet and scented well. Shall you travel from Greenland to Norway and thence on to Iceland and will farm in Iceland. There shall you settle and shall you have longer life than him. You shall journey out and go south[70] and come back after to Iceland to your farm and shall there a church raised be and shall you there be and take nun's consecration and there shall you die.' But then fell Þorstein back and was prepared his body and taken to the ship.[71]

Þorstein the farmer fulfilled well with Guðríð all that which he had sworn. He sold in the spring all his land and farm animals and travelled by ship with

Fig 100. Excavated Norse Church foundations at Qassiarsuk.

Guðríð and all her possessions prepared the ship and obtained men and then travelled to Eirikssfjord.[72] Were now the bodies interred at the church. Guðríð went to Leif at Brattahlíð but Þorstein the black made his farm in Eirikssfjord and settled there for the rest of his life and was thought to be a clever man.

Kapituli 7

That same summer came a ship from Norway to Greenland. A man was called Þorfinn karlsefni[73] who was the ship's captain. He was the son of Þórð Horse-Head, son of Snorri, son of Þórð of Hofði. Þorfinn Karlsefni was greatly endowed with wealth and was a winter at Brattahlíð with Leif Eiriksson. Quickly felt he compassion[74] for Guðríð and asked her[75] but she turned to Leif to answer for her. Afterwards was she fastened to him[76] and were they married the following winter.

Same was the discussion of Vínland journeys as before, and encouraged men Karlsefni to lead a group, both Guðríð and other men. Thus was caused his journey and readied he the ship's crew: six tens of men and five women. Karlsefni created an agreement[77] with his oarsmen that evenly should they have all that which they obtained with good fortune.[78] They took with themselves all kinds of domestic animals because they desired to settle the land if they could accomplish that. Karlsefni bade Leif for the houses in Vínland. He declared to lend the houses but to give not. Afterwards steered they over sea the ships and came to Leif's Booths both safety and heartiness and bore there up their hide-boxes.[79]

Quickly brought at hand to them were great provisions and good because a rorqual was there up driven both big and good. They travelled then and scored the whale, then there was no food shortage. The animals went there to the land but that was the way that the male stock were riled up and difficult it became with them. They had brought with them a bull. Karlsefni caused to be felled wood to fill his ship and lay the wood on a rock for drying. They had all used the land's resources, those that there were, both grapes and kinds of hunting game and goods.

After that winter had come to summer then encountered they the Skræling when travelled there out of the trees a great flock of men. There were nearby their stock but the bull took to bellowing and yelled so greatly that it frightened the Skræling and they lay out from there with their loads, and that was furs and sables and all kinds of skins, and headed for the buildings of Karlsefni and attempted there to get in the houses. Karlsefni ordered the doors barred. Neither could understand the other's words.[80]

Then took the Skrælings off their packs[81] and opened them and offered goods to them but desired weapons in exchange at first but Karlsefni banned them from selling weapons. And now the council came into his head so that he bade the women to bear out milk at them. Once they saw the milk then wished they to purchase that and naught else. Now was the trade journey of the Skrælings that they bore away their goods in their stomachs but Karlsefni and his crew held after their packs and skins travelled they to a position away.[82]

From this point it is said that Karlsefni caused to be built a palisade well-built around his farm and settled themselves there in. Around this time birthed Guðríð a boy child, the woman of Karlsefni, and called the boy Snorri. It was early the following winter then came the Skrælings back near then and were in a greater flock than before and had with them the same goods as before. Then spoke Karlsefni with the women, 'Now shall you bear out the same goods, same as before was demanded, but naught else.' But when they saw that, then cast they their packs in over the palisade.

But Guðríð sat in the doorway with the cradle of Snorri her son then bore a shadow across the doorway and then went there in a woman in a black close-kirtle. She was rather short and had a band around the head and was bright in hair, pale and greatly eyed, so that never had bigger eyes been set in a man's head. She went there, where Guðríð sat, and spoke, 'What are you called?' said she.

'I am called Guðríð; but what are you called?'

'I am called Guðríð,' said she.

Then motioned Guðríð the housewife her hand towards her so that she would sit next to her but at the same moment then heard Guðríð a noise great and was then the woman gone and that was when killed a Skræling was by a man of Karlsefni because he had attempted to take their weapon. And they went now away quickly but clothing theirs lay there after and trade goods. No man had this woman seen except for Guðríð alone.

'Now must we come up with a council to take,' said Karlsefni, 'because I expect that they shall visit us a third time with un-peace and more men. Now

Fig 101. The Eirikssfjord, looking towards Qassiarsuk in the right of the shot.

shall we take this council ten men will go forth on the headland and there make themselves seen but the rest of the group shall go into the trees and hew there a clearing out for our stock where the group comes from the woods. We shall take the bull restrained and have him go before us.' It was there intended, to have their fight, a lake was on the one side while wooded the other way. Now were these councils played out, where Karlsefni had laid in. Then came the Skrælings to that place where Karlsefni had chosen to fight. Now was there fighting and fell there many forms of Skrælings. One man was greatly tall and handsome amongst the group of Skrælings and thought Karlsefni that he must be their chieftain. Now had one of those Skrælings taken up an axe and looked at it for a time and swung at his group and hewed he so fell one then dead. Then took the big man possession of the axe and looked at it for a bit and threw it far into the sea, far as he could. Afterwards flew they into the woods travelling quick and stopped[83] there now their dealings. Were they and Karlsefni there that winter all but it was then announced Karlsefni that he willed to not be there longer and wished to travel to Greenland. Now prepared they for their journey and had much good fortune in vines and grapes and fur skins. Now sailed they over sea and came to Eiríkssfjord their ship safe and were there a winter.

Kapituli 8

At this point discussion resumed about Vínland travels, because these travels commanded both fame and worth.[84] That same summer came a ship from Norway to Greenland when Karlsefni came from Vínland. That ship was steered by two brothers, Helgi and Finnbogi, and they were there a winter in Greenland. Those brothers were Icelandic by birth and came from the East fjords.

Then it occurred, that Freydís Eiriksdottir went forth from her home at Garðr and travelled to meet with those brothers. Helgi and Finnbogi, and bid then that they travel to Vínland with her conveyance. They would have had a good share of all with her those there that might be obtained. Now agreed they to this. Then travelled she to meet with Leif, her brother, and asked if he would give her those houses which he had built and lay in Vínland. But he responded the same manner, declaring he shall lend the houses, but give not. So made an agreement between those brothers and Freydís that each should have three tens of men on the ship and women as well. But Freydís broke from this early on and had five men extra and hid them. Aware the brothers were not before they had come to Vínland.

Now did lay they over sea and had before agreed, that they should have a flotilla if it was so possible. There was a little space between the ships but came the brothers shortly before and had up born their goods.

Then spoke Freydís: 'why bore your goods in here?'

'Because we had believed,' said they, 'that the agreement should be an-honored between us.'

'To me lent Leif these houses,' said she, 'but not you.'

Then spoke Helgi: 'match not us brothers in meanness with you.' Bore now out their goods and built themselves a hall inland from a lake's edge and settled well there. But Freydís ordered felled wood for her ship.

That was one morning early that Freydís stood up inner space and dressed herself except for her foot-cIothes. The weather was so that it happened that dew had fallen greatly. She took the cloak of her husband and went out immediately went she to the hall of the brothers and to the door. A man had out gone a little before and locked the door after unevenly. She opened up the door and stood in the opening for a time then and without speech but Finnbogi lay the furthest in the hall and was awake.

He spoke: 'What are you at, Freydís?'

She answered: 'I wish that you stand up and go out with me, and will I talk with you.'

He did thus. They went out to a tree, which lay near the house walls, and set themselves there down. 'How do you like things?' said she.

He answered: 'Good think I this land's resources, but ill it seems to me this, that is between us, because I can find no cause of it.'

'That you say is correct, 'said she, 'and so it seems to me. That reason I have visited you, because I desire to trade ships with you brothers as you have the bigger ship than I and desire I to go away hence.'

'That shall I allow to occur, 'said he, 'if you like that well.'

Now they parted with that and went she home and Finnbogi went to his bed space. She took the path and came to the room with cold feet and awoke Þorvarð with that and asked why she was so cold and wet.

She replied with great resentment, 'I was walking,' said she, 'to those brothers to offer to purchase their ship, and wished I to buy a bigger ship. This sat with them so ill-ly that they beat me and was I roughly handled. You miserable man would avenge neither my disgrace nor thine and must I that now discover that I am away from Greenland. Shall I get split from you unless you avenge this.'

And now he could stand the jibes from her no more and bade the men to stand up quickly and take their weapons and so did they and went they to the hall of the brothers and went in while they slept and took them and bound their feet and dragged thus out and bound were but Freydís ordered killed each as out they came. Now were there all the men killed but the women were left after and wished none to them kill.

Then spoke Freydís: 'Find me a hand-axe.' So that was done. After killed she those women five who there were and thus they went to death. Now went they back to their hall after those ill-works, and obvious that was, that Freydís thought herself having had good council and spoke with her group, 'If words of this is heard to come to Greenland,' said she, 'then shall I take the life of any who speak out these actions.' Now shall we say this, that here after they settled, then when we had went away.

Now prepared they the ship early in the spring that which those brothers had owned, with all the goods, amounts as much as the ship could bear. Thereafter they sailed over sea and went well the journey until came into Eirikssfjord the ship in early summer. There was Karlsefni from before, and had completely prepared his ship for sea and waited for good wind but it is spoken of by men that there was no other richly laden ship that went over sea from Greenland than that, which he steered.

Kapituli 9

Freydís travelled now back to her farm[85] which had flourished while she was gone. She gave great wealth to all of her journey-crew because she wished to keep her misdeeds secret. Settled she now on her farm. But her crew was not all word-holding to say nothing of these ill-deeds and keep them from being known. Now came this information before Leif her brother and thought he this tale the worst.[86] Then took Leif three men from the group of Freydís and the tortured them into telling the events they had committed together, and each spoke the same tale.

'Not willing am I' said Leif, 'to do that which Freydís, my sister, seems to deserve, but I predict this, that those who come from her shall never have worth.' And from that time, no one thought anything of her and hers but ill.

Now it is said at this time, that Karlsefni prepared his ship and sailed over sea. He travelled well and came to Norway both safe and hale and stayed there a winter and sold his goods and had there good overturning and then he and his woman were lauded by the noblest of men in Norway but the spring after prepared the ship for Iceland. And when he was all-ready and his ship lay ready to set out before the jetty then came there at him a Southern man, by birth from Bremen in Saxland.[87] He offered to buy the gable-end of Karlsefni.

'I will not sell,' said he.

'I shall give you a half mark of gold,' said the Southern man.

Karlsefni thought this was a good deal, and afterwards the bargain was made. Travelled the Southern man away with the gable-end, but Karlsefni knew not what kind of tree it was but that was hard-wood[88] which came from Vínland.

Now sailed Karlsefni over sea and came the ship before northern lands, in Skagafjord, and up there set his ship over winter. The following spring purchased he lands in Glaumby and built a farm there, and settled for the rest of his life and was considered a noble man. Many men come from him and Guðríð, his woman, and were goodly descendents. And when Karlsefni died, took Guðríð over the farming and Snorri, her son, who was born in Vínland. And when Snorri was married, then travelled Guðríð east and went to the south[89] and came back after to the farm of Snorri, her son, and had he by then built a church at Glaumby. Afterwards was Guðríð a nun and anchoress and was there the rest of her life.[90]

Snorri was descended [from] thusly by his son, who was Þórgeir called. He was the father of Yngvild, the mother of Brand the Bishop. The daughter of Snorri Karlsefnisson was called Hallfríð. She was the woman of Runólf, father of Þorlák the Bishop. Bjorn was called the other son of Karlsefni and Guðríð.[91] He was the father of Þorunn, the mother of Bjarni the Bishop. Many men have come from Karlsefni and has he become the kin-ancestor of a strong line. It was Karlsefni who told men all of the events of these voyages all which now here some words have come.

Appendix B

Norse Place Name Elements

Element	Alternative Element	Description
Aergi-	argi-, ergi-, ærgi-, airigh-, -ary, sel–	Farm location where there was originally a grazing place. This term is actually Gaelic in origin and is absorbed into the north Atlantic toponymic lexicon within the Irish Sea Region. This term is mostly found in the west of the region.
Ávellir		The flat lands associated with a river – a flood plain in modern terms.
-ay	-ey, -a, øy	Island.
Bakki	----	A banked up area in the landscape.
Bekkr	----	Stream.
Bjoð	----	Multiple fields.
Bolstaðr	-bister	These are later farms formed from a division of an older farm's home-fields. Place names including this element are sometimes associated with the extended settlements around the Bu's
Borg	----	A stronghold. In the east this is more likely to be fortified. In the west this description is placed on natural landscape features.
Bœr	----	The Norse term for house and its affiliated wider farmstead.
Brekka	----	Hillside or slope.
Bu	----	Place name associated with high status farms that include in a hall. These are associated most with the Orcadian Jarldom.
Dalr	----	Valley. This is a common element in Icelandic place names.
Dýr	----	Animals both domestic and wild.
Efja	----	Mud or mire.
Eið	aith-, eye-, ed	An isthmus that is specifically used for portage. The Gaelic equivalent of this is *tairm-bert* or *tarbert* meaning over-bringing.
Eik	----	Oak.
Eng	----	A meadow specifically used as a pasture for livestock.

Eyða	---	To be laid waste to. This is used in combination with physical description terms – ie *eyði-dalr*.
Eyrr	---	This is a banked up area of gravel or sand in the landscape that is associated with water.
Fé	---	This is a term for domestic animal-based wealth.
Fen	---	A marsh or bog in the landscape.
Fjall	fell	Hill. This is sometimes translated to *–val* in Gaelic speaking areas. An example of this would be *hvalr*.
Fjord	---	Glacially formed marine inlets into the landscape known for their steep sides.
Garðr	garth	A farm where there was an earlier enclosure. This is sometimes translated to *–achadh* in Gaelic speaking areas. An example of this is *gearraidh*.
Gil	---	Ravine.
Gren	---	Fox lair. These are rocky places that provide shelter while being slightly remote.
Hagi	---	Pasture – land for livestock grazing.
Haugr	---	Grave mound. These can be assumed as well when excavation proves such mounds to be naturally formed.
Helgar	Heilagr	Holy or sacred. A place of sanctuary.
Hestr	---	Horse-linked names.
Hlíð	---	Mountain or hill-side.
Hof	---	A heathen place of worship.
Holr	hol	A hollow or hole in the landscape.
Holt	---	A woodland.
Holmr	holm	A low-lying island when viewed from aboard a ship.
Hross	ross	A horse or mare.
Hult	---	A sacred grove of trees.
Hváll	---	A knoll, hill or hillock in the landscape.
Hýlr	---	Pool or water-filled hole.
Kirkja	Kirk	The site of either a church or church-owned lands.
Korn	---	Grain.
Kví	Akr, quoy	Farm where there originally was a field or fold for the stock such as sheep or cattle.
Lauf	---	Leaf.
Laug	---	Bath.
Leir	---	Mud. This is used with *–vik* in two notable occasions – this may imply coastal mud specifically.
Lœkr	Lækr	Stream.
Mosi	---	Moss.

Møl	----	Gravel.
Mørk	----	Forested area in the landscape.
Møsurr	----	Maple.
Muli	----	A ridge located between valleys.
Nes	----	Coastal promontory.
Ørfiris	----	Tidal.
Óss	----	Estuary water way in the landscape.
Sæter	Setter	Farm where there originally was a grazing place. These are most often found in the Northern Isles of Scotland. In Gaelic speaking regions this is sometimes Gaelicized to –*shader*.
Setr	----	A human dwelling in the landscape.
Skali	----	Later established farms with a high status hall. This sometimes includes hall, a sleeping hall and outbuildings.
-sker	----	Rock. In Gaelic speaking areas this is found as –*sgeir*.
Skógar	----	Wood or forest in the landscape.
Smiðja	----	Smithy.
Staðir	----	Dwelling, place and location in the landscape. Farm names that may have personal name elements, such as the farms of freemen.
Støng	----	A standing pole or staff. This is sometimes an element in assembly site construction.
Stora	Stori	Greater or larger in comparison to another feature.
Strand	----	Shore or beach suitable for landing upon.
Tré	----	Tree specifically used as lumber.
Tun	----	The inner fields affiliated with a farm unit.
Þing	Ting, thing	Assembly location for the *þing*.
Vaða	----	Specifically to wade. In the landscape an area to ford across water.
Vatn	----	Water of any type in a landscape.
-vellir	----	Fields or flat lands in a landscape.
Vík	----	A bay – both an area to turn a ship and a safe place to wait out storms on the open sea.

Glossary

Term	Description
Activity	With regards to identity this is identification by who you are. How activities are undertaken is influenced by the habitus of the individual.
Byre	A building that is meant to hold livestock. It may or may not have stalls or drains to deal with excrement build-up.
Capabilities	In relation to identity this is part of identification by what you are. This encompasses both the action of activity but also the skill carried as potential activities.
Clinker-built	This term refers to a form of ship construction that is flexible and makes economic use of lumber. It is based upon a central keel that is then built up.

Clinker construction consists of over-lapping plank strakes that compose the walls. Once set the ribs of the vessel strengthen and solidify the vessel's walls as a unit. They are then stuffed with fibre known as luting to waterproof the gaps in between.

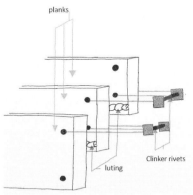

Daughter longhouse	Essentially the same features as home farm yet will be located quite physically close to the home farm's initial location if not actual structure. Still located within the initial infield. The multitude of activities which occurred within the home farm can of course occur on a daughter farm but they are more likely to occur in the widest variety of forms in the home farm associated architecture.

Dispositions	The transposable habitual tendencies of individuals to act and react in certain ways. The dispositions that are available to an individual or group will depend upon the constituent elements of the habitus.
Dorset	The indigenous inhabitants of Newfoundland and south-eastern Canada who were potentially living in the area upon Norse arrival circa AD 1000.
Doxa	The elements of culture which appear to be obviously self-evident and unchanging, essentially the known cultural world. This is composed of the habitus and what is possible to be known.
Emic	Anthropological term that assumes a position internal to a cultural group.
Etic	Anthropological term that assumes a position external to a cultural group.
Færing	A vessel rowed by four oars. They are sometimes used in north Atlantic ship burials.
Fær-øy	The Faroe Islands.
Farmyard	The portion of a farm existing between the main domicile and the outbuildings required for farm functions.
Gift exchange	Social reciprocity of goods and services that serves to facilitate hierarchical interactions between individuals and groups.
Grænland	Greenland.
Habitus	The embodied dispositions that are the domain of habit, which is at once individual and collective. The individual habitus is dependent upon the collective habitus of the wider population to which they belong.
Hayfields	The farm associated fields that supply livestock with their over-winter fodder.
Helluland	Literally Flat Rock-land. Modern Baffin Island.
Hérjolfsnes	Famous Greenlandic cemetery site with associated saga references and archaeological excavation. One of the most spectacular instances of textile conservation comes from this site.
Hiberno-Norse	Irish-Norse material.
Hjaltland	Literally Hilt-land or Hjalti's-land. Shetland. This portion of the Northern Isles was held by Norway far after Orkney had become part of Scotland.
Home fields	The fields closest to a main farm unit.
Hvalsey	The last named site in Norse Greenlandic texts. This was the site of a wedding important enough to be noted amongst the Diplomaticum Islandicae kept by the medieval church. Archaeologically this is also the site of a very well preserved medieval stone chapel.
Identification	Identification is possible in the medieval period by defining who one is, what one is and who you belong to. When all of these are considered together this creates the spectrum of identities present on site and within a network. Each of these means of identification are impacted by space and time differentially, depending on their context.

Identity	Identity is the complex collection of habitus, doxa and practice that humans express in accordance to all of their contexts. This can express in tangible and intangible forms.
Identity prioritization	This refers directly to choices made to promote certain elements of identity in response to the context. This assesses the amount of risk inherent to actions and choices made during existence.
Iron-blooms	The result of smelting iron ore. This is before the iron is shaped into a workable ingot.
Ísland	Iceland.
Kin	The extended family unit.
Kin group	With regards to identification this is who you belong to – most often blood relations of extended consanguinity.
Knórr	Deep drafted clinker-built vessel that is capable of both open ocean voyages and carrying a substantial amount of cargo.
Landing sites	Natural features of shallow sandy bays which are suitable for the easy approach of shallow clinker-built shallow draft vessels. This was a vial part of the system on a variety of levels. It provided the location for wider communication with the region and world. It provided the location for exchange to occur through. It provided a large number of relatively low-effort species – a vital part of a marginal environment's subsistence pattern.
Landnám	Literally land-naming. This is a process involving
Langskip	Literally this translates to long-ship. They are perhaps the most famous of the Norse vessels occurring as named vessels in some medieval texts. These vessels are best suited for coastal voyages.
Littoral	Physically this is a shore area that encompasses both terrestrial and marine elements. In a social sense this is an in-between designation.
Longhouse	This is a term used for both Norse farm buildings of the medieval period and later Thule Inuit domiciles. Norse buildings have few fixed internal features. Early forms held both humans and animals, maximizing upon the body heat of livestock to reduce the amount of fuel needed to heat the building. Later forms see more efficient forms of heating and animals removed to byres. Thule longhouses are widely different in form.
Marine	Oriented on water-based activities, particularly those involving open ocean travel.
Markland	Literally Forest-land. These are the forests of the eastern Canadian coast. These forests formed a source of driftwood for the Davis Strait settlements of Greenland.
Midden	Refuse deposits found on during archaeological excavation. In north Atlantic populations these can prove very good sources for environmental exploitation on site.
Norðreyr	Orkney and Shetland, located to the north coast of Scotland.
Norðsetr	The northern hunting fields for Arctic and marine goods in Greenland.

Norse	Cultural group closely affiliated with the Scandinavian peninsula that expand their sphere of influence dramatically during the Migration Era and Medieval Period in Europe.
Outbuildings	Buildings in the outfield depend on the utilization of the space – there must be a need for storage primarily and possibly shelter for animals and humans on a small scale. These functioned as stations of procurement for the farm buildings, both home and daughter.
Papar	Norse term for an Irish Christian cleric. There is a small but varied amount of evidence supporting the presence of these clerics in the north Atlantic prior to Norse *landnám* taking place. What seems to be apparent is that from a biological point of view there was not enough people to support a population.
Practice	The collective dispositions and choices that result from the habitus interacting with cultural doxa. This functions upon the premise that habitus and doxa are recreated and reinforced through the dispositions of the individual and group.
Primary longhouse	Human and animal habitation year-round, although this may not actually be the pattern in true day-to-day practice, also secondary outbuildings separate from either the habitation or the byre, which housed a wider variety of activities such as weaving and smithing. This is public and private at once as it is not only the domestic site for many in this period but also as the local node for trade and exchange in both economic and socially linked goods but also ritual and spiritual elements as well.
Risk	This address the amount of inherent threat. It can be physical or social. With regards to identity it is influential as whether confirmed or perceived this influences choices made in practice.
Runes	The lexicon of symbols utilized for writing within Norse regions. These were originally carved into wood and often hidden from direct view when placed on objects. This is reflected by the dominant presence of vertical elements to the symbols themselves. Runes were later used to carve more permanent public declarations onto stone.
Shieling	A main farm's subsidiary unit for summer maintenance of livestock. This fits within a system of animal transhumance that shifts domestic stock away from the growing fields during the summer season. There are several types that are described by their farm function. Dairy shielings will hold the dairy stock within easy travel of the home farm. Other shielings holding sheep, for instance, would have been located farther away from the home farm so as to spare the fields.
Ship's boat	Ship's boats are primarily coastal, short distance vessels used for a variety of jobs that other vessels were too large to do.
Suðreyr	The Inner and Outer Hebrides, located off the western coast of Scotland.
Terrestrial	Oriented on land-based activities. This can include domestic tasks, agricultural and pastoralism.

Thule Inuit	Populations originating in north–western Alaska who specifically exploit the marine resources of the high Arctic. During the Medieval Optimal kin groups of Thule followed bowhead whales eastwards along newly open seaways in the North American pack ice. They began to arrive in the Davis Strait region around AD 1100.
Long Distance Trader	The upper level of north Atlantic medieval social hierarchy associated with taking on physical risk, most often associated with long distance voyages. In order to be successful at this endeavour wealth, weather, technology, network and opportunity combined to provide goods to a guaranteed market at every stop along the network.
Vester um haf	Literally 'West over sea '. This becomes a signal trope in sagas for expensive voyages that enhanced the social worth of the subject family.
Warrior	The upper level of medieval social hierarchy associated with taking on physical risk, most often associated in battle. This is a long studied concept with regards to Viking studies in general due to the portrayal of historical evidence over time. It also ties into an earlier Germanic tradition found in northwest Europe where power consolidation amongst local magnates was based upon physical achievement of chieftains. Hierarchy was maintained by gift exchange and social reciprocity of action in battle. Dynasties were difficult to maintain at this time.

Appendix D

Sampling and Analysis

SAMPLING STRATEGY

Given the large geographic area in combination with the variety of evidence under consideration for this study sampling has been required. Sites have been chosen as a focus based upon several aspects. The first is that reliable dating evidence is known to exist. The second aspect is that there are complete artefact placement maps and lists, preferably with photographs, in relation to site buildings. The third is that excavations have been conducted to the highest standards possible for the time conducted, ideally with full site survey. These three criteria alone make the north Atlantic collection of viable sites relatively small with certain areas such as Orkney and Iceland being much better represented than others. The utilization of zones also allows for certain textual sources to be considered in relation to the regions, particularly in the case studies and analysis of this work. The case study for Zone 1 is concerned with the evidence provided by Shetland and the Faroe Islands. In Chapters 6, 7 and 8 the full zone is considered in relation to macroscale concepts of identity. The case study for Zone 2 is concerned with the evidence provided by the Southern and Eastern Quarters of Iceland as well as any recent excavations in the Northern and Western Quarters of Iceland and Mývatnssveit – the region of the Northern Quarter most extensively excavated and widely published in recent years. These Quarters were established in relation to the regional spring things officially established in AD 930 to be held before the Icelandic Alþing during the Icelandic Free State period. In Chapters 6, 7 and 8 all Quarters of Iceland are considered and evidence from throughout the country is referenced. The case study for Zone 3 is concerned with the Eastern Settlement of Greenland, New World sites on the North American eastern coast as well as the modern excavation of the Farm under the Sand as the site most extensively excavated and widely published in recent years. In Chapters 6, 7 and 8 both Settlements of Greenland, the New World and the hunting region of Norðsetr are considered.

Data Creation and Compilation

Data tables have been created which compiles a variety of early Norse farm settlements. This includes both archaeological evidence and textual material. These tables were derived from excavation publications from Borg in the Lofoten

Small finds

Gold

Silver

Coins

Weights and balances

Weaponry

Horse harness

High artistic quality

Semi-precious stones

Religious objects

Glass vessels

Copper alloy vessels

Luxury pottery

Production of luxuries

Production of weaponry

Steatite

Bone

Ivory

Wooden objects

Iron

Settlement Structure

Large settlement

Large building

Large enclosed yard, >15m

Stock pen, <15m

Hall house

Cemetery

Wealthy grave

Rune stone

Landing site, shallow often sandy bay

Boat house

Fortification

Court site

Infield/outfield system

Shieling/saeter associated in some way

Outbuildings including stables/byre

Cave utilization

Multi-cellular farm dwelling

Landscape setting

Rich resources

Commanding position

Placed in power landscape

Placed near communication route

Medieval church

Ready fresh water supply

Whaling area

Relatively flat arable lands for agriculture/
animal husbandry

Written sources

Evidence of royal estate

Evidence of manorial estate

Sacral place name

Organizational place name

Direct mention in saga

Religious written material concerning

Excavation reports

Survey reports

Fig 102. Criteria used in data creation.

Islands, from the Birsay region of Orkney, Sandwick and Sandwick North in Shetland, Toftanes and Argisbrekka in the Faroe Islands, Hofstaðir in Iceland, The Farm Under the Sand in Greenland and L'Anse aux Meadows in Newfoundland. Examined first were site and artefact placement maps and diagrams followed by artefact placement maps and diagrams followed by artefact presence lists and tables. Of subsequent importance is associated textual material such as law-codes and sagas. Fig 16 presents the resultant data tables used to analyze data for this bipartite consideration of identity construction and maintenance in the Norse north Atlantic. By seeing elements present on a site quickly in comparison to similar elements on other sites, aspects of what constitutes the Norse maritime farm identity can be highlighted as microscale and macroscale elements.

In order to collect this evidence a variety of techniques has been used. Much of the evidence for this study has been derived from archaeological excavation publications including articles, excavation reports as well as excavation websites where available. All archaeological sources examined have been utilized in the creation of comparative categorizations and tables where all relevant site data is compiled for consideration. This is possible due to the homogenous nature of much of the Norse settlement period material throughout the north Atlantic, particularly about architecture and construction.

Sites were subjected to a two-stage process of tables that are analytically and logistically derived. The first is a qualitative table detailing site directors, excavation years, major publications, and a site description including major details. It is categorized by Zone as well as by archipelago or Quarter. This is mainly a brief list of site material so that information can be found quickly within the evidence. This allows for analysis and comparison to be made in relation to known historical biases on the part of the excavators.

The second table is both qualitative and quantitative in nature and like the first table is site based. This table details key artefact types, structure presence and absence as well as any associated reliable texts. This has been derived from a combination of archaeological excavation and publications of high status farm sites, and localized regional networks such as Mývatnssveit in Iceland and Birsay in Orkney that provides information on network affiliations and economics as well as burials. It is based on site commonalities but also a range of variation is represented such as the size of stock pens. The table allows for raw material replacement such as iron forms that would be executed in bone. Also included are imports, which provide commentary upon trade and exchange networks. This table provides an equitable means of consideration of a wide variety of source material during analysis.

This also allows a relative ranking of poor, neutral or rich of site information to be made via the assignment of a point to each category ticked per site. This allows for graphs and pie charts to be included on site evidence available and published on all four aspects. These tables have drawn the diverse array of evidence for this consideration of identity construction and maintenance to allow for the more generalized discussion, presentation of evidence and analysis in case study chapters. When relevant portions of the second presence and absence table has been included within the chapter text. The full raw data tables have been included on an accompanying disc in Appendices A and B.

Aspects	Small finds (19)	Settlement morphology (17)	Landscape context (10)	Written sources (8)
Poor	0–6	0–5	0–3	0–3
Neutral	7–13	6–12	4–7	4–6
Rich	14–19	13–17	8–10	7–8
Total Point Range	Poor 0–20	Neutral 21–41	Rich 42–54	

Fig 103. Table detailing the relative ranking system applied to site evidence.

Each of these data sets provides different insights and perceptions of the past. The integration of diverse data sets has been encouraged particularly with reference to identity and social structure reconstruction. The products of such diverse data set analysis inherently are evidence that speaks of differing temporal and spatial scales. A multi-layered framework that employs complementary theories at relevant levels such as Practice Theory requires the direct integration of data sets and in order to keep this a critical analysis there should be separate interrogation of the data sets followed by correlation and comparison. Each source has been considered in terms of the impact of contemporary context, type and, when applicable, in terms of the author/scribe, theoretical basis and audience. Once the written texts have been excavated and the archaeological data compiled then correlative analysis and corroboration can be accomplished. It is at this stage that evidence on the microscale and macroscale should be the most visible,

Notes

Chapter 1

1. Jenkins, 2008.
2. Bourdieu, 1990, pp. 52–58.
3. Jenkins, 2008.
4. Bourdieu, 1990, pp. 441–446; Jenkins, 2010, pp. 16–18.
5. Amorosi, et al., 1997.
6. Peel, et al., 2007.
7. After Schmitz 1996, p. 15, figure 1–10.
8. Peel, et al., 2007.
9. Crowley & Lowery, 2000; Fagan, 2000, p. 7.
10. Crowley & Lowery, 2000; Steffensen, et al., 2008.
11. Fagan, 2000
12. Steffensen, et al., 2008
13. Amorosi, et al., 1997, p. 486; Steffensen, et al., 2008
14. (McGovern, et al., 1988
15. Bloch, 2007, pp. 11–12; Szabo, 2008, pp. 93–94
16. Barrett, 2008
17. Peel, et al., 2007
18. Barrett, et al., 2008; Lindquist, 1994 [unpublished]; Szabo, 2008
19. Bill, 2010; Stylegar & Grimm, 2005
20. Lindquist, 1994 [unpublished]; Dugmore, et al., 2005, pp. 28–29
21. CIA World Factbook, accessed 21/12/2010).
22. Buckland, et al., 2009, p. 114
23. Buckland, et al., 2009
24. Mahler, 1995
25. Mahler, 1995
26. Keller, 2010
27. Mahler, 1995; Albrethsen & Keller, 1986
28. Albrethsen & Keller, 1986; Sveinbjarnardottir, 1991
29. Albrethsen & Keller, 1986; Mahler, 1995; Sveinbjarnardottir, 1991
30. Malmros, 1991; Lindquist, 1994 [unpublished]
31. Frieman, 2008, pp. 135–136; Lindquist, 1994 [unpublished]
32. Fagan, 2000, p. 21
33. Finsens, 1974; Durrenberger, 1989
34. Fagan, 2000, pp. 3–21
35. Bill, 2010; Christiansen, 2002; Crumlin-Pedersen, 1995
36. Stylegar & Grimm, 2005; Bill, 2010; Crumlin-Pedersen, 1995
37. Barrett, 2008; Bagge, 2010
38. Barrett, 2008; Bagge, 2010; Sawyer & Sawyer, 2003, p. 39; Derry, 1979, p. 41
39. Sigurdsson, 2007, pp. 286,295; Sorensen, 2000, pp. 26–28; Quinn, 2000, pp. 30–31; Whaley, 2000, pp. 167–169

40. Crumlin-Pedersen, 1995
41. Barrett, 2008; Amorosi, et al., 1997; Dugmore, et al., 2005; McGovern, 1991
42. Friðriksson, 1994, p. 182
43. McGovern, 1991, pp. 333–334; Svanberg, 2003, pp. 36–38
44. Stummann Hansen, 2002; Svanberg, 2003
45. Svanberg, 2003; Friðriksson, 1994
46. Dahl, 1955; Dahl, 1970, p. 67
47. MacGregor, 1986 [unpublished]; Lane, 1983 [unpublished]
48. See McGovern 1991; Bigelow, ed. 1991; Samson, ed. 1991; Morris and Rackham, eds. 1992; Batey, Jesch and Morris, eds. 1993.
49. Mortensen and Arge, eds, 2005
50. Wawm and Sigurðardóttir, eds 2001
51. See Ballin Smith, Taylor and Williams, eds 2007 for the most intensive of these.
52. Svanberg, 2003, pp. 111–112; Friðriksson, 1994, p. 184
53. Barrett *et al* 2008: unpublished conference information materials
54. Kowaleski 2010: personal comment
55. Brink 2011: personal comment; Lee 2011: personal comment; Friðriksson 2011: personal comment; Hines 2011: personal comment; Jesch 2011: personal comment; Abrams 2011: personal comment
56. Friðriksson, 1994, pp. 184–185; Svanberg, 2003, pp. 93–94
57. Cunliffe, 2001, pp. 66–67; Greenhill & Morrison, 1995, p. 92
58. MacDonald, 2002, p. 15; Dumville, 2002, p. 125
59. Blakely, 2008, p. 18
60. Jenkins, 2010, pp. 37–48
61. Bourdieu, 1990, pp. 441–442; Jenkins, 2008, pp. 198–199; Jenkins, 2010, pp. 58–64; Jones, 2007; Sahlins, 1985, pp. 144–145
62. Sawyer & Sawyer, 2003, p. 163
63. Sawyer & Sawyer, 2003, p. 163; Gaimster, 2005, p. 410
64. Svanberg, 2003, pp. 111–112
65. Friðriksson, 1994

Chapter 2
1. Jenkins, 2008; Jenkins, 2010
2. Jones, 2007
3. Jenkins, 2010, pp. 16–18
4. Jenkins, 2010, p. 18
5. Jenkins, 2010, pp. 200–201
6. Jenkins, 2010, pp. 158–159
7. Jenkins, 2010, pp. 35–48
8. Jones, 2007
9. Meskell, 2007, p. 24
10. Meskell, 2007, p. 24
11. Meskell, 2007, p. 24
12. Bourdieu, 1990
13. Jenkins, 2010, pp. 76–81; Bourdieu, 1990, p. 165
14. Jenkins, 2008, pp. 169–170; 2010, pp. 200–206; Jones, 2007, pp. 52–53
15. Sindbaek, 2008, p. 174; Sindbaek, 2007
16. Jones, 1997, pp. 117–118
17. Friðriksson, 1994, pp. 181–182; Jenkins, 2010, pp. 76–81; Jones, 1997, pp. 116–117; Svanberg, 2003, pp. 98–99

18. Graeburn 2002: personal comment
19. Graeburn 2002: personal comment
20. Meskell, 2007, pp. 24–25
21. Jones, 2007, p. 53
22. Jones, 2007, p. 53
23. Silliman, 2001, p. 381; Silliman, 2001, pp. 204–205
24. Bedos-Rezak, 2000
25. Braudel, 1981
26. Jones, 2007, pp. 44–46; Jones, 1997, p. 110; Hodder, 1993
27. Jones, 1997, p. 117; Sindbaek, 2008, pp. 172–173
28. Bourdieu, 1990, p. 163; O'Sullivan, 2008
29. Weber, 1949
30. Mauss, 2000
31. Braudel, 1981, p. 562
32. Jones, 1997, pp. 111–112; Jones, 2007, p. 45; Earle, 1987, pp. 290–291; Jenkins, 2008, pp. 58–64; Steane, 2001, pp. 251–275
33. Trigger, 2009, pp. 166–210
34. Braudel, 1981, p. 561; Knapp, 1992, p. 11
35. Braudel, 1981, p. 3
36. Braudel, 1981; Knapp, 1992, p. 16
37. Braudel, 1981, pp. 26–27; Knapp, 1992, p. 11
38. Braudel, 1981, p. 560; Knapp, 1992, p. 2
39. Bourdieu, 1990
40. Giddens, 1979, pp. 4–5
41. Latour, 2005
42. Sindbaek, 2007; Sindbaek, 2008
43. Sahlins, 1985
44. Giddens, 1979, pp. 64–65
45. Bourdieu, 1990; Braudel, 1981; Farr, 2006; Jenkins, 2010; 2008
46. Bourdieu, 1990, pp. 162–163
47. Joyce, 2008, p. 78; Lightfoot, 1995, p. 209
48. Silliman, 2001, p. 194; Silliman, 2001, p. 364
49. Silliman, 2001, pp. 191–192; Silliman, 2001, p. 380; Lightfoot, 1995, p. 201
50. Sindbaek, 2007, p. 120
51. Latour, 2005, pp. 131–133; Sindbaek, 2008, p. 172; Sindbaek, 2007, pp. 70–71
52. Sindbaek, 2007, pp. 65–66; Sindbaek, 2008, p. 172; Latour, 2005, p. 33
53. Sindbaek, 2007, p. 120
54. Sindbaek, 2009, p. 72
55. Sindbaek, 2007, p. 128; Sindbaek, 2008
56. Bourdieu, 1990, p. 445
57. Lightfoot & Martinez, 1995
58. Lightfoot & Martinez, 1995, p. 473; Rice, 1998, pp. 45–46
59. Frieman, 2008, p. 145
60. Frieman, 2008, p. 145
61. Frieman, 2008, p. 144
62. Jenkins, 2008, pp. 51–53; Jenkins, 2010, pp. 37–48; Jones, 1997, pp. 92–93; Latour, 2005, p. 33
63. Sindbaek, 2009, p. 105
64. Wallerstein, 1974
65. Wallerstein, 1974, p. 38; Wolf, 1984, p. 397

66. Rice, 1998, p. 478
67. Rice, 1998, pp. 228–230; Lightfoot & Martinez, 1995, p. 488
68. Lightfoot & Martinez, 1995
69. Joyce, 2008, p. 77; Lightfoot, 1995, p. 199; Parker Pearson & Richards, 1997
70. Parker Pearson & Richards, 1997
71. Friðriksson, 1994; Svanberg, 2003
72. Sigurdsson, 2007
73. Sahlins, 1985, p. xi
74. Sigurdsson, 2007
75. Gelsinger, 1970, p. 107; Marcus, 1955, p. 603
76. Frieman, 2008, pp. 146–147
77. Sindbaek, 2009, p. 96
78. Stummann Hansen, 2002; Stummann Hansen, 2001
79. Roussell, 1934
80. Bedos-Rezak, 2000

Chapter 3

1. Johansen, 1985, pp. 93–95; MacGregor, 1986 [unpublished]
2. Faulkes & Barnes, 2007, p. 104
3. Owen & Lowe, 1999, p. 7
4. Eithun, et al., 1994, p. 9
5. Stummann Hansen & Waugh, 1998
6. Buttler, 1984 [unpublished]
7. Frieman, 2008, pp. 137–138
8. Bigelow, 1995
9. Stummann Hansen & Waugh, 1998
10. Stummann Hansen & Waugh, 1998; MacGregor, 1986 [unpublished]
11. Hamilton, 1956, pp. 96, 106 facing page
12. Stummann Hansen & Waugh, 1998
13. Stummann Hansen & Waugh, 1998
14. MacGregor, 1986 [unpublished]
15. Stummann Hansen & Waugh, 1998
16. Small, 1966
17. McKenzie, 2007; MacGregor, 1986 [unpublished]
18. McKenzie, 2007
19. Owen & Lowe, 1999; Sharples, 2002; Sharples, 1998
20. Carter & Frasier, 1996
21. Ballin Smith, 2007
22. Buttler, 1984 [unpublished]; Ballin Smith, 2005; Smith, 2007; Crawford & Ballin Smith, 1999
23. Small, 1966; Buttler, 1984 [unpublished]; Hamilton, 1956; MacGregor, 1986 [unpublished]
24. Moffat & Buttler, 1986, pp. 102–103; Buttler, 1984 [unpublished]
25. Stummann Hansen & Waugh, 1998, pp. 129–130; Stummann Hansen, 2000, p. 99
26. Stummann Hansen & Waugh, 1998, p. 130
27. Fenton, 1985, pp. 164–168
28. Eithun, et al., 1994, p. 89
29. MacGregor, 1986 [unpublished]; Stummann Hansen & Waugh, 1998
30. Crawford & Ballin Smith, 1999
31. Eithun, et al., 1994, p. 88

32. Eithun, et al., 1994, pp. 108–109
33. Moffat & Buttler, 1986; Buttler, 1984 [unpublished]
34. Ballin Smith, 2007
35. Stummann Hansen & Waugh, 1998
36. Lane, 1983 [unpublished]
37. Buttler, 1984 [unpublished]
38. Stummann Hansen, 1996
39. Barrett, 2007, personal comment
40. Arge, et al., 2009; Olsen & Svanberg, 2004
41. Eithun, et al., 1994
42. Ahronson, 2007
43. Arge, et al., 2009
44. Stummann Hansen, 2005
45. Stummann Hansen, 2005
46. Arge, 2005
47. Stummann Hansen, 2005
48. Dahl, 1970
49. Stummann Hansen, 1991
50. Mahler, 1995
51. Mahler, 1995; 1991
52. Mahler, 1995, p. 487
53. Arge, 2005
54. Dahl & Rasmussen, 1956; Dahl, 1970
55. Stummann Hansen, 2009, personal comment
56. Stummann Hansen, 2002
57. Vickers, et al., 2005
58. Stummann Hansen, 1991
59. Stummann Hansen, 2005; Stummann Hansen, 1991
60. Johansen, 1985
61. Thorsteinsson, 2008
62. Thorsteinsson, 2008; Mahler, 1995; Mahler, 1991; Thomsen, et al., 2005
63. Thomsen, et al., 2005
64. Mahler & Malmros, 1990; Thomsen, et al., 2005
65. Thorsteinsson, 2008; Thomsen, et al., 2005
66. Stummann Hansen, 2005
67. Dahl, 1955
68. Resi, 1987
69. Mahler, 1991; Stummann Hansen, 1991; MacGregor, 1986 [unpublished]
70. Dahl, 1970; Stummann Hansen, 2005
71. Stummann Hansen, 1996
72. Stummann Hansen, 1991; Malmros, 1991; Small, 1992
73. Malmros, 1991
74. Small, 1992; Malmros, 1991; Arge, 2005
75. Vickers, et al., 2005
76. Thorsteinsson, 2008
77. Arge, et al., 2009
78. Vickers, et al., 2005
79. Arge, 1991; Mahler, 1991
80. Stummann Hansen, 1996
81. Fenton, 1985; Roussell, 1934

82. Eithun, et al., 1994, p. 89
83. MacGregor, 1986 [unpublished]
84. Stummann Hansen, 2005; Vickers, et al., 2005
85. Vickers, et al., 2005
86. Roussell, 1941
87. Eithun, et al., 1994
88. S. Crawford 2011: personal comment
89. Arge, et al., 2009
90. Malmros, 1991
91. Stummann Hansen, 1991; Mahler, 1991; Arge, 1989
92. Arge, et al., 2009; Ballin Smith, 2007; Hamilton, 1956; Stummann Hansen, 1991
93. Vickers, et al., 2005
94. Johansen, 1985
95. Lane, 1990; Small, 1966; Buttler, 1984 [unpublished]; Forster & Bond, 2004
96. Johansen, 1985
97. Eithun, et al., 1994
98. Brink, 2012
99. Eithun, et al., 1994
100. McKenzie, 2007
101. Eithun, et al., 1994
102. Hamilton, 1956
103. Stummann Hansen, 1991
104. Stummann Hansen, 2005
105. Thorsteinsson, 2008; Mahler, 1991; Mahler & Malmros, 1990
106. Mahler, 1995
107. Mahler & Malmros, 1990
108. Eithun, et al., 1994
109. Eithun, et al., 1994
110. Mahler, 1991
111. Mahler, 1995
112. Thorsteinsson, 2008; Mahler, 1995
113. Carter & Frasier, 1996; Ballin Smith, 2007
114. Carter & Frasier, 1996
115. Ballin Smith, 2007; Arge, 2005
116. Mauss, 2000
117. Smith, 2007
118. Eithun, et al., 1994
119. Stummann Hansen, 1991; Stummann Hansen & Waugh, 1998
120. Mahler, 1991; Mahler & Malmros, 1990; Eithun, et al., 1994
121. Bloch, 2007; Lindquist, 1994 [unpublished]
122. Eithun, et al., 1994
123. Eithun, et al., 1994
124. Mauss, 2000
125. Brink, 2012
126. Jesch, 2001, pp. 40–41
127. Arge, et al., 2009

Chapter 4
1. Lucas, 2009
2. Thorlaksson, 2000

3. Sigmundsson & Saemundson, 2008
4. Thorarinsson, 1981; Dugmore, 1989
5. Ahronson, 2002; Sveinbjarnardottir, 2002
6. Fríðriksson, 1994; Svanberg, 2003
7. Fríðriksson, 1994; Svanberg, 2003
8. Thorlaksson, 2007
9. Lucas, 2009; Ascough, et al., 2007; Brown, 2010 [unpublished]
10. Fríðriksson, 1994
11. Svanberg, 2003
12. Fríðriksson, 1994; Eldjarn & Fridriksson, 2000
13. Lucas, 2009; Stenberger, 1943; Einarsson, 2008
14. Dennis, et al., 1980
15. Thorlaksson, 2007
16. Sawyer & Sawyer, 2003; Fríðriksson, 1994
17. McTurk, 2007
18. Sigurdsson, 2007; Sorensen, 2000; Quinn, 2000; Whaley, 2000
19. Eldjarn & Fridriksson, 2000
20. Eldjarn & Fridriksson, 2000
21. Hermanns-Audardottir, 1991; Snaesdottir, 1991
22. Hermanns-Audardottir, 1991
23. Hermanns-Audardottir, 1991
24. Einarsson, 2008
25. Faulkes & Barnes, 2007
26. Einarsson, 2008
27. Snaesdottir, 1991; Milek, 2006 [unpublished]
28. Snaesdottir, 1991
29. Einarsson, 2008
30. Hermanns-Audardottir, 1991; Milek, 2006 [unpublished]
31. Snaesdottir, 1991; Hermanns-Audardottir, 1991; Einarsson, 2008; Bertelsen & Lamb, 1995
32. Snaesdottir, 1991; Milek, 2006 [unpublished]
33. Snaesdottir, 1991
34. Snaesdottir, 1991; Milek, 2006 [unpublished]; Bertelsen & Lamb, 1995
35. Hermanns-Audardottir, 1991
36. Milek, 2006 [unpublished]; Einarsson, 2008
37. Snaesdottir, 1991; Bertelsen & Lamb, 1995
38. Snaesdottir, 1991
39. Milek, 2006 [unpublished]
40. Berson, 2002
41. Berson, 2002
42. Vesteinsson, 2007
43. Berson, 2002
44. Milek, 2006 [unpublished]
45. Einarsson, 2008
46. Eldjarn & Fridriksson, 2000
47. Eldjarn & Fridriksson, 2000
48. Eldjarn & Fridriksson, 2000
49. Eldjarn & Fridriksson, 2000
50. Einarsson, 2008
51. Einarsson, 2008

52. Milek, 2006 [unpublished]
53. Buttler, 1984 [unpublished]; 1991; Forster & Bond, 2004
54. Hermanns-Audardottir, 1991
55. Berson, 2002
56. Vesteinsson, 2007
57. Eldjarn & Fridriksson, 2000
58. Eldjarn & Fridriksson, 2000
59. Byock, et al., 2005; Sverrisdottir, 2006
60. Stenberger, 1943
61. Vesteinsson, 2007
62. Sverrisdottir, 2006
63. Sverrisdottir, 2006
64. McGovern, et al., 1988
65. Sverrisdottir, 2006
66. Milek, 2006 [unpublished]
67. Stenberger, 1943
68. Stenberger, 1943, p. illustration after
69. Milek, 2006 [unpublished]
70. Stenberger, 1943, p. illustration after
71. Church, et al., 2007
72. Arnalds, 1987; Caseldine, et al., 2004; Erlendsson, 2007 [unpublished]
73. Church, et al., 2007
74. Bathurst, et al., 2010
75. Bathurst, et al., 2010
76. Buckland, et al., 1991
77. Arnalds, 1987; Erlendsson, 2007 [unpublished]; Eysteinsson & Blondal, 2003
78. Dennis, et al., 1980
79. Dennis, et al., 1980
80. Gronlie, 2006
81. Dennis, et al., 1980
82. Dugmore, 1989
83. Gudmundsson, 1996
84. Stenberger, 1943, p. illustration after
85. Bruun, 1928
86. Stenberger, 1943; Stummann Hansen, 2001
87. Berson, 2002
88. Sveinbjarnardottir, 1991; Berson, 2002
89. Sveinbjarnardottir, 1991
90. Milek, 2006 [unpublished]
91. Sveinbjarnardottir, 1991
92. Berson, 2002
93. Sverrisdottir, 2006
94. Dennis, et al., 1980, p. 110
95. Dennis, et al., 1980
96. Eldjarn & Fridriksson, 2000
97. Sveinbjarnardottir, et al., 1982; Eysteinsson & Blondal, 2003
98. Dennis, et al., 1980
99. Stenberger, 1943; Bruun, 1928
100. Sveinbjarnardottir, 1991
101. Roussell, 1941

102. Berson, 2002
103. Thorgeirsson, 2004; Durrenberger, 1991
104. Gudmundsson, 1996
105. Eysteinsson & Blondal, 2003
106. Buttler, 1991
107. Forster & Bond, 2004
108. Szabo, 2008; Lindquist, 1994 [unpublished]
109. Lindquist, 1994 [unpublished]
110. Sveinbjarnardottir, 1991; Amorosi, 1991
111. Szabo, 2008; Amorosi, 1991
112. Brown, 2010 [unpublished]
113. Ascough, et al., 2007
114. Friðriksson & Vesteinsson, 1997; Lucas, 2009
115. Lucas, 2009; Brown, 2010 [unpublished]; Milek, 2006 [unpublished]
116. Lucas, 2009
117. Lucas, 2009; Brown, 2010 [unpublished]; Friðriksson & Vesteinsson, 1997
118. Lucas, 2009
119. Lucas, 2009
120. Lucas, 2009
121. McGovern, et al., 2007
122. Bolender, 2006 [unpublished]; Brown, 2010 [unpublished]
123. Eysteinsson & Blondal, 2003
124. Dennis, et al., 1980
125. Adderley, et al., 2008; McGovern, et al., 2007
126. Lucas, 2009
127. Buttler, 1991; Forster & Bond, 2004
128. Lucas, 2009
129. McGovern, et al., 2007
130. Sveinbjarnardottir, 1991
131. Dennis, et al., 1980
132. Eldjarn & Fridriksson, 2000
133. McGovern, et al., 2007
134. Milek, 2006 [unpublished]; Brown, 2010 [unpublished]
135. Friðriksson, 1994
136. Friðriksson, 1994
137. Lucas, 2009
138. Milek, 2006 [unpublished]; Byock, et al., 2005
139. Svanberg, 2003; Stummann Hansen, 2001
140. Eldjarn & Fridriksson, 2000
141. Stenberger, 1943; Lucas, 2009
142. Bruun, 1928
143. Bathurst, et al., 2010
144. Bathurst, et al., 2010
145. Bathurst, et al., 2010
146. Eysteinsson & Blondal, 2003
147. Byock, 2001; Gordon, 1957
148. Bathurst, et al., 2010
149. Milek, 2006 [unpublished]
150. Sverrisdottir, 2006
151. Larson, 1917, pp. 140–141

152. Dennis, et al., 1980
153. Dennis, et al., 1980
154. Stenberger, 1943; Stummann Hansen, 2001
155. after Thorrson 2000
156. McGovern, et al., 2007; Sverrisdottir, 2006
157. Eithun, et al., 1994
158. Dennis, et al., 1980
159. Sadler, 1991; Milek, 2006 [unpublished]
160. Eldjarn & Fridriksson, 2000
161. Marcus, 1955
162. Snaesdottir, 1991
163. Dennis, et al., 1980
164. Ascough, et al., 2007
165. Sveinbjarnardottir, 1991; Adderley, et al., 2008
166. Mauss, 2000
167. Stenberger, 1943
168. Dennis, et al., 1980
169. Jesch, 2001
170. Durrenberger, 1991; Durrenberger, 1989
171. Quinn, 2000
172. Quinn, 2000
173. Gudmundsson, 1996
174. Lucas, 2009
175. Amorosi, 1991
176. Lucas, 2009; Ascough, et al., 2007

Chapter 5
   1. McGovern, 1991; McGovern, et al., 1988; Keller, 1989 [unpublished]
   2. McGovern, 1991
   3. Buckland, et al., 1996
   4. Morcken, 1968
   5. Schledermann & McCullough, 2003
   6. Albrethsen & Keller, 1986
   7. Maxwell, 1981
   8. Ross, 1997 [unpublished]
   9. Buckland, et al., 1996; Ross, 1997 [unpublished]
  10. Krogh, 1967
  11. Guldager, et al., 2002
  12. Ingstad, 1997; Wallace & Fitzhugh, 2000
  13. DI, 1876
  14. Keller, 2010
  15. Guldager, et al., 2002; Stenberger, 1943
  16. Svanberg, 2003
  17. Bruun, 1928
  18. Guldager, et al., 2002
  19. Albrethsen & Keller, 1986; Buckland, et al., 1996
  20. Sanmark, 2010
  21. Hoegsberg, 2009
  22. Hoegsberg, 2009
  23. Guldager, et al., 2002

24. Adderley & Simpson, 2006
25. Guldager, et al., 2002
26. Norlund, 1936
27. Norlund, 1936, p. 63
28. Guldager, et al., 2002
29. Amorosi, 1991; Adderley & Simpson, 2006
30. Albrethsen & Keller, 1986
31. Smiarowski, 2008
32. Albrethsen & Keller, 1986
33. Adderley & Simpson, 2006
34. Sanmark, 2010
35. Albrethson, 2003, p. 106
36. Smiarowski, 2008
37. Ostergard, 2009
38. Norlund, 1936
39. Norlund, 1936; Buttler, 1991
40. Smiarowski, 2008; Buckland, et al., 1994
41. Albrethsen & Keller, 1986; Norlund, 1936; DI, 1876
42. McManis, 1969; Perkins, 2004; Wallace, 1991
43. Perkins, 2004
44. Wallace, 2000
45. Rode, 1993; Sigurdsson, 2000
46. Sutherland, 2000
47. McGhee, 1981
48. Lightfoot, 1995
49. Miller, 2008
50. Wallace, 2000, pp. 218, Figure 9.9
51. Friesen, 2007; Kirch, 1992; Silliman, 2001
52. Maxwell, 1980
53. Pringle, 2012
54. Pringle, 2012
55. Wallace, 1991
56. Friesen, 2007
57. Wallace, 1991; Ingstad, 1997; Pringle, 2012
58. Friesen, 2007
59. Pringle, 2012
60. Wallace, 2009; 1991
61. Davis, et al., 1988
62. Davis, et al., 1988
63. Wallace, 1991
64. Wallace, 1991
65. Wallace, 2000
66. Davis, et al., 1988
67. Wallace, 1991
68. Wallace, 2000
69. Davis, et al., 1988
70. Wallace, 2009; 2000
71. Wallace, 1991
72. Wallace, 2000
73. Davis, et al., 1988; Ingstad, 1997

74. Wallace, 2009
75. Wallace, 2009
76. Davis, et al., 1988
77. Rowlett, 1982
78. Wallace, 1991
79. Pringle, 2012
80. Pringle, 2012
81. Renouf & Bell, 2008; Pringle, 2012
82. Pringle, 2012
83. Pringle, 2012
84. Wallace, 1991; Davis, et al., 1988
85. Davis, et al., 1988
86. Pringle, 2012
87. Wallace, 2009
88. Davis, et al., 1988
89. Berglund, 2000
90. Berglund, 2000
91. Ross, 1997 [unpublished]
92. Hoegsberg, 2009
93. Berglund, 2000; Panagiotakopulu, 2004
94. Albrethson, 2003
95. Albrethson, 2003; Ross, 1997 [unpublished]
96. Berglund, 2000
97. Albrethson, 2003; Hoegsberg, 2009
98. Berglund, 2000; Buckland, et al., 1994
99. Buckland, et al., 1994
100. Berglund, 2000
101. Panagiotakopulu, 2004
102. Berglund, 2000
103. Hoegsberg, 2009
104. Berglund, 2000
105. Ross, 1997 [unpublished]
106. Ross, 1997 [unpublished]
107. Panagiotakopulu, 2004
108. Buckland, et al., 1994
109. Berglund, 2000
110. Ostergard, 2009
111. Berglund, 2000
112. Panagiotakopulu, 2004
113. Buckland, et al., 1994
114. Berglund, 2000
115. Buckland, et al., 1994
116. Berglund, 2000
117. Ostergard, 2009
118. Berglund, 2000
119. Berglund, 2000
120. Ross, 1997 [unpublished]
121. Berglund, 2000; Buckland, et al., 1994
122. Wallace & Fitzhugh, 2000
123. Wallace, 2000; 2000

124. Pringle, 2012
125. Pringle, 2012
126. Sutherland, 2000; Rowlett, 1982
127. Hoegsberg, 2009; Pringle, 2012
128. Adderley & Simpson, 2006
129. Albrethsen & Keller, 1986; Hoegsberg, 2009; Wallace, 2000
130. Rowlett, 1982
131. Hoegsberg, 2009
132. Hoegsberg, 2009
133. McGovern, 1980
134. Keller, 1989 [unpublished]; Roussell, 1941; Norlund, 1936
135. Davis, et al., 1988; Wallace, 1991; Pringle, 2012; Guldager, et al., 2002
136. McGovern, 1980
137. Albrethsen & Keller, 1986; Davis, et al., 1988
138. Buckland, et al., 2009
139. Ross, 1997 [unpublished]
140. Albrethsen & Keller, 1986
141. Hoegsberg, 2009; Roussell, 1941; Norlund, 1936
142. Sanmark, 2010; Berlin, 1932
143. Gjerland & Keller, 2010
144. Abrams, 2009
145. Norlund, 1936; Gjerland & Keller, 2010
146. Andren, 2007; Gjerland & Keller, 2010
147. Krogh, 1967
148. Sigurdsson, 2007
149. Sanmark, 2010; Gjerland & Keller, 2010
150. Albrethsen & Keller, 1986
151. Arneborg, 2003
152. Faulkes & Barnes, 2007
153. Arneborg, 2003
154. Krogh, 1967
155. Bruun, 1928; Norlund, 1936; Roussell, 1941
156. Abrams, 2009; Strombeck, 1997
157. Arneborg, 2003
158. Arneborg, 2003

Chapter 6
 1. Oka & Kusimba, 2008
 2. Oka & Kusimba, 2008
 3. Braudel, 1981
 4. Cunliffe, 2001
 5. Sindbaek, 2009
 6. Cunliffe, 2001
 7. Sindbaek, 2009
 8. Sindbaek, 2007; Sindbaek, 2009
 9. Oka & Kusimba, 2008
10. Bill, 2010
11. Crumlin-Pedersen, 1995
12. Bill, 2010; Crumlin-Pedersen, 1995
13. Greenhill & Morrison, 1995; Bill, 2010

14. Westerdahl, 2008
15. Westerdahl, 2008; Crumlin-Pedersen, 1995
16. Westerdahl, 2008
17. Westerdahl, 2008
18. Westerdahl, 2008
19. Bill, 2010; Crumlin-Pedersen, 1995
20. Bill, 2010
21. Bill, 2010
22. Unger, 1980
23. Morcken, 1968
24. Bill, 2010; Westerdahl, 2008
25. Unger, 1980; McGovern, et al., 2007
26. Roesdahl, 2005; Seaver, 1996
27. Miller, 2008
28. Seaver, 1996; Bill, 2010
29. Quinn, 2000
30. Sveinsson & Þórðarson, 1935
31. Unger, 1980
32. Bill, 2010
33. Westerdahl, 2008
34. Unger, 1980
35. McGovern, 1980
36. Greenhill & Morrison, 1995
37. MacDonald, 2002; Dumville, 2002; Ahronson, 2002
38. Dr D Gray, DVM: personal comment
39. Dr D Gray, DVM: personal comment
40. Sindbaek, 2009
41. Lightfoot & Martinez, 1995
42. Larson, 1917; Grove, 2009
43. Larson, 1917, pp. 83–84
44. Gelsinger, 1970; Bill, 2010
45. Dugmore, et al., 2005
46. Unger, 1980; Seaver, 1996
47. Vesteinsson, 2007
48. Durrenberger, 1989
49. Bill, 2010; Seaver, 1996
50. Mauss, 2000
51. Roesdahl, 2005; Seaver, 1996
52. Gjerland & Keller, 2010
53. McGovern, et al., 1988
54. Fagan, 2000
55. Unger, 1980; Vesteinsson, 2007
56. Quinn, 2000
57. Hastrup, 1989
58. Mauss, 2000
59. Fojut, 1996
60. Challinor, 2004
61. Buttler, 1984 [unpublished]
62. Challinor, 2004
63. Cunliffe, 2001

64. Buckland, et al., 1991
65. Barrett, et al., 2008
66. Farr, 2006
67. McGovern, 1980
68. Ostergard, 2009
69. Arneborg, 2003
70. Keller, 2010
71. Magnus, 1998; Szabo, 2008
72. Magnus, 1998
73. Larson, 1917
74. Doyle, 2008; Magnus, 1998
75. Magnus, 1998; Keller, 2010
76. Buckland, et al., 1996
77. Englert, 2007
78. Roesdahl, 2005
79. Roesdahl, 2005; Roesdahl, 2010; Keller, 2010
80. Keller, 2010
81. DI, 1876
82. Mauss, 2000
83. Page, 1998
84. Bill, 2010
85. Sindbaek, 2007
86. Mauss, 2000
87. Brink, 2012
88. Farr, 2006
89. Eithun, et al., 1994; Dennis, et al., 1980; DI, 1876
90. Durrenberger, 1991
91. Barrett, 2007
92. Barrett & Slater, 2009
93. Sindbaek, 2009
94. Williams, 1996 [unpublished]
95. Bill, 2010
96. Miller, 2008; Dennis, et al., 1980
97. Keller, 2010

Chapter 7
1. Andersson, 2008
2. Andersson, 2008; Quinn, 2000
3. Quinn, 2000
4. Andren, 2007
5. Andren, 2007
6. Schjodt, 2008
7. Lucas & McGovern, 2007
8. Andren, 2007; Eldjarn & Fridriksson, 2000
9. Eldjarn & Fridriksson, 2000
10. Lund, 2005
11. Quinn, 2000; Lindow, 2001
12. Lindow, 2001
13. Lund, 2005
14. Eldjarn & Fridriksson, 2000; Carter & Frasier, 1996

15. Carter & Frasier, 1996; Owen & Dalland, 1994
16. Larson, 1917
17. Ahronson, 2002
18. Ahronson, 2002; MacDonald, 2002
19. Knight, 2007 [unpublished]
20. Cunliffe, 2001
21. Ahronson, 2007
22. Arge, 1991; Debes, 1995
23. Ahronson, 2007; Ahronson, 2002
24. Ahronson, 2007; Ahronson, 2002; Sveinbjarnardottir, 2002
25. Fríðriksson, 1994
26. Knight, 2007 [unpublished]
27. MacDonald, 2002
28. Knight, 2007 [unpublished]
29. Fisher, 2002; Cunliffe, 2001
30. Ahronson, 2002; MacDonald, 2002; Sveinbjarnardottir, 2002
31. Arge, 1991; Debes, 1995
32. Arge, 2005; Arge, 1991; Debes, 1995
33. Stummann Hansen & Sheehan, 2006
34. Sveinbjarnardottir, 2002; Ahronson, 2002
35. Svanberg, 2003; Fríðriksson, 1994
36. Ahronson, 2002
37. Sveinbjarnardottir, 2002
38. Helgason, et al., 2001
39. Ahronson, 2007
40. Stummann Hansen & Sheehan, 2006
41. Stummann Hansen & Sheehan, 2006
42. Stummann Hansen & Sheehan, 2006
43. MacDonald, 2002, p. 19
44. Dumville, 2002
45. Ahronson, 2007
46. Strombeck, 1997
47. Quinn, 2000
48. Morris, 1995
49. Abrams, 2009; Strombeck, 1997
50. Stummann Hansen & Sheehan, 2006
51. Eldjarn & Fridriksson, 2000
52. Eldjarn & Fridriksson, 2000
53. Gronlie, 2006
54. Bagge, 2010
55. Derry, 1979; Sawyer & Sawyer, 2003
56. Solli, 1996
57. Graslund, 1987
58. Solli, 1996
59. Antonsson, 2007
60. Gronlie, 2006
61. Quinn, 2000
62. Eldjarn & Fridriksson, 2000
63. Sveinsson & Þórðarson, 1935
64. Arneborg, 2003; Guldager, et al., 2002

65. Norlund, 1936
66. Guldager, et al., 2002
67. Stummann Hansen, 2009: personal comment
68. Stummann Hansen & Sheehan, 2006; Guldager, et al., 2002
69. Abrams, 2009
70. Guldager, et al., 2002
71. Solli, 1996
72. Bagge, 2010
73. Bagge, 2010; Sawyer & Sawyer, 2003
74. Bagge, 2010
75. Mauss, 2000
76. Strombeck, 1997
77. Eldjarn & Fridriksson, 2000
78. Quinn, 2000
79. Solli, 1996
80. Quinn, 2000
81. Quinn, 2000
82. Mauss, 2000

Chapter 8
1. Bill, 2010
2. Ogilvie, et al., 2009
3. Sigurdsson, 2007; Bagge, 2010
4. Seibert, 2008
5. Quinn, 2000
6. Roesdahl, 2005
7. Keller, 2010
8. Roesdahl, 2005
9. Sverrisdottir, 2006
10. McGovern, 1980
11. Roesdahl, 2010; Dugmore, et al., 2007
12. MacDonald, 2002
13. Svanberg, 2003
14. Fríðriksson, 1994; Svanberg, 2003
15. Oma, 2010
16. Stummann Hansen, 1996
17. Stummann Hansen & Waugh, 1998
18. McGovern, et al., 2007
19. Albrethsen & Keller, 1986
20. Farr, 2006
21. Bill, 2010
22. Cooke, et al., 2002
23. Svanberg, 2003
24. Fríðriksson, 1994; Svanberg, 2003
25. Dr D Gray, DVM: personal comment
26. Kirch, 1992
27. Cunliffe, 2001
28. Stummann Hansen & Waugh, 1998
29. Sveinsson & Þórðarson, 1935

Appendix A

1. Sveinsson & Þórðarson, 1935, p. 241
2. Jæderen, Norway
3. They were outlawed for murder.
4. Literally 'obtained'
5. This could be related to 'leacherous' or being from a western Icelandic settlement named Saurbœr.
6. This is direct acknowledgement by the saga-author that this portion of the source material at least post-dates Eiríksaga.
7. A group of small islands located between north-western Iceland and eastern Greenland.
8. A glacier in western Greenland.
9. A glacier in western Greenland most likely named due to the vivid colors found in Greenland's glaciers.
10. Modern Igdlotalik.
11. Literally 'took there his farm'.
12. Small islands off the coast of Cape Farewell, Greenland.
13. Modern Agdluitsok.
14. Eirik had apparently only been outlawed for three years, if he had been outlawed completely he would never have been allowed to return safely to Iceland. This is signified by the legal term *alsekr* which does not occur in this saga.
15. Possibly Qassiarsuk, Greenland.
16. This passage gives important contextual information for the discovery and settlement of Greenland.
17. Modern Amitsuarssuk.
18. Modern Ikigiat.
19. Modern Tasermiut.
20. Modern Agdluitsok.
21. At the head of the Kangikitsok fjord.
22. Modern Sermilik.
23. Modern Unartok.
24. Modern Igaliku.
25. Modern Ekaluit.
26. Ingólf Arnarsson, the first settler of Iceland.
27. Literally 'those of Herjólf'.
28. This is evidence of recognition of differences being tied to location between Norse inhabitants of the north Atlantic archipelagos.
29. The inclusion of this poem is to help situate the voyage within a wider context – a form of medieval referencing by the saga author.
30. Note the present tense – this text was written at the time of **living** Greenlandic settlements, or at least the saga-author believes so. Greenland existed in the eyes of the Church long after the settlements themselves actually failed.
31. Greenland was settled subsequent to the Icelandic conversion to Christianity.
32. These winds came from the north thus blowing Bjarni's ship off course towards the south for several days as opposed to being able to maintain similar latitude for a more direct voyage to Greenland.
33. This can be taken one of two ways. 1) Bjarni and the crew actually make landfall at some unknown location in North America, perhaps along the shores of Labrador. 2) Bjarni and crew sail in as close as possible to the shore, but do not actually get off of the ship, rather getting close enough to see what exists on the land but still being able to make a reasonably quick getaway should the unknown situation turn dangerous.

34. This appears to be a description of the coast of southern Baffin Island or Labrador.
35. This appears most likely to be a description of the coast of northern Baffin Island or another of the northern arctic islands.
36. A storm at sea, from the description a very strong one. This could also imply that Bjarni had made a crossing between Iceland and Greenland late in the safe sailing season and so was caught by stiff north Atlantic storms.
37. Cape Farewell, Greenland.
38. Jarl in Norway, AD 1000–1014.
39. Leif has requested Eirik to lead the expedition.
40. From the Continent – in this respect the Norse of the north Atlantic were still utilizing a system of referencing based upon their Scandinavian homelands as the continent of Europe is physically located to the south for someone who is in Scandinavia.
41. Launched the ship's boat – Bjarni's (now Leif's) ship must have been fairly deep drafted, making beaching the vessel to unload the cargo much more difficult. As this was supposed to have been a long distance trading vessel, or knórr, this is unsurprising.
42. Modern Baffin Island.
43. Wallace, 1991, pp. 169, figure 1.
44. Modern Labrador.
45. Modern Belle Isle.
46. This is commonly accepted as the archaeological site at L'Anse aux Meadows discovered and initially excavated by the Ingestaads during the 1960s.
47. This reflects the differences found in salmon species available in comparison to the types previously known by the Norse. It is important to remember, however, that these resources are also sources of exaggeration in order to artificially create greater worth for the discovered lands amongst the saga's literate audience.
48. This can be taken as evidence of a location lower in latitude than 60°N, the latitude of much of the north Atlantic archipelagos.
49. 'Southern' in relation to the location of the Scandinavia homelands – somewhere on the European continent.
50. This may imply that Tyrkir was either a domestic servant in Eirik's household or was a retainer of Eirik's.
51. Literally 'foster-er.'
52. The lack of a common language within the sources can be a major acknowledgement of non-Norse identities within the textual resources.
53. This reflects the fact that this was not merely a voyage of discovery of new lands – it was a voyage of discovery of closer natural resources for Greenland, and possibly Iceland as well.
54. Skerries are rocky tidal islands. Traditionally these are islands which are exposed at low tide but covered with water at high time. There are some which are more substantial and do not become covered, such as a sea stack, but that does not seem to be the case here.
55. Along the coast.
56. Literally 'Keel-headland'.
57. Turning over a skin-hulled boat would make a very effective tent for a small number of men and removed the necessity for carrying shelter along on longer voyages. Utilization of skin umiaks in such a manner has been documented in early ethnological paintings of regional descendents during the sixteenth and seventeenth centuries.
58. Þorvald's crew.
59. The sleepiness episode may be a residual from oral transmission of the original source material. The ghostly voice warning of life-threatening danger is a folkloristic trope found in tales from around the world (Dundes 2003: personal comment).

60. Advanced to attack.
61. Set shields on the gunwales of the ship.
62. Indigenous peoples of North America and Greenland.
63. Literally 'Cross-headland'.
64. Þorvald had split the crew into two groups during the spring to explore further inland.
65. Had been married to.
66. Norwegian.
67. This stylized phrasing points to common literary formulas used by Christian clerics involved with compiling sagas, in this case the concept of the *noble pagan*.
68. Illnesses transported by long distance trade ships going between Europe and Iceland and Greenland would have been increasingly more potent amongst the north Atlantic populations as time passed as the increasingly virulent diseases of Europe began and were introduced fully developed.
69. The bed where she had died.
70. To go on pilgrimage in Europe.
71. The more fantastic elements of this episode are linked to later information found within the saga concerning Guðrið and her later devotion to God. The reinforcement of the idea that Guðrið's fate was fore-ordained by God shows that the original intended audience was probably connected to Guðrið's home convent. The fact that religion plays a small role within this work points to the former rather than the latter.
72. Þorstein the black had to do this socially as a host, but he would have also benefitted greatly from the action by raising his social standing amongst the Greenlandic population through good deed.
73. Literally 'man-makings.'
74. Fell in love.
75. Asked her to marry.
76. Betrothed.
77. Literally 'settlement'.
78. This is quite similar to the agreements which Norwegian captains of smaller fishing vessels engaged their crews.
79. Some translate this as hammocks.
80. A clear indication that these were foreign people to the Norse settlers.
81. This would have been a commonality between them, but is also a common literary formula for this genre.
82. Milk may well have been an exchange good between Norse and indigenous people, especially of the more northerly latitudes, as milk is a ready energy source which is high in fat. A concern for this, however, is the fact that lactose intolerance is quite high in descendent populations as well as New World indigenous populations in general.
83. Literally 'locked'.
84. An important aspect of any exploration expedition.
85. At Garðar.
86. Literally 'all–ill'.
87. In Saxony. Yet another example of reference to the European continent via direction.
88. E.V. Gordon lists this as being maple wood.
89. Guðrið appears to have gone first to Norway then on pilgrimage in Continental Europe. Jerusalem would had been named specifically had she made her pilgrimage there.
90. This paragraph provides closure to the prophecy given by Þorstein Eiríksson shortly after his death, an obvious folkloristic trope (Dundes 2003: personal comment).
91. Bjorn had not yet been previously mentioned due to the fact that he was born after his father's Vínland journey and so didn't dirently figure into the primary storyline of the saga.

Bibliography

Abrams, Lesley. "Early Religious Practice in the Greenland Settlement." *Journal of the North Atlantic* Special Volume 2 (2009): 52–65.

Adderley, W Paul, and Ian Simpson. "Soils and Palaeo-climate based evidence for irrigation requirements in Norse Greenland." *Journal of Archaeological Science* 33 (2006): 1666–1679.

Adderley, W Paul, Ian Simpson, and Orri Vesteinsson. "Local-Scale Adaptations: A Modeled Assessment of Soil, Landscape, Microclimatic and Management Factors in Norse Home-Field Activities." *Geoarchaeology* 23, no. 4 (2008): 500–527.

Ahronson, Kristjan. "Testing the Evidence for Northern North Atlantic Papar: a Cave Site in Southern Iceland." In *The Papar in the North Atlantic: Environment and History*, edited by Barbara Crawford, 107–120. St Andrews: St John's House Papers, 2002.

———. *Viking-Age Communities: Pap – names and Papar in the Hebridean Islands.* Vol. 450. Oxford: British Archaeological Reports, British Series, 2007.

Albrethsen, Svend, and Christian Keller. "The Use of the Saeter in Medieval Norse Farming in Greenland." *Arctic Anthropology* 23, no. 1&2 (1986): 97–107.

Albrethson, Svend. "The Early Norse Farm Buildings of Western Greenland: Archaeological Evidence." In *Vinland Revisited: The Norse World at the Turn of the First Millenium*, edited by Shannon Lewis-Simpson, 97–110. St John's: Historic Sites Association, 2003.

Amorosi, Thomas. "Icelandic Archaeofauna: A Preliminary Review." *Acta Archaeologica* 61 (1991): 273–291.

Amorosi, Thomas, Paul Buckland, Andrew Dugmore, Jon Ingimundarson, and Thomas McGovern. "Raiding the Landscape: human impact in the Scandinavian North Atlantic." *Human Ecology* 25, no. 3 (1997): 491–518.

Andersson, Theodore. "From Tradition to Literature in the Sagas." In *Oral Art Forms and Their Passage into Writing*, edited by Else Mundal and Jonas Wellendorf, 7–17. Copenhagen: University of Copenhagen Press, 2008.

Andren, Andres. "Behind Heathendom: Archaeological Studies of Old Norse Heathendom." *Scottish Archaeological Journal* 27, no. 2 (2007): 105–138.

Antonsson, Haki. *St. Magnús of Orkney: A Scandinavian Martyr-Cult in Context.* 1st. Leiden: Brill, 2007.

Arge, Simun. "Cultural Landscapes and Cultural Environmental issues in the Faroes." In *Vikings and Norse in the North Atlantic*, edited by Andras Mortensen and Simun Arge, 22–38. Torshavn: Annales Societatis Scientiarum Faeroensis, 2005.

Arge, Simun. "Naer Foroyar vordu bygdar." *Mondal* 15, no. 3 (1989): 2–31.

Arge, Simun. "The landnam in the Faroes." *Arctic Anthropology* 28, no. 2 (1991): 101–120.

Arge, Simun, Michael Church, and Seth Brewington. "Pigs in the Faroe Islands: An Ancient Facet of the Islands' Palaeoeconomy." *Journal of the North Atlantic* 2 (2009): 19–32.

Arnalds, Andres. "Disturbance in Iceland." *Arctic and Alpine Research* 19, no. 4 (1987): 508–513.

Arneborg, Jette. "Norse Greenland: Reflections on Settlement and Depopulation." In *Contact, Continuity and Collapse: The Norse Colonization of the North Atlantic*, edited by James Barrett, 163–181. Turnhout: Brepols, 2003.

Ascough, Paul, et al. "Reservoirs and Radiocarbon: 14C Dating Problems in Myvatnssveit, Northern Iceland." *Radiocarbon* 49, no. 2 (2007): 947–961.

Bagge, Sverre. *From Viking Stronghold to Christian Kingdom*. 1st. Copenhagen: Museum Tusculanum Press, 2010.

Ballin Smith, Beverley. *Catpund: a prehistoric house in Shetland*. Edinburgh: Scottish Archaeological Internet Report, 2005.

Ballin Smith, Beverley. "Norwick: Shetland's First Viking Settlement?" In *West Over Sea*, edited by Beverley Ballin Smith, Simon Taylor and Gareth Williams, 287–297. Leiden: Brill, 2007.

Barrett, James. "The Pirate Fisherman: The Political Economy of A Maritime Society." In *West Over Sea*, edited by Beverley Ballin Smith, Simon Taylor and Gareth Williams, 299–340. Leiden: Brill, 2007.

Barrett, James. "What Caused the Viking Age?" *Antiquity* 82 (2008): 671–685.

Barrett, James, and Adam Slater. "New Excavations at the Brough of Deerness: Power and Religion in Viking Age Scotland." *Journal of the North Atlantic* 2 (2009): 81–94.

Barrett, James, et al. "Detecting the Medieval Cod Trade: a new method and first results." *Journal of Archaeological Sciences* 35 (2008): 850–61.

Bathurst, Rhonda, Davide Zori, and Jesse Byock. "Diatoms as bioindicators of site use: locating turf structures from the Viking Age." *Journal of Archaeological Science* 37 (2010): 2920–2928.

Bedos-Rezak, Brigitte. "Medieval Identity: A Sign and a concept." *The American Historical Review [online]* 105, no. 5 (2000).

Berglund, Joel. "The Farm Beneath the Sand." In *Vikings: The North Atlantic Saga*, edited by William Fitzhugh and Elizabeth Ward, 295–303. Washington: Smithsonian Institution Press, 2000.

Berlin, Knud. *Denmark's Right to Greenland*. 1st. Copenhagen: Nyt Nordisk Forlag, 1932.

Berson, Bruno. "A Contribution to the Study of the Medieval Icelandic Farm: The Byres." *Archaeologica Islandica* 2 (2002): 37–64.

Bertelsen, Reidar, and Raymond Lamb. "Settlement Mounds in the North Atlantic." In *The Viking Age in Caithness, Orkney and the North Atlantic*, edited by Colleen Batey, Judith Jesch and Christopher Morris, 544–554. Edinburgh: Edinburgh University Press, 1995.

Bigelow, Gerald. "Archaeological and Ethnohistorical Evidence of a Norse Island Food Custom." In *The VIking Age in Caithness, Orkney and the North Atlantic*, edited by Colleen Batey, Judith Jesch and Christopher Morris, 441–453. Edinburgh: Edinburgh university Press, 1995.

Bill, Jan. "Viking Age ships and seafaring in the West." In *Viking Trade and Settlement in Continental Western Europe*, edited by Klaesoe, 19–39. Copenhagen: Museum Tusculanum, 2010.

Blakely, Michael. "An Ethical Epistemology of Publicly." In *Evaluating Multiple Narratives*, edited by Junko Habu, Clare Fawcett and John Matsunaga, 17–28. New York: Springer, 2008.

Bloch, Dorete. *Faeroernes grindefangst*. Torshavn: Foroya Natturugripasavn, 2007.

Bolender, Douglas. "The Creation of a Propertied Landscape: Land Tenure and Agricultural Investment in Medieval Iceland." Evanston: Northwestern University, 2006 [unpublished].

Bourdieu, Pierre. *The Logic of Practice*. 1st. Vol. 7. Stanford: Stanford University Press, 1990.

Braudel, Fernand. *The Structures of Everyday Life: Civilization and Capitalism 15th-18th Century*. 1st . New York: Harper and Row, 1981.

Brink, Stefan. *Vikingarnas slavar*. 1st. Riga: Atlantis, 2012.

Brown, Jennifer. "Human responses, resiliances and vulnerability: an interdisciplinary approach to understanding past farm success and failure in Myvatnssheit, northern Iceland." Stirling: University of Stirling, 2010 [unpublished].

Bruun, Daniel. *Fortidsminder og Nutidshjem paa Island.* 1st. Copenhagen: Gyldendalkse, 1928.

Buckland, Paul, Andrew Dugmore, Donald Perry, Daniel Savory, and Gudrun Sveinbjarnardottir. "Holt in Eyjafjallasveit, Iceland: A Paleoecological Study of the Impact of landnam." *Acta Archaeologica* 61 (1991): 253–271.

Buckland, Paul, et al. "Bioarchaeological and Climatological Evidence for the Fate of Norse Farmers in Medieval Greenland." *Antiquity* 70 (1996): 88–96.

Buckland, Paul, Kevin Edwards, Eva Panagiotakopulu, and J Edward Schofield. "Palaeoecological and Historical Evidence for manuring and irrigation at Gardr (Igaliku), Norse Eastern Settlement, Greenland." *The Holocene* 19, no. 1 (2009): 105–116.

Buckland, Paul, Thomas McGovern, Jon Sadler, and Paul Skidmore. "Twig layers, floors and middens. Recent palaeoecological Research in the Western Settlement, Greenland." In *Developments Around the Baltic and North Sea in the Viking Age*, edited by Bjorn Ambrosiani and Helen Clarke, 132–143. Stockholm: Twelfth Viking Congress, 1994.

Buttler, Simon. "Steatite in the Norse North Atlantic." *Acta Archaeologica* 61 (1991): 228–232.

———. "The Steatite Industry in Norse Shetland." Liverpool: University of Liverpool, 1984 [unpublished].

Byock, Jesse. *Viking Age Iceland.* 1st. London: Penguin, 2001.

Byock, Jesse, et al. "A Viking-Age Valley in Iceland: The Mosfell Archaeological Project." *Medieval Archaeology* 69 (2005): 195–218.

Carter, Stephen, and David Frasier. "The Sands of Breckon, Yell, Shetland: archaeological survey and excavation in an area of wind-blown sand." *Proceedings of the Society of Antiquarians of Scotland* 126 (1996): 271–301.

Caseldine, Christopher, Mark Dinnin, Dawn Hendon, and Pete Langdon. "The Holocene Development of the Icelandic Biota and its Palaeoclimatic Significance." In *Atlantic Connections and Adaptations*, edited by Rupert Housley and Geraint Coles, 182–190. Oxford: Oxbow, 2004.

Challinor, Christopher. "Butter as an Economic Resource in the Northern Isles." In *Atlantic Connections and Adaptations*, edited by Rupert Housley and Geraint Coles, 163–174. Oxford: Oxbow Books, 2004.

Christiansen, Axel. "Dark Age naval power: superb seamanship or not?" *International Journal of Nautical Archaeology* 31, no. 1 (2002): 134–136.

Church, Michael, et al. "Charcoal Production during the Norse and early medieval periods in Eykafjallahreppur, Southern Iceland." *Radiocarbon* 49, no. 2 (2007): 659–672.

Cooke, Bill, Carol Christensen, and Lena Hammarlund. "Viking Woollen square-sails and fabric cover factor." *International Journal of Nautical Archaeology* 31, no. 2 (2002): 202–210.

Crawford, Barbara, and Beverley Ballin Smith. *The Biggings, Papa Stour, Shetland. The History and Excavation of a Royal Norwegian Farm.* Edinburgh: Society of Antiquaries of Scotland Monograph Series, 1999.

Crowley, Thomas, and Thomas Lowery. "How warm was the Medieval Warm Period?" *Ambio* 29, no. 1 (2000): 51–54.

Crumlin-Pedersen, Ole. "Ship Types and Sizes AD 800–1400." In *Aspects of Maritime Scandinavia AD 200–1200*, edited by Ole Crumlin-Pedersen, 69–82. Roskilde: The Viking Ship Museum, 1995.

Cunliffe, Barry. *Facing the Ocean. The Atlantic and its Peoples, 8000 BC to AD 1500.* Oxford: Oxford University Press, 2001.

Dahl, Sverri. "The Norse Settlement of the Faroe Islands." *Medieval Archaeology* 15 (1970): 60–73.

Dahl, Sverri. "The Norse Settlement of the Faroe Islands." *Medieval Archaeology* 14 (1970): 60–73.

Dahl, Sverri. "Um tidarfesting av foroyaskum fitisteinsfundum." *Frodskaparit* 4 (1955): 61–84.

Dahl, Sverri, and Joannas Rasmussen. "Vikingaldergrov i Tjornuvik." *Frodskaparit* 5 (1956): 153–167.

Davis, Andrew, John McAndrews, and Birgitta Wallace. "Palaeoenvironmental and the Archaeological Record at the L'Anse aux Meadows site, Newfoundland." *Geoarchaeology* 3, no. 1 (1988): 53–64.

Debes, Hans. "Problems concerning the Earliest Settlement of the Faroe Islands." In *The Viking Age in Caithness, Orkney and the North Atlantic*, edited by Colleen Batey, Judith Jesch and Christopher Morris, 454–464. Edinburgh: University of Edinburgh, 1995.

Dennis, Andrew, Peter Foote, and Richard Perkins. *Laws of Early Iceland: Gragas.* Winnipeg: University of Manitoba, 1980.

Derry, Thomas. *A History of Scandinavia.* St Paul: University of Minnesota, 1979.

DI. *Diplomatarium Islandicum volume 1 .* Kaupmannahofn: SL Mullers, 1876.

Doyle, Alison. "Ruins may be Viking hunting outpost in Greenland." *San Diego Union-Tribune*, July 28, 2008.

Dugmore, Andrew. "Icelandic volcanic ash in Scotland." *Scottish Geographical Journal* 105, no. 3 (1989): 168–172.

Dugmore, Andrew, Christian Keller, and Thomas McGovern. "Norse Greenland Settlement: Reflections on Climate, Trade, and the Contrasting Fates of Human Settlements in the North Atlantic Islands." *Arctic Anthropology* 44, no. 1 (2007): 12–36.

Dugmore, Andrew, et al. "The Norse landnam on the North Atlantic Islands: an environmental impact assessment." *Polar Record* 41, no. 1 (2005): 21–37.

Dumville, David. "The North Atlantic Monastic Thalassocracy: Sailing into the Desert in Early Medieval Insular Spirituality." In *The Paper in the North Atlantic: Environment and History*, edited by Barbara Crawford, 121–131. St Andrews: St John's House Papers, 2002.

Durrenberger, E. Paul. "Anthropological Perspectives on the Commonwealth Period." In *The Anthropology of Iceland*, edited by E Paul Durrenberger and Gisli Palsson, 228–246. Iowa City: University of Iowa Press, 1989.

Durrenberger, Paul. "Production in Medieval Iceland." *Acta Archaeologica* 61 (1991): 14–21.

Earle, Timothy. "Chiefdoms in Archaeological and Ethnohistorical Perspective." *Annual Review of Anthropology* 16 (1987): 279–308.

Einarsson, Bjarni. "Blot houses in Viking Age farmstead cult practices." *Acta Archaeologica* 79 (2008): 145–184.

Eithun, Bjorn, Magnus Rindal, and Tor Ulset. *Den Eldre Gulatingslova.* Oslo: Riksarkivet, 1994.

Eldjarn, Kristjan, and Adolf Fridriksson. *Kuml and haugfe.* 2nd. Reykjavik: Mal og menning, 2000.

Englert, Antone. "Ohthere's Voyage seen from a Nautical Angle." In *Ohthere's voyages: a late 9th-century account of voyages along the coasts of Norway and Denmark and its cultural context*, 117–129. 2007.

Erlendsson, Egill. "Environmental Change around the settlement of Iceland." Aberdeen: University of Aberdeen, 2007 [unpublished].

Eysteinsson, Throstur, and Sigurdur Blondal. "The Forests of Iceland at the Time of Settlement: Their Utilisation and eventual fate." In *Vinland Revisited: The Norse World at the time of the New Millenium*, edited by Shannon Lewis-Simpson, 411–415. St John's: Historic Sites Association, 2003.

Fagan, Brian. *The Little Ice Age.* New York: Basic Books, 2000.

Farr, Helen. "Seafaring as Social Action." *Journal of Marine Archaeology* 1 (2006): 85–99.

Faulkes, Anthony, and Michael Barnes. *A New Introduction to Old Norse: Part III Glossary and Index of Names.* 4th. London: Viking Society for Northern Research, 2007.

Fenton, Alexander. "Building Tradition in Shetland: The Vernacular Evidence." In *Shetland Archaeology*, edited by Brian Smith, 159–174. Lerwick: The Shetland Times, 1985.

Finsens, Vilhjalmur. *Gragas: Konungsbok.* re-release. Odense: Universitetsforlag, 1974.

Fisher, Ian. "Crosses in the Ocean: some papar sites and their sculpture." In *The Papar in the North Atlantic: Environment and History*, edited by Barbara Crawford, 39–57. St Andrews: St John's House Papers, 2002.

Fojut, Noel. "Not Seeing the Wood: an Armchair Archaeology of Shetland." In *Shetland's Northern Links: Language and History*, edited by Doreen Waugh and Brian Smith, 103–116. Edinburgh: Scottish Society for Northern Studies, 1996.

Forster, Amanda, and Julie Bond. "North Atlantic Networks: Preliminary Research into the Trade of Steatite in the VIking and Norse Periods." In *Atlantic Connections and Adaptations*, edited by Rupert Housley and Geraint Coles, 218–229. Oxford: Oxbow, 2004.

Frieman, Catherine. "Islandscapes and 'Islandness': The Prehistoric Isle of Man in the Irish Seascape." *Oxford Journal of Archaeology* 27, no. 2 (2008): 135–151.

Friesen, T Max. "Hearth rows, hierarchies and Arctic hunter-gatherers: the construction of equality in the Late Dorset Period." *World Archaeology* 39, no. 2 (2007): 194–214.

Friðriksson, Adolf. *Sagas and Popular Antiquarianism in Icelandic Archaeology.* Aldershot: Avebury, 1994.

Friðriksson, Adolf, and Orri Vesteinsson. "Hofstadir Revisited." *Norwegian Archaeological Review* 30, no. 2 (1997): 103–112.

Gaimster, David. "A Parallel History: The Archaeology of Hanseatic Urban Culture in the Baltic, c.1200–1600." *World Archaeology* 37, no. 3 (2005): 408–423.

Gelsinger, Bruce. "The Norse 'Day's Sailing'." *Mariner's Mirror* 56 (1970): 107–109.

Giddens, Anthony. *Central Problems in Social Theory.* London: Macmillan, 1979.

Gjerland, Berit, and Christian Keller. "Graves and Churches in the North Atlantic: A Pilot Study." *Journal of the North Atlantic* Special Volume 2 (2010): 161–177.

Gordon, Eric. *An Introduction to Old Norse.* 2nd. Oxford: Oxford University Press, 1957.

Graslund, Anne-Sofie. "Pagan and Christian in the Age of Conversion." In *Proceedings of the Tenth Viking Congress*, edited by James Knirk, 81–94. Oslo: Universitetets Oldsaksamlings Skrifter, 1987.

Greenhill, Basil, and John Morrison. *The Archaeology of Boats and Ships: an introduction.* London: Conway Maritime Press, 1995.

Gronlie, Sian. *Islendingabok, Kristni Saga.* London: Viking Society for Northern Research, 2006.

Grove, Jonathan. "The Place of Greenland in Medieval Icelandic Saga Narrative." *Journal of the North Atlantic* Special Volume 2 (2009): 30–51.

Gudjonsson, Elsa. "Some Aspects of the Icelandic Warp-Weighted Loom, Vefstadur." *Textile History* 21, no. 2 (1990): 165–179.

Gudmundsson, Gardar. "Gathering and Processing of lyme-grass (Elymus arenarius L.) in Iceland, an ethnohistorical account." *Vegetation History and Archaeobotany* 5 (1996): 13–23.

Guldager, Ole, Steffen Stummann Hansen, and Simon Gleie. *Medieval Farmsteads in Greenland.* 1st. Copenhagen: Danish Polar Center, 2002.

Hamilton, John. *Excavations at Jarlshof, Shetland*. 1st. Edinburgh: Her Majesty's Stationary Office, 1956.

Hastrup, Kirsten. "Saeters in Iceland 900–1600." *Acta Borealia* 6, no. 1 (1989): 72–85.

Helgason, Agnar, et al. "mtDNA and the Islands of the North Atlantic: Estimating the Proportions of Norse and Gaelic Ancestry." *American Journal of Human Genetics* 68 (2001): 723–737.

Hermanns-Audardottir, Margret. "The Early Settlement of Iceland." *Norwegian Archaeological Review* 24, no. 1 (1991): 1–33.

Hodder, Ian. "The Narrative and Rhetoric of Material Cultural Sequences." *World Archaeology* 25, no. 2 (1993): 268–282.

Hoegsberg, Moegens. "Continuity and Change: The Dwellings of the Greenland Norse." *Journal of the North Atlantic* Special Volume 2 (2009): 82–101.

Ingstad, Anne. *The Discovery of a Norse Settlement in America. Excavations at L'Anse aux Meadows, Newfoundland 1961–1968*. Bergen: Universitetsforlaget Oslo., 1997.

Jenkins, Richard. *Rethinking Ethnicity*. 2nd. London: SAGE, 2008.

——. *Social Identity*. 3rd. London: Routledge, 2010.

Jesch, Judith. *Women in the Viking Age*. Woodbridge: The Boydell Press, 2001.

Johansen, Johannes. *Studies in the Vegetational histories of the Faroe and the Shetland Islands*. 1st. Torshavn: Foroya Frodskaparfelag, 1985.

Jones, Sian. "Discourses of Identity in the Interpretation of the Past." In *Tha Archaeology of Identities*, edited by Timothy Insoll, 44–58. London: Routledge, 2007.

——. *The archaeology of Ethnicity*. London: Routledge, 1997.

Joyce, Rosemary. "Critical Histories of Archaeological Practice: Latin American and North American Interpretations in a Honduran Context." In *Evaluating Multiple Narratives: Beyond Nationalist, Colonialist, Imperialist Archaeologies*, edited by Junko Habu, Clare Fawcett and John Matsunaga, 56–68. New York: Springer, 2008.

Keller, Christian. "Furs, Fish and Ivory: Medieval Norsemen at the Arctic Fringe." *Journal of the North Atlantic* 3 (2010): 1–23.

——. "The Eastern Settlement Reconsidered: some analyses of Norse Medieval Greenland." Oslo: University of Oslo, 1989 [unpublished].

Kirch, Patrick. *The Archaeology of History: The Anthropology of History in the Kingdom of Hawai'i, volume 2*. Chicago: University of Chicago Press, 1992.

Knapp, A Bernard. "Archaeology and Annales: time space, and change." In *Archaeology, Annales and Ethnohistory*, edited by A Bernard Knapp, 1–21. Cambridge: Cambridge University Press, 1992.

Krogh, Knud. *Viking Greenland: With a supplemental of saga texts*. Copenhagen: National Museum, 1967.

Lane, Alan. "Dark-Age and Viking-Age Pottery in the Hebrides, with special reference to the Udal, North Uist." London: University College London Press, 1983 [unpublished].

——. "Dark-Age and Viking-Age Pottery in the Hebrides, with special refernec to the Udal, North Uist." London: University College, London, 1983 [unpublished].

Lane, Alan. "Hebridean Pottery: Problems of definition, chronology, presence and absence." In *Beyond the Brochs*, edited by Ian Armit, 108–130. Edinburgh: Edinburgh University Press, 1990.

Larson, Lars. *The King's Mirror*. New York: American-Scandinavian Foundation, 1917.

Latour, Bruno. *Reassembling the Social*. Oxford: Oxford University Press, 2005.

Lightfoot, Kent. "Culture Contact studies: Redefining the Relationship between prehistoric and Historical Archaeology." *American Antiquity* 60, no. 2 (1995): 199–217.

Lightfoot, Kent, and Antoinette Martinez. "Frontiers and Boundaries in Archaeological Perspective." *Annual Review of Anthropology* 24 (1995): 471–492.

Lightfoot, Kent, Antoinette Martinez, and Ann Schiff. "Daily Practice and Material Culture in Pluralistic Social Settings: An Archaeological study of culture change and Persistence from Fort Ross, California." *American Antiquity* 63, no. 2 (1998): 199–222.

Lindow, John. *Norse Mythology: A Guide to the Gods, Heroes, Rituals, and Beliefs.* New York: Oxford University Press, 2001.

Lindquist, Ole. "Whales, Dolphins and Porpoises in the Economy and Culture of Peasant Fisherman in Norway, Orkney, Shetland, Faeroe Islands and Iceland, ca 900–1900 AD, and Norse Greenland, ca 1000–1500." St Andrews: University of St Andrews, 1994 [unpublished].

Lucas, Gavin. *Hofstadir: Excavation of a Viking Age feasting hall in North-Eastern Iceland.* 1. Reykjavik: Fornleifastofnun Islands, 2009.

Lucas, Gavin, and Thomas McGovern. "Bloody Slaughter: Ritual Decaptiation and Display at the Viking Settlement of Hofstadir, Iceland." *European Journal of Archaeology* 10, no. 1 (2007): 7–30.

Lund, Julie. "Thresholds and Passages: The Meanings of Bridges and Crossings in the Viking Age and Early Middle Ages." *Viking and Medieval Scandinavia* 1 (2005): 109–135.

MacDonald, Aiden. "The papar and some problems: a brief review." In *The Papar in the North Atlantic: Environment and History*, edited by Barbara Crawford, 13–29. St Andrews: St John;s House Papers, 2002.

MacGregor, Lindsay. "The Norse Settlement of Shetland and Faroe, c800 –c1500." St Andrews: University of St Andrews MA dissertation, 1986 [unpublished].

Magnus, Olaus. *Historia de Gentibus Septentrionalibus.* Edited by Peter Foote. Translated by Peter Fisher and Humfrey Higgens. London: The Haklyut Society, 1998.

Mahler, Ditlev. "Argisbrekka: new Evidence of Shielings in the Faroe Islands." *Acta Archaeologica* 61 (1991): 60–72.

Mahler, Ditlev. "Shielings and their role in the Viking-Age economy." In *The Viking Age in Caithness, Orkney and the North Atlantic*, edited by Colleen Batey, Judith Jesch and Christopher Morris, 487–505. Ediburgh: Ediburgh University Press, 1995.

Mahler, Ditlev, and Claus Malmros. "Nytt tilfar um aergid undir Argisbrekku." *Mondal* 16, no. 2 (1990): 12–31.

Malmros, Claus. "Exploitation of local, drifted and imported wood by the Vikings of the Faroe Islands." *Botanical Journal of Scotland* 46 (1991): 552–559.

Marcus, Geoffrey. "Hafvilla: A Note on Norse Navigation." *Speculum* 30, no. 4 (1955): 601–605.

Mauss, Marcel. *The Gift.* 2nd. New York: Routledge, 2000.

Maxwell, Moreau. "A Southeastern Baffin Thule House with Ruin Island Characteristics." *Arctic* 34, no. 2 (1981): 133–140.

Maxwell, Moreau. "Dorset Site Variation on the Southeast Coast of Baffin Island." *Arctic* 33, no. 3 (1980): 505–516.

McGhee, Robert. "The Timing of the Thule Migration." *Polarforsch* 54, no. 1 (1981): 1–7.

McGovern, Thomas. "Climate, Correlation and Causation in Norse Greenland." *Arctic Anthropology* 28, no. 2 (1991): 77–100.

McGovern, Thomas. "Cows, Harp seals and Church Bells: Adaption and Extinction in Norse Greenland." *Human Ecology* 8, no. 3 (1980): 245–275.

McGovern, Thomas, et al. "Lanscapes of settlement in northern Iceland: historical ecology of human impact and climate fluctuation on the millenial scale." *American Anthropologist* 109, no. 1 (2007): 27–51.

McGovern, Thomas, Gerald Bigelow, Thomas Amorosi, and Daniel Russell. "Northern Islands, Human Error, and Environmental Degradation: A View of Social and Economic Change in the North Atlantic." *Human Ecology* 16, no. 3 (1988): 225–270.

McKenzie, Jo. "Manuring Practices in Scotland: Deep Anthropogenic Soils and the Historical Record." In *West Over Sea*, edited by Beverley Ballin Smith, Simon Taylor and Gareth Williams, 401–417. Leiden: Brill, 2007.

McManis, Douglas. "The Traditions of Vinland." *Annas of the Association of American Geographers* 59, no. 4 (1969): 797–814.

McTurk, Rory. *A Companion to Old Norse-Icelandic Literature and Culture.* Edited by Rory McTurk. Oxford: Blackwell, 2007.

Meskell, Lynn. "Archaeologies of Identity." In *The Archaeology of Identity*, edited by Timothy Insoll, 21–43. London: Routledge, 2007.

Milek, Karen. "Houses and Households in Early Icelandic Society: Geoarchaeology and the interpretation of social space ." Cambridge: University of Cambridge, 2006 [unpublished].

Miller, William Ian. *Audun and the Polar Bear: Luck, Law and Largesse in a Medieval Tale of Risky Business.* 1st. Leiden: Brill, 2008.

Miller, William Ian. "Choosing the Avenger: Some Aspects of the Bloodfeud in Medieval Iceland and England." *Law and History Review* 1 (1986): 159–204.

Moffat, David, and Simon Buttler. "Rare Earth Element Distribution Patterns in Shetland Steatite – consequences for artifact provenancing studies." *Archaeometry* 28, no. 1 (1986): 101–115.

Morcken, Roald. "Norse Nautical Units and Distance Measurements." *The Mariner's Mirror* 54 (1968): 393–401.

Morris, Christopher. "The Birsay Bay Project: A Resume." In *The Viking Age in Caithness, Orkney, and the North Atlantic*, edited by Colleen Batey, Judith Jesch and Christopher Morris, 286–307. Edinburgh: Edinburgh University Press, 1995.

Norlund, Poul. *Viking Settlers in Greenland and their Descendents During Five Hundred Years.* 1st. Copenhagen: GEC Gads Forlag, 1936.

Ogilvie, Astrid, et al. "Seals and Sea Ice in Medieval Greenland." *Journal of the North Atlantic* 2 (2009): 60–80.

Oka, Rahul, and Chapurukha Kusimba. "The Archaeology of Trading Systems, Part 1: Towards a New Trade Synthesis." *Journal of Archaeological Research* 16 (2008): 339–395.

Olsen, Osva, and Ingvar Svanberg. "Nalbinding in the Faroe Islands." *Frodskaparit* 51 (2004): 190–199.

Oma, Kristin Armstrong. "Between Trust and Domination: social contracts between humans and animals." *World Archaeology* 42, no. 2 (2010): 175–187.

Ostergard, Else. *Woven into the Earth: Textiles from Norse Greenland.* 2nd. Aarhus: Aarhus University Press, 2009.

O'Sullivan, Aiden. "Early Medieval Houses in Ireland: Social Identity and Dwelling Space." *Peritia* 20 (2008): 225–256.

Owen, Olwyn, and Christopher Lowe. *Kebister: The Four-Thousand Year-Old Story of One Shetland Township.* Edinburgh: Society of Antiquaries of Scotland Monograph Series, 1999.

Owen, Olwyn, and Magnar Dalland. "Scar, Sanday: a Viking Boat Burial from Orkney. An Interim Report." In *Developments around the Baltic and the North Sea in the Viking Age*, edited by Bjorn Ambrosiani and Helen Clarke, 159–172. Stokholm: Statens Historiska Museer, 1994.

Page, Raymond. *Chronicles of the Vikings.* Toronto: University of Toronto Press, 1998.

Panagiotakopulu, Eva. "Dipterous remains and archaeological interpretation." *Journal of Archaeological Science* 31 (2004): 1675–1684.

Parker Pearson, Michael, and Charles Richards. "Architecture and Order: Spatial Representation and Archaeology." In *Architecture and Order: Approaches to Social Space*, edited by Michael Parker Pearson and Charles Richards, 38–72. London: Routledge, 1997.

Peel, M, B Finlayson, and T McMahon. "Updated world map of the Koppen-Geiger climate lassification." *Hydrology and Earth System Sciences Discussion* 4 (2007): 439–473.

Perkins, Richard. "Medieval Norse Visits to North America: Millenial Stocktaking." *Saga Book* 28 (2004): 29–69.

Perkins, Richard. "The Furdutsrandir of Eiriks saga rauda ." *Medieval Scandinavia* 9 (1976): 51–98.

Pringle, Heather. "Evidence of Viking Outpost Found in Canada." *National Geographic News*, October 19, 2012.

Quinn, Judy. "From Orality to Literacy in Medieval Iceland." In *Old Icelandic Literature and Society*, edited by Margaret Clunies Ross, 30–60. Cambridge: Cambridge University Press, 2000.

Renouf, M A Priscilla, and Trevor Bell. "Dorset Palaeoeskimo skin processing at Phillip's Garden, Port aux Choix, Northwestern Newfoundland." *Arctic* 61, no. 1 (2008): 35–47.

Resi, Heid. "Reflections on Viking Age Local trade in Stone Products." In *Proceedings of the Tenth Viking Congress*, edited by James Knirk, 95–102. Oslo: Universitets Oldsaksamlings Skrifter, 1987.

Rice, Prudence. "Contexts of Contact and Change: Peripheries, Frontiers and Boundaries." In *Studies in Culture Contact: Interactions, Culture Change and Archaeology*, 44–66. Chicago: Southern Illinois University, 1998.

Rode, Eva. "The Vinland Sagas and their Manuscripts." In *Viking Voyages to North America*, edited by Birthe Clausen, 22–30. Roskilde: The VIking Ship Museum, 1993.

Roesdahl, Else. "Viking Art in European Churches." In *Viking Trade and Settlement in Continental Western Europe*, edited by Iben Skibsted Klaesoe, 149–164. Copenhagen: University of Copenhagen, 2010.

Roesdahl, Else. "Walrus ivory – demand, supply, workshops, and Greenland." In *Viking and Norse in the North Atlantic*, edited by Andras Mortensen and Simun Arge, 182–191. Torshavn: Annales Societatis Scientiarum Faeroensis, 2005.

Ross, Julie. "A Palaeoethnobotanical Investigation of Garden Under Sandet, a Water-logged Norse Farm site, Western Settlement, Greenland." Edmonton: University of Alberta, 1997 [unpublished].

Roussell, Aage. "Farms and Churches in the Medieval Norse Settlements of Greenland." *Meddelelesrom Gronland* 89, no. 1 (1941).

——. *Norse Building Customs in the Scottish Isles*. 1st. London: Williams and Norgate, 1934.

Rowlett, Ralph. "1,000 Years of New World Archaeology." *American Antiquity* 47, no. 3 (1982): 652–654.

Sadler, Jon. "Beetles, Boats and Biogeography: Insect invaders in the north Atlantic." *Acta Archaeologica* 61 (1991): 199–211.

Sahlins, Marshall. *Islands of History.* Chicago: University of Chicago Press, 1985.

Sanmark, Alexandra. "The Case of the Greenlandic Assembly Sites." *Journal of the North Atlantic* Special Volume 2 (2010): 178–192.

Sawyer, Birgit, and Peter Sawyer. *Medieval Scandinavia.* 6th. Minneapolis: University of Minnesota Press, 2003.

Schjodt, Jens. *Initiation between Two Worlds: Structure and Symbolism in Pre-Christian Scandinavian Religion.* 1st. Copenhagen: University of Southern Denmark, 2008.

Schledermann, Peter, and Karen McCullough. "Inuit-Norse Contact in the Smith Sound Region." In *Contact, Continuity, and Collapse: The Norse Colonization of the North Atlantic*, edited by James Barrett, 183–205. Turnhout: Brepols, 2003.

Seaver, Kirsten. *The Frozen Echo.* Stanford: Stanford University Press, 1996.

Seibert, Sebastian. *Reception and Construction of the Norse Past in Orkney.* 1st. Frankfurt: Peter Lang, 2008.

Sharples, Niall. *Scalloway.* Oxford: Oxbow , 1998.

Sharples, Niall. *Scalloway Supplementary Data.* Cardiff: Archaeological Data Service, 2002.

Sigmundsson, Freystein, and Kristjan Saemundson. "Iceland: a window on North Atlantic Divergent Plate Tectonics and Geologic Processes." *Episodes* 31, no. 1 (2008): 92–97.

Sigurdsson, Gisli. "Orality Harnessed: How to Read Written Sagas from an Oral Culture?" In *Oral Art Forms and their Passage into Writing*, edited by Else Mundal and Jonas Wellendorf, 19–28. Copenhagen: Museum Tusculanum, 2007.

Sigurdsson, Gisli. "The Quest for Vinland in Saga Scholarship." In *Vikings: The North Atlantic Saga*, edited by William Fitzhugh and Elizabeth Ward, 232–237. Wasington: Smithsonian Institution Press, 2000.

Sigurdsson, Jon. "The Appearance and Personal Abilities of Godar, Jarlar, and Konungar: Iceland, Orkney and Norway." In *West Over Sea*, edited by Beverley Ballin Smith, Simon Taylor and Gareth Williams, 95–109. Leiden: Brill, 2007.

Sigurdsson, Jon. "The Appearance and Personal Abilities of Godr, Jarlar and Konungar: Iceland, Orkney and Norway." In *West Over Sea*, edited by Beverly Ballin Smith, Simon Taylor and Gareth Williams, 95–109. Leiden: Brill, 2007.

Silliman, Stephen. "Agency, practical politics and the archaeology of culture contact." *Journal of Social Archaeology* 1, no. 2 (2001): 190–209.

Silliman, Stephen. "Theoretical Perspectives on Labor and Colonialism: Reconsidering the California Missions." *Journal of Anthropological Archaeology* 20 (2001): 379–407.

Sindbaek, Soren. "Networks and Nodal Points: the emergence of towns in early Viking Age Scandinavia." *Antiquity* 81 (2007): 119–132.

Sindbaek, Soren. "Open Access, Nodal Points, and Central Places." *Estonian Journal of Archaeology* 13, no. 2 (2009): 96–109.

Sindbaek, Soren. "Routes and long-distance traffic: the nodal points of Wulfstan's Voyage." In *The Baltic Sea Region in the Early Viking Age as Seen from Shipboard.*, edited by Anton Englert and Athena Tradakas, 72–78. Roskilde: The Viking Ship Museum, 2009.

Sindbaek, Soren. "The Lands of Denemearc:Cultural Differences and Social Networks of the Viking Age in South Scandinavia." *Viking and Medieval Scandinavia* 4 (2008): 169–208.

Small, Alan. "Excavations at Underhoull, Unst, Shetland." *Proceedings of the Society of Antiquaries of Scotland* 98 (1966): 225–248.

Small, Alan. "The Juniper Decline during the Norse landnam in the Faroe Islands." *Acta Borealia* 9, no. 1 (1992): 3–7.

Smiarowski, Konrad. *Archaeological Excavations in Vatnahverfi, Greenland 2008 Preliminary Excavation Report.* Northern Science and Education Center: North Atlantic Biocultural Organization, 2008.

Smith, Brian. "Stobister, Sinnabist and Starrapund: Three Wilderness Settlements in Shetland." In *West Over Sea*, 419–430. Leiden: Brill, 2007.

Snaesdottir, Mjoll. "Storaborg – an Icelandic farm mound." *Acta Archaeologica* 61 (1991): 116–119.

Solli, Brit. "Narratives of Encountering Religions." *Norwegian Archaeological Review* 29, no. 2 (1996): 92–114.

Sorensen, Preben. "Social Institutions and belief systems of medieval Iceland (c870–1400) and their relations to literary production." In *Old Icelandic Literature and Society*, edited by Margaret Clunies Ross, 8–29. Cambridge: Cambridge University Press, 2000.

Steane, John. *The Archaeology of Power.* 1st. Stroud: Tempus, 2001.

Steffensen, J, et al. "High Resolution Greenland Ice Core Data Show Abrupt Climate Change Happens in a Few Years." *Science* 321 (2008): 680–684.

Stenberger, Marten. *Forntida Gardar i Islands.* 1st. Copenhagen: Munksgaard, 1943.

Strombeck, Dag. *The Conversion of Iceland: A Survey.* London: Viking Society for Northern Research, 1997.

Stummann Hansen, Steffen. "A Dane and the Dawning of Faeroese Archaeology." *Frodskaparit* 50 (2002): 11–32.

Stummann Hansen, Steffen. "Aspects of Viking Society in Shetland and the Faroe Islands." In *Shetland's Northern Links: Language and History*, edited by Doreen Waugh and Brian Smith, 117–135. Lerwick: The Shetland Times, 1996.

Stummann Hansen, Steffen. "Settlement Archaeology in Iceland: The race for the Pan-Scandinavian Project in 1939." *Acta Archaeologica* 72, no. 2 (2001): 115–127.

——. *Toftanes – a Viking-Age Farm at Leirvik.* 1st. Leirvik: Sporamork, 2005.

Stummann Hansen, Steffen. "Toftanes: A Faroese Viking Age Farmstead from the 9–10th centuries AD." *Acta Archaeologica* 61 (1991): 44–53.

Stummann Hansen, Steffen. "Viking Settlement in Shetland: Chronological and Regional Contexts." *Acta Archaeologica* 71 (2000): 87–103.

Stummann Hansen, Steffen, and Doreen Waugh. "Scandinavian Settlement in Unst, Shetland: Archaeology and Place-names." In *The Uses of Place Names*, edited by Simon Taylor, 120–146. Edinburgh: Scottish Cultural Press, 1998.

Stummann Hansen, Steffen, and John Sheehan. "The Leirvík 'Bønhústoftin' and the Early Christianity of the Faroe Islands, and beyond." *Archaeologia Islandica* 5 (2006): 27–54.

Stylegar, Frans-Arne, and Oliver Grimm. "Boathouses in Northern Europe and the North Atlantic." *International Journal of Nautical Archaeology* 72, no. 2 (2005): 253–263.

Sutherland, Patricia. "The Norse and Native North Americans." In *Vikings: The North Atlantic Saga*, edited by William Fitzhugh and Elizabeth Ward, 238–247. Washington: Smithsonian Institution Press, 2000.

Svanberg, Frederik. *Decolonizing the Viking Age.* Lund: Acta Archaeologica Ludensia, 2003.

Sveinbjarnardottir, Gudrun. "Shielings in Iceland: an archaeological and historical survey." *Acta Archaeologica* 61 (1991): 73–96.

Sveinbjarnardottir, Gudrun. "The Question of papar in Iceland." In *The Papar in the North Atlantic: Environment and History*, edited by Barbara Crawford, 97–106. St Andrew's: St John's House Papers, 2002.

Sveinbjarnardottir, Gudrun, Paul Buckland, and Anthony Gerrard. "Landscape change in Eyjafjallasveit, Southern Iceland." *Norwegian Journal of Geography* 36, no. 2 (1982): 75–88.

Sveinsson, Einar Ól., and Matthías Þórðarson, . *Íslenzk fornrit. Eyrbyggja saga: Brands þáttr Qrva, Eiríks saga Rauða Groenlendinga saga, Groenlendinga þáttr.* 1st. Reykjavik: Hið íslenzka fornritafélag, 1935.

Sverrisdottir, Bryndis. *Reykjavik 871+-2: The Settlement Exhibition.* Reykjavik: Reykjavik City Museum, 2006.

Szabo, Vicki. *Monstrous Fishes and the Mead-Dark Sea.* Leiden: Brill, 2008.

Thomsen, Amanda, Ian Simpson, and Jennifer Brown. "Sustainable Rangeland grazing in Norse Faroe." *Human Ecology* 33, no. 5 (2005): 737–761.

Thorarinsson, Sigurdur. "Greetings from Iceland: Ash-falls and volcanic Aerosols in Scandinavia." *Geografiska Annaler Series A Physical Geography* 63, no. 3/4 (1981): 109–118.

Thorgeirsson, Bergur. *From Excavation to Interdisciplinary Perspective: The Reykholt Project.* Tübingen: Universität Tübingen, 2004.

Thorlaksson, Helgi. "Historical Background: Iceland 870–1400." In *A Companion to Old Norse-Icelandic Literature and Culture*, edited by Rory McTurk, 136–154. Oxford: Blackwell, 2007.

Thorlaksson, Helgi. "The Icelandic Commonwealth Period." In *Vikings!: The North Atlantic Saga*, edited by William Fitzhugh and Elisabeth Ward, 175–185. Washington: Smithsonian Institution Press, 2000.

Thorsteinsson, Arne. "Land division, land ownership and land rights in the Faeroe Islands." In *Nordic Landscapes: Region and Belonging on the Northern Edge of Europe*, edited by Michael Jones and Kenneth Olwig, 77–105. St Paul: University of Minnesota Press, 2008.

Trigger, Bruce. *A History of Archaeological Thought*. 2nd. Cambridge: Cambridge University Press, 2009.

Unger, Richard. *The Ship in the Medieval Economy 600–1600*. London: Croom Helm, 1980.

Vesteinsson, Orri. "Archaeology of Economy and Society." In *A Companion to Old Norse-Icelandic Literature and Culture*, edited by Rory McTurk, 7–26. Oxford: Blackwell, 2007.

Vickers, Kim, Joanna Bending, Paul Buckland, Kevin Edwards, Steffen Stumman Hansen, and Gordon Cook. "Toftanes: the Palaeoecology of a Norse landnam Farm." *Human Ecology* 33, no. 5 (2005): 685–710.

Wallace, Birgitta. "An Archaeologist's Interpretation of the Vinland Sagas." In *Viking: The North Atlantic Saga*, edited by William Fitzhugh and Elizabeth Ward, 225–231. Washington: Smithsonian Institution Press, 2000.

Wallace, Birgitta. "L'Anse aux Meadows, Leif Eriksson's Home in Vinland." *Journal of the North Atlantic* Special Volume 2 (2009): 114–125.

Wallace, Birgitta. "L'Anse aux Meadows: Gateway to Vinland." *Acta Archaeologica* 61 (1991): 166–197.

Wallace, Birgitta. "The Viking Settlement at L'Anse auxMeadows." In *Vikings: The North Atlantic Saga*, edited by William Fitzhugh and Elizabeth Ward, 208–216. Washington: Smithsonian Institution Press, 2000.

Wallace, Birgitta, and William Fitzhugh. "Stumbles and pitfalls in the search for Viking America." In *Vikings: The North Atlantic Saga*, edited by Birgitta Wallace and Fitzhugh Ward, 374–384. Washington: Smithsonian Institution Press, 2000.

Wallerstein, Immanuel. *The modern world-system*. New York: Academic Press, 1974.

Weber, Max. *The Methodology of the Social Sciences*. 1st. Glencoe: Free Press, 1949.

Westerdahl, Christer. "Boats Apart. Building and Equipping an Iron-Age and Early-Medieval Ship in Northern Europe." *International Journal of Nautical Archaeology* 37, no. 1 (2008): 17–31.

Whaley, Diana. "A Useful Past: historical writing in medieval Iceland." In *Old Icelandic Literature and Society*, edited by Margaret Clunies Ross, 161–202. Cambridge: Cambridge University Press, 2000.

White, Tim. *Human Osteology*. 2nd. San Francisco: Academic Press, 2000.

Williams, Daniel Gareth. *Land Assessment and Military Organization in the Norse Settlements in Scotland, 900–1266*. St Andrews: University of St Andrews, 1996 [unpublished].

Wolf, Eric. "Culture: Panacea or problem?" *American Antiquity* 49, no. 2 (1984): 393–400.

Index

Á Sondum 51, 68
activity, identity 182, 187, 221
Actor-Network Theory 33
Aðalstraeti 93–94, 97–99, 104, 107, 181
Adam of Bremen 162
Adómnan 17
affiliation 23, 27, 183, 185–187, 196
    Religious 160, 169, 170
    Sampling 228
    Trade 153, 156
    Zone 1 44,
    Zone 2 74, 85, 88
    Zone 3 119, 133
aisle 62, 127, 130
Alfred the Great 181
Álptafjord 200–201
Althing 105–107
Anahulu 122. See Hawai'i.
angelica 56
animal
    cull 70
    husbandry 8, 50, 78, 130, 146, 151, 160,
        191, 227
Annales School 1, 32
anthropogenic landscape 111, 116
anthropology 14
antiquarian 12
    Iceland 86, 89, 93, 96, 103
    Greenland 112, 115
arable land 8, 227
archaeological survey 3, 13, 18, 45, 83, 89,
    116, 118, 185
archipelago 1, 3, 5, 10, 14, 18, 20, 23, 30, 36,
    37, 41, 181, 182, 186, 196
    Religion 169, 170
    Sampling 228
    Trade 141, 142, 144, 148, 150, 151, 155
    Zone 1 44, 49, 51, 52, 60, 63, 69, 71, 72, 78
Arctic fox 116
Argisbrekka 51, 54, 56–58, 65, 68, 72, 76, 227
Ari Þorgilsson 2, 87, 168
artefact 7, 8, 15, 21, 25, 28, 33, 35, 39–40, 42,
    162, 197

Sampling 226–228
    Zone 1 47–49, 55–58, 60, 68
    Zone 2 87, 98, 107, 108, 110
    Zone 3 121, 125, 134
Asgard 158
ash 48, 55, 68, 97, 100
Áslakstunga fremri 94–97
Áslakstunga innri 95
assemblages 23, 27, 28, 33–35, 177, 181–182,
    195
    Religious 162, 167
    Zone 1 49, 57, 59, 72
    Zone 2 87, 90, 92, 99–101, 103, 110
    Zone 3 112, 119, 125–126, 134
Assembly 83, 93, 117, 119, 133, 178, 220
Atlantic Current 4, 5, 6, 18, 84
Auðun Vestfiska 156
auk 90, 101, 103, 105, 149, 186, 200
Avayalik Islands 123, 126
axe 68, 93, 120, 214, 216

Baffin Island 121, 125, 128
Baltic Sea 137
barn 97, 117, 118, 119, 160
basalt 8, 169
bench 47, 48, 53, 55, 56, 62, 64, 100, 129,
    200, 210
Bergen 61, 118
Bessastaðir 94
Betula spp. 95, 151
Bifrost Bridge 158
bird 8, 10, 16, 37, 42, 198
    Religion 160
    Trade 151
    Zone 1 57, 61, 65, 66, 67, 80
    Zone 2 98, 101, 110
    Zone 3 119
birding cliff 57, 110, 160
Bjarni Hérjólfssonr 143, 202, 203, 204, 217
Black Duck Brook 124, 125
blóthus 90
bog iron 92, 124, 125
bone 50, 87, 92, 99, 110, 128, 227

Bónhústoftin 166, 167, 169, 172
Bornais 2
boundaries 36, 38, 68, 98, 124, 160
Bourdieu 23, 26, 31, 32
bowl 48, 128
Brattahlið 115, 117, 172, 196, 201, 202, 204, 207, 212
Breckon Cullivoe 45
Breckon Sands 47, 74, 163, 173
Breiðabólstaðir 200
Breiðafjord 200, 201
broch 45
Brøgger 42
Brough of Birsay 42, 120, 155, 169, 227, 228
Brú 91
Bruun 42, 100, 114, 118
bulk goods 134, 138–141, 144, 153–155, 179, 181, 183–184, 192
burial 11, 180, 186, 192
    Religious 141, 160, 162, 163, 169, 170, 171, 173, 175, 176
    Sampling 228
    Zone 1 47, 49, 52, 54, 74
    Zone 2 86, 88, 89, 91, 92, 93, 98, 99, 101, 102, 103, 108
    Zone 3 121
butter 75
butternut 125
byre 29, 39, 160
    Sampling 227
    Zone 1 46, 47, 48, 53, 54, 62, 64, 66, 68, 69
    Zone 2 91, 97, 101
    Zone 3 124

Caithness 13
capability, identity 65, 81, 135, 140, 178, 187
cargo drayage 141
caribou 9
Carolingian 153
carrying capacity 10, 72
Castle of Strom 45
Catpund 45, 48, 49, 68
cattle 47, 50, 54, 59, 61, 66, 68, 72, 97, 101, 113, 219
Celtic fields 164
cemetery 74, 120, 121, 124, 169
childhood identity 27, 34
Christian 13, 16, 47, 133, 135, 145, 179, 189
    Grænlendinga Saga 202, 209
    network 157, 169, 174
    Religion 157, 159, 161, 163, 166, 169, 170–174, 176, 178

Christianity 11, 47, 74, 111, 179, 189–190, 192
    Grænlendinga Saga 201, 209
    Religion 161–162, 170–175
church 17, 29, 52, 53, 74, 109, 119, 133, 179, 184, 190, 196, 198
    Trade 150, 153, 156
    Religion 157, 164, 169, 170, 173, 174, 175, 176
    Grænlendinga Saga 211, 212, 217, 219
    Sampling 227
Church Island 164
cleric 161, 163, 224
Clibberswick 45, 48–49, 74, 151
clinker built 11, 49, 67, 139, 141–142, 153, 187
coastline 10, 112, 142
cog 141
Commonwealth Period 88, 95
conjecture 31
consolidation into kingdoms 11, 153, 179, 197, 198
conversion 11, 74, 135, 157, 161, 162, 169, 170, 171, 174, 175, 176, 178, 187, 192
cooking 26, 92, 120, 127
core 36–39, 147, 149–150, 179
corner hearth 127–128
cultural identity 10, 26, 29
cultural structures 1, 19, 22, 31
Cunningburgh 49
Curle 46
current 5, 6, 16, 18, 30–31, 42, 83–84, 151, 177, 186

Da Biggins 45, 47
daily domestic 21, 137
dairy processing 50, 56, 65–66, 69, 72–73, 80, 119
daughter longhouse 66
Davis Strait 113, 122, 128, 130,
deeper draft 132, 139, 141–143
Denmark 11, 12, 42, 44, 52, 115, 118, 139, 153, 175, 177
diaspora 11
Dicuil 17
Dingle Peninsula 164
Diplomaticum Islandicae 115
dispositions 32
Dorset 123, 125–126, 128–130,
doxic practice 22, 26–27, 32, 36
drain 8, 46, 48, 53, 56, 62, 69, 89, 93, 123, 127, 132, 167

drainage 8, 46, 53, 56, 62, 93, 123, 167
Drepstokk 143, 202
driftwood 5, 10, 47, 50, 58–59, 95–96, 99,
    104, 107, 113, 119, 128, 130, 133

East Greenland Current 6
Eastern Quarter 4, 18, 88–91, 93, 103
Eastern Settlement 5, 19, 113, 117–120, 186,
    200
ecclesiastical 29, 84, 115, 119, 153, 167, 169,
    175
ecofacts 8, 40, 107
ecological environment 5, 7
efficiency in travel 187
egGraenlendinga Saga 66, 101, 107
Einarsfjord 202
Eingjartoftum 51
Einholt 93
Eirík Þorvaldsson rauda 200–202, 207
Eiriksfjord 200, 209–210, 213
Eirikssaga Rauða (ESR) 115, 121, 171, 130,
    133, 134, 135
Eiríksstaðir 200
Eldjárn 88, 89
environmental determinism 10
Epaves Bay 124
Episcopal 118, 119, 133, 175, 176
erosion 13, 37, 49, 52, 53, 54, 86, 88, 89, 90,
    93, 114, 115, 127, 163
ESR see Eirikssaga Rauða.
Esturoy 54
ethnicity 1, 22, 23, 26, 27, 40
European market 137, 181
evénmentielle 31
excavation 4, 5, 12, 13, 14, 18, 20, 32, 39, 40,
    42
    Religious 166, 167, 172, 197, 199, 219
    report 40, 227, 228
    Sampling 226, 227, 228
    Zone 1 46, 47, 48, 49, 50, 52, 53, 54, 55,
        57, 58, 59, 60, 62, 65, 80
    Zone 2 83, 85, 86, 88, 89, 90, 91, 93, 96,
        97, 98, 99, 100, 101, 102, 103
    Zone 3 112, 114, 116–121, 123–127, 129,
        131, 133–136

Færeyinga saga 52, 164, 166
færing 144–145
Fair Isle 155
farm 5, 10, 11, 18, 19, 21, 25, 28, 29, 42,
    178–180, 182, 184–186, 191–192, 196–198
    complex 5, 18, 56, 67, 70, 76, 87, 118, 126,
        128

Grænlendinga Saga 200, 202, 208, 212–213,
    216, 219
    high status 70–72, 74, 110, 132, 218, 228
    religious 159–161, 169, 171–172, 173–175
    sampling 226, 227, 228
    trade 146–151, 154–156
    unit 160, 178, 182, 184, 185, 186, 191
    Zone 1 46, 47, 60, 63, 66, 68, 70, 73, 75,
        76, 77
    Zone 2 91, 98, 101, 102, 105, 110
    Zone 3 111, 119, 130, 131, 133
    Trade 150, 154, 155, 156
    Zone 1 46–49, 52–60, 63–80
    Zone 2 84–95, 97–110
    Zone 3 111, 114–115, 118–121, 124,
        126–136
farmyard 65, 80, 90, 97, 160
Faroe Islands 1, 3, 7, 8, 9, 12, 13, 17, 18, 42,
    44, 51–56, 58–62, 68, 74, 76, 78, 180, 185
    Religion 164, 166, 167, 168, 172, 173
    Sampling 226, 227
    Trade 138, 143, 144, 146, 151
Fetlar 49
Fifth Thule Expedition 116
fire utilization 92, 124, 128
fish 7, 8, 10, 37, 42, 198, 208
    Trade 151, 160, 163
    Zone 1 49, 50, 55, 57, 58, 59, 60, 61, 65,
        67, 68, 69, 79, 80
    Zone 2 92, 101, 110
    Zone 3 135
fishing 7, 8, 49, 50, 57, 65, 69, 79, 80, 110,
    160, 163
fodder 8, 10, 49, 54, 56, 66, 72, 73, 74, 76, 97,
    119, 132, 146, 191, 206, 222
forest 121, 130, 151
Forntiða Gårdar í Ísland 97
Fourteenth Viking Conference 15
fox 9, 116, 219
Frankia 153
Free State 83, 178, 193, 226
fresh water 8, 46, 53, 89, 94, 123, 124, 128,
    227
Freydís Eiríksdóttir 202, 214, 215, 216
Friðríksson 86, 89
Frobisher 123
frontier 23, 36, 37, 38
Fyrkat 42

Gadids 8
Gård Under Sandet (GUS) 20, 126
Garðabær 97
Gardie 45, 46, 47, 69

Garm 162
garment 121
geos 8
Giddens 26, 31, 32
gift exchange 75, 145, 150, 153, 154, 176, 182, 183, 189
  network 150, 153, 183
Giljanes 51, 54
Gjáskógar 97
Gjógvara 51
goat 47, 50, 128
Goðatættur 88, 91
Grænlendinga Saga 20, 41, 115, 121, 126, 127–129, 143, 171, 200–217
Gragás 40, 87, 95–96, 98, 101, 103, 105, 107, 109, 110, 154, 156, 160
grain 50, 65, 68, 75, 83, 103, 105, 142, 151, 182–183, 219
granite 8
grass-hay 132
Greenland 1, 2, 5, 6, 8, 12, 14, 19, 20, 42, 186, 187, 196, 197
  Evidence 113–115, 117–120, 122–123, 126–133, 135
  Grænlendinga Saga 201–204, 206, 209, 211–212, 215–216
  Religion 163, 167, 171–172
  Sampling 226, 227
  Trade 142, 151–153
Greenlander 5, 19
group identity 1, 23, 26, 30, 36, 42, 195
Guðrið Þorbjorndóttir 207, 209–213, 217
Gulathing 44, 61
Gulatingslova 44, 48–49, 51
GUS see Gård Under Sandet.

habitus 5, 10, 19, 22–23, 26–28, 32, 35–36, 40–42, 44, 63, 88, 108, 148, 151, 154, 157, 174, 181, 186–188, 198
Háfgrímsfjord 202
Hamar 45–47, 76
Hamilton 45
Hansea 20
Hanúsa 51
hare 9, 125, 126
Haukadale 200
Hawai'i 196
hay-making 9
heathen 170, 203, 219
Hebrides 3, 8, 16, 18, 44, 138, 146, 185, 187
Hedeby 141
heimrust 47, 54, 59
Heimskringla 161, 166

Hel 162
Helluland 121, 204
Hérjólfsdalur 88–90, 92
Hérjólfsfjord 201
Hérjólfsnes 118, 133
Hesta Ness 45, 49, 68, 151
hexagonal pin 125
Hiberno-Norse 32, 125, 164, 167, 222
hierarchy 23, 26, 28, 38, 179–180, 183, 185–186
  Religious 157, 169, 175, 179
  Trade 135, 150
  Zone 1 64, 72–75, 77, 80, 82
  Zone 3 116, 133
high status farm 70–72, 74, 110, 132, 218, 228
Historia Norwegiae 15, 168
Hjaltland 44, 222
Hófstaðir 87, 100, 101, 102, 103, 111, 127
hogback 104, 167, 169
Hólar 175
Hólmur 87, 89, 90, 91, 92, 103, 107
homefield 160
homespun 128
homogeneity 177
horn 128
horses 50, 91, 93, 95, 101, 142, 146, 162, 204, 212, 219, 227
Hrafnsfjord 201
Hrífunes 92–93, 98
Hrísbru 95, 97
human exploitation 4, 18
human lice 105, 127
Hvalsey 118, 222
Hvítarholt 94

iceberg 113, 142
ice-core 7
Iceland 1, 2, 3, 4, 5, 8, 10, 11, 12, 16, 18, 19, 40, 42, 61, 182, 186–187, 189, 196
  Evidence 83, 85–89, 91–93, 96–102, 104, 107–108, 110–111
  Grænlendinga Saga 200, 201, 206, 211, 216
  Religion 161, 164, 166–168, 170, 176
  Sampling 226, 227, 228
  Trade 131, 133, 135, 141, 157
Icelander 5, 16, 19
identity 1, 2, 3, 5, 10, 18–30, 32–34, 36, 37, 39–43, 179, 180, 182, 183, 184, 185, 186, 187, 188, 189, 191, 192, 193, 195, 196, 197, 198
  activity 182, 187, 221
  capability 65, 81, 135, 140, 178, 187

childhood 27, 34
cultural 10, 26, 29
group 1, 23, 26, 30, 36, 42, 195
medieval 30, 188
national 197
religious 169, 170, 171, 175, 177
sampling 226, 228–229
Scandinavian 1, 112, 180
trade 137, 143, 147, 148, 149, 150, 154,
   156, 157
Zone 1 49, 60, 61, 62, 64, 69, 70, 77, 78,
   90, 81, 82
Zone 2 85, 86, 87, 88, 89, 91, 92, 105, 109
Zone 3 111, 112, 124, 128, 129, 130, 131,
   134, 135, 136
Igaliku 117–119, 121, 133, 156, 172, 175, 181,
   202
Ikigiat 118, 121
immrama 16
indigenous 5, 19, 33, 36, 38, 41, 46–47, 58,
   63, 116, 121, 123, 125–126, 128–130, 155,
   164, 168, 169
individual actor 1, 22–23, 26–27
infield 8, 47, 54, 66, 97, 124, 160
Inoqquassaq 169
international markets 142, 149
Iona 164
Irish Sea 3, 11, 16, 17, 137, 138, 151, 164,
   166, 181, 218
Irminger Current 5, 6, 151
iron 142
   Sampling 227, 228
   Zone 1 49, 57, 58, 66, 72
   Zone 2 87, 92, 99, 110
   Zone 3 120, 124–126, 128, 132
iron blooms 92, 142
island group 1, 3, 8, 13, 17, 18, 44–45, 53, 60,
   138, 193
island resources 11, 78
islandscape 36, 55, 72, 74, 174
Íslendingabók 87, 96, 133
ivory 142, 149, 152, 156, 181, 227

jarl 62, 155, 187, 204, 248
Jarlshof 42, 44–48, 68, 71, 113
Jónsbók 154
Jotunheim 158
Juniper 47, 58
Junkárinsflótti 51, 53, 58, 59, 65, 68, 81

Karlsefni 212, 213, 214, 216, 217
Kebister 44, 45, 47
keds 127

Kensington Rune Stone 128
Ketilsfjord 201
kin 25, 28, 38, 77, 133, 178–179, 183–184,
   186, 192
   Grænlendinga Saga 202, 204, 217
   group 25, 133, 155, 175, 223
   Religion 169, 174–175
   Trade 147–148, 155
   unit 179
kingdom consolidation 176
Kirch 122
Kirki geo 45
Kirkjubær 74
Kirkjubøur 51–53, 172–173, 175
Kirkjugard 51, 74
Kirkwall 15, 174
Kjálarnes 208
knives 92–93, 120
knörr 12, 139, 141–144, 154, 187
Konungsbók 87
Koppen-Geiger 6, 7, 8
Krístni saga 171
Króssanes 209
Kvívík 13, 53, 114

La Purisma 122
Labrador Current 6, 151
LAM *see* L'Anse aux Meadows.
Lambhófða 96
lamp 48, 55, 92, 101, 120
land naming 2, 107
landing site 8, 37, 67, 227
landnám 2, 3, 4, 5, 10, 13, 18
   Religion 166–167
   Zone 1 44, 51, 56, 63, 71, 76
   Zone 2 87–88, 93, 105, 107
   Zone 3 111, 117, 132
Landnámabók 87
Landslog 51
land-taking 2, 164
langskip 139, 142, 223
L'Anse aux Meadows (LAM) 5, 8, 19, 115,
   122–125, 128, 131–132, 151, 186, 205, 227
Latour 22, 31, 33
Law Ting Holm 45
legal treatise 25
Leifr Eiriksson 15, 196–197
Leifsbuðr 115, 121, 128
Lewis 17, 142, 162, 185
Lewis chessman 17, 162, 185
Lightfoot 122
liminality 37
Lítla Dímun 59

Little Ice Age 7, 10, 74, 78, 150, 151
littoral zone 7, 8, 13, 42, 49, 57, 64, 67, 77, 79, 80, 110, 123, 126, 135, 137, 160, 186, 223
livestock 49, 56, 57, 64, 80, 98, 146, 148, 186, 191, 218, 221, 222, 223, 224
long distance trader 225
long hearth 47, 48, 55, 62, 127, 159, 161
longhouse 13, 42, 185
    daughter longhouse 66
    Grœnlendinga Saga 201
    primary longhouse 66
    Religion 159, 161, 169, 172, 173
    Trade 143
    Zone 1 46–48, 53–56, 58, 60–66, 68, 71–72, 76, 80
    Zone 2 86, 90, 91, 92, 94–95, 97, 100, 102, 104–105, 108–109
    Zone 3 118, 120, 123, 126–132, 135
longue durée 23, 30
luxury goods 75, 139, 140, 142, 153, 155, 156, 176, 182, 188, 227
lyme grass 96, 105

macroscale 21, 25, 26, 27, 28, 29, 34, 40, 177, 179, 186, 188, 197, 198
    Religion 157, 162, 169, 170, 174, 176
    Sampling 226, 228, 229
    Trade 149, 154, 156,
    Zone 2 74, 78, 82, 109,
    Zone 3 111, 112, 119, 121, 133, 136
Magnus Erlingsson 44
Magnus Hakónsson 51
Mainland 45, 49
marginal 5, 9, 10, 11, 36, 37, 38, 56, 60, 67, 73, 74, 75, 76, 78, 89, 104, 119, 125, 130, 132, 136, 137, 151, 169, 173, 174, 177, 185, 186, 223
marine mammal 7, 8, 10, 37, 61, 99, 151
maritime
    environment 16, 36, 41, 42, 144, 198
    technology 11
Maritime Subarctic Climate 7
Maritime Temperate Climate 7
Markland 121, 205, 223
material culture 19, 25, 92, 120, 125, 198
meadow 8, 95, 104, 123, 132, 218
medieval identity 30, 188
Medieval Optimal 7, 50, 63, 83, 177
Medieval Period 1, 10, 20, 26, 60, 76, 85, 89, 94, 117, 125, 128, 137, 142, 143, 169, 175, 177, 183, 185, 187, 188, 197
Merovingian 153

microscale 21, 24, 25, 27, 28, 29, 35, 40, 177, 179, 188, 191, 198
    Religion 163, 171
    Sampling 228, 229
    Trade 143, 147, 149, 150, 154
    Zone 1 49, 60, 62, 63, 69, 70, 74, 78, 80, 81
    Zone 2 85, 91, 92, 102, 105, 109
    Zone 3 111, 112, 118, 119, 120, 121, 127, 128, 129, 130, 131, 133, 135, 136
midden 25, 47, 49–50, 54, 56, 59, 65, 67–68, 72, 76, 87, 97, 100–101, 107, 120, 124–125, 160
Middles Ages 3, 18, 182
Midgard 158
migration 5, 7, 116, 143, 151, 177–178, 191, 197, 199
Migration Era 143, 224
milking 56, 65, 80
Mosfellssveit 93
Mousa 2, 45
musk oxen 9
Mývatnssveit 5, 18, 83, 86, 99, 100, 103, 107, 112, 120, 226, 228

NABO *see* North Atlantic Biocultural Organization.
North Atlantic Biocultural Organization (NABO) 14, 15, 16, 83, 100, 116
Nanook 125, *see* Tanefield.
Narsaq 129, 132
Narsarsuaq 115, 117, 151
national identity 197
naust 8, 11
need for human work 70, 77
Neolithic 3, 18, 45, 137
network
    Christian 157, 169, 174
    gift exchange 150, 153, 183
    North Atlantic trade 20, 141, 146, 148, 156
    power 3, 18, 23
    trade 20, 36, 61, 88, 102, 137–138, 141, 143, 146, 148, 150, 151, 155–157, 169, 179, 181, 192
New World 5, 19, 20, 115, 121–126, 129–130, 133, 167, 196, 226
Newfoundland 5, 14, 19, 115, 123, 128, 205, 222
Niðaros 187–188
Niðri í Toft 51
Niðri við Hus 51
Noðuri í Forna 51
Norland 114, 118

Norse 1,3, 4, 5, 10, 11, 12, 13, 15, 16, 17, 18, 19, 20, 21, 22, 25, 28, 32, 33, 39, 41, 42, 178, 180, 185, 195–197
    Grænlendinga Saga 206, 211, 216, 219
    Hiberno-Norse 32, 125, 164, 167, 222
    North Atlantic 1, 16, 20, 28, 32, 33, 41, 42, 77, 86, 118, 125, 152, 160, 162, 197, 228
    Religion 157–164, 167, 169, 171–173
    Sampling 226, 228
    Trade 139, 141, 142, 146, 152, 153
    Zone 1 44–51, 54–55, 58–61, 64–65, 68, 70, 72, 74, 77–81
    Zone 2 84, 86, 89, 92–93, 108
    Zone 3 114, 116–118, 120–134, 136
North Atlantic Current 6, 18, 84
North Atlantic Drift Current 6
North Atlantic trade network 20, 141, 146, 148, 156
North Cape Current 6
North Sea 3, 16, 17, 44, 61, 137, 138, 153, 181, 183
Northern Hemisphere 7
Northern Isles 222
Norway 3, 18, 20, 44, 49, 51–52, 58, 61–62, 64, 78, 83, 85, 108, 115, 131, 156, 161, 175, 178, 181, 187, 197, 202, 211, 212, 214, 216
Norwegian Atlantic Current 5, 6
Norwick 45, 47, 68, 74
Nunguvik 123, 126

ocean travel 155, 160
oðal 10, 44, 61
Oðinn 162
Ohthere 152, 181
Olavus Magnus 152
Old Devonian Red Sandstone 8
Old Norse 20, 41, 196
Old Scatness 44, 45, 65
Old Scatness 44, 45, 65
Old World 126, 137
Orkney 3, 8, 15–16, 18, 42, 44, 61, 75, 138, 146, 151, 155–156, 167–169, 173–174, 178, 180, 185, 187, 227–228
Orkneyinga Saga 75
Ormsstaðir 93
outbuilding 8, 9, 173, 227
    Zone 1 47, 48, 54, 56, 60, 62–64, 66, 72, 76
    Zone 2 91, 94, 97, 100–101, 104, 108
    Zone 3 119–121, 124–125, 127, 132
outfield 8, 66, 91, 97, 124, 132, 160, 227
over-winter 9, 101, 184, 203, 222
Øxney 200

pagan 2, 13, 91, 103, 133, 157–159, 161–163, 169–171, 173–174, 176, 179, 187
palaeobotanical 5, 18
Papa Stour 45
Papa Westray 167–169
Papar 11, 17, 51, 53, 84, 145, 163–169
Paparókur 53
Papurhálsur 53
pasture 8, 9, 49, 56, 72–73, 76, 218, 219
peat 66, 127
periphery 14, 23, 36–39, 85, 125, 137, 147, 177, 179
Peti-names 168
Phase 1 146–149
Phase 2 148–149
Phase 3 149
Phase 4 149–150
Phase 5 150
Pict 120, 142, 155, 164, 168
Pierowall 163, 173
pigs 47, 50, 61
platter-style 58
polar bear 116, 142, 156
Portugal Current 6
pottery 49, 120, 227
power networks 3, 18, 23
practical drivers 78
practicality 91, 136, 148, 192
Practice Theory 23–24, 31–32, 35, 188, 229
primary longhouse 66
prioritization 177, 190
protein 9, 67, 90, 131, 151
puffin 49, 101

Qassiarsuk 115–118, 129, 132–133, 151, 156, 171–172, 175, 196–197, 201, 211, 213
Qinngua 172
Quarter Courts 103

Rafn 166
Rangá 91, 93
raw material 9, 114, 142, 155, 175, 228
recycling 59, 68, 92, 99, 110, 125
Reformation 88
re-supply 146, 149, 154, 191
Reykjasel 92, 98
Reykjavík 93, 94, 98
roof construction 53, 62, 89, 90, 94, 95, 96, 100, 104, 111, 119, 130, 153, 169
Roskilde Fjord 139
Roussell 42, 114, 118, 133
rune 128, 227

saeter 119, 121, 124, 132, 133, 186, 227
saga 4, 11–12, 15–16, 18, 20, 25, 40–41, 52,
    75, 85–86, 88, 103, 105, 107, 115, 121, 128,
    143, 154, 161, 164, 166, 168, 171, 196, 227
saga-scribe 25
sail 3, 17, 18, 44, 69, 70, 108, 139, 143, 148,
    149, 151, 153, 156, 177, 183, 187, 191,
    200–209, 214, 216–217
sailing, see sail.
sailors 69, 70, 108, 151, 154
Sáksun 53
Sámsstaðir 9, 96
Sandoy 53, 81
Sandur 53, 58
Sandwick 45–47, 68, 227
Scandinavian homeland 3, 11, 17–18, 147,
    152, 157, 168
Scandinavian identity 1, 112, 180
Scar 141, 153, 163
schist baking plate 48, 55, 58
Sea of Human Consciousness 30–31
seasonality 140
Setters 45, 76
settlement 1–3, 5–6, 9–14, 16, 19–22, 25,
    28–29, 33, 42, 178, 180–183, 186–189,
    191–192, 195, 197–199
    Grænlendinga Saga 200, 202, 208, 209, 218
    Religion 157, 162, 171, 174, 175, 177
    Sampling 226–229
    Trade 138, 139, 141, 142, 145, 146, 147,
        148, 149, 150, 151, 152, 153, 154, 156
    Zone 1 44–45, 47–48, 51–53, 60–63,
        71–72, 74, 77
    Zone 2 87–90, 93–96, 99, 102, 104–105,
        108–110
    Zone 3 111, 113–114, 117–120, 123,
        126–127, 129–133
Settlement Period 2, 3, 20, 71, 104, 110, 150,
    156, 182, 189, 228
Seyðabrævið 40, 52, 64, 154
shearing 65, 80
sheep 47, 50–51, 54, 59–61, 66, 68, 98, 101,
    108, 113, 121,127–128, 151, 219
sheep lice 68, 108, 127
Shelf Edge Current 6
shellfish 7–8
Shetelig 42
Shetland 2–3, 8, 16, 18, 42, 44–50, 53, 58,
    60–62, 68, 74, 78, 138, 146, 151, 155, 173,
    180, 185, 196, 227
shieling 47, 54, 56, 64, 66, 68, 69, 72–73, 76,
    97, 101, 160, 227

shipping
    female stock 191
    livestock 146
    stress 146, 191
Siglufjord 202
Skáholt 93, 103, 175
Skaldskarpismál 161
skali longhouse 118, 129–130, 132, 220
Skallakót 94, 97
Skeljastaðir 97–98, 103
skin rope 149, 152–153, 156, 182
skræling 208, 212–214
Skuledev 139
Sleipnir 162
small finds 48, 55, 76, 227, 229
smith 66, 99, 160, 220
Snjáleifartottir 97
Snorri Sturlusson 88, 161
soapstone 121, 125, 128
social
    space 36, 40, 159–161
    world 1, 74
Soil sampling 86, 118–120
Solvadale 201
Soterberg 45
South Whiteness 45
Southern Quarter 4, 18, 83, 86, 93, 94,
    96–98, 103, 111, 186
spear 120
spectrum 27, 28, 32, 37, 72, 78, 116, 161,
    180, 222
spice 182
spindle whorl 54, 60, 99, 120
spinning 98
Spitsbergen Current 6
St Boniface 168, 169
St Columcille's Chapel 169
St Magnus 156, 174
St Ninian's Isle 45
St Olaf of Norway 156
Standibrough 45
steatite 45, 48–50, 55, 58, 61–62, 68, 92, 99,
    101, 108, 120–121, 151, 227
Stöng 82, 93–94, 96–98, 103, 106, 118
Stoora Toft 45
Stórhóshlið 97
Straumer 92, 98
Streymoy 52–54, 175
Strobister 45
Structure and Event Theory 31
Sturlung 193
subsistence strategy 10, 135

Suðurgata 94
supply and demand 75
Svalbard 181
Sweden 11, 163
symbolic estate 26

Tanefield 123, 125–126, 128, 132
text 2, 11, 13–14, 16, 20–21, 40–41, 88, 105, 111, 113, 115, 121, 128, 131, 143, 147, 162–163, 168, 171, 176, 181, 196–197, 200, 228, 229
textiles 59, 68, 98, 108, 120, 125, 127, 149, 151, 154, 182,
textual sources 2, 3, 18, 26, 29, 42, 80, 85, 87, 89, 94, 105, 115–116, 118, 121–122, 131, 135, 169, 178, 187, 195, 226
Theory
    Actor-Network 33
    Practice 23–24, 31–32, 35, 188, 229
    Structure and Event 31
Þingvellir 83, 93
Þjóhlíð Jorundóttir 200
Þorsádalur 91, 93–94, 96–98, 103, 106, 108, 114, 118, 120
Þorstein Eiríksson 202, 209–212
Þorvald Ásvaldsson 200
Þorvald Eiríksson 202, 207–209
Thule Inuit 114, 122, 125–126, 128–129, 152, 172, 182
Tinganes 51–52
tithe barn 118, 119
Tjørnuvík 54, 121
Toftanes 51, 53–54, 58, 65, 68–69, 72, 76, 227
toponymic 5, 17, 18, 90, 163–164, 218
Torshavn 15, 52, 59, 144
trade 4, 10–11, 16, 18, 20, 25, 28–30, 36, 137–139, 141–146, 148–151, 153, 154–156, 178, 180–184, 187, 189–190, 192, 198
    agreement 4, 18
    Grænlendinga Saga 208, 213, 215
    network 20, 36, 61, 88, 102, 137–138, 141, 143, 146, 148, 150, 151, 155–157, 169, 179, 181, 192
    Religion 157, 169–170, 177
    Sampling 228
    Zone 1 61, 65–66, 70, 79–80
    Zone 2 88, 102, 105,
    Zone 3 113, 123, 132, 135
trader 154, 178, 181–183
transport 5, 36, 79, 101, 137, 138, 139, 140, 146, 147, 148, 150, 171
Trelleborg 42

Trondheim 118, 121, 187, 188
turf
    block 95, 97, 104, 123–125, 127, 167
    construction 46–48, 53–54, 60, 62, 66–67, 71, 76, 81, 86, 89–91, 94–95, 97–98, 100, 104, 116, 119, 123–128, 130, 132, 160, 167, 169, 172–173, 185–186
    wall 71, 91, 104, 127, 128, 130, 160, 169, 186
Tyrkir 134–135, 204, 206, 207

Uist 2
Underhoull 44–45, 47–48, 68
Underworld 158
Unst 45–47, 49, 185, 196
Upper Scalloway 45, 47
Úppistóvubeitum 68
útlaga 10

Vað 92, 98
Vágar 51
Vatnahverfi 118–119, 132
Vector 12, 22, 25–26, 29, 38, 75, 78, 85, 122, 133, 137, 149, 150, 157, 170, 178, 180, 183–184, 186–187
vertical loom 109, 127–128
Vestmanna 53
Viking Age 1, 3, 14–15, 17, 22, 26, 40–42, 50, 62–64, 130, 143, 155, 162, 176, 190, 201
Vinland 121, 207
    Map 128
voe 5, 45
Voluspä 161
Vorbasse 42

walrus 8, 99, 103, 105, 112–113, 119, 142, 149, 152, 156, 177, 181–182, 186
Ward Hill 45
Watlee 45
weaving 65–66, 72, 80, 97, 99, 109–110, 160
West Greenland Current 6
Western Isles 1, 3, 13, 17, 42, 151, 155, 163, 164, 168
whale 10, 49, 55, 65, 67, 76, 80, 99, 110, 212
White Sea 181
wics 138
Willows Island 123, 126
Winter 7, 9–11, 47, 49, 56, 64, 66, 70, 74, 76, 101–102, 119, 132, 140, 143, 172, 184, 186, 200–203, 206–210, 212–214, 216–217
wood 3, 18, 44, 49–50, 54, 58–59, 64–67, 71, 87, 92, 96, 98–99, 101, 104–105, 107, 120,

124–128, 130, 160, 162, 169, 173, 203, 207, 208, 212, 214–216, 219
World Tree 158–159, 161

Yvíri í Troð 173

Zone 1 3–4, 13, 170 18, 44–83, 88–99, 106, 108, 110–111, 113–115, 118, 120, 122, 124, 133–136, 138, 143, 145–146, 151, 153, 155, 161–163, 169–170, 175–176, 180, 185–188, 192, 198, 226

Zone 2 4, 13, 18, 83, 112–115, 118, 120, 122, 124, 131, 133, 135–136, 148, 150–151, 155, 156, 158, 161–163, 167, 170, 171, 175–177, 180–182, 186–189, 196–198, 226
Zone 3 4, 5, 9, 13, 19, 83, 113–136, 148–151, 155–156, 164, 167, 173, 175, 177, 181–182, 186–187, 198, 226
Zones of settlement 2–3, 5, 17, 20, 38, 57, 114, 117, 121, 126, 127, 129–130, 133, 136, 146, 150–151, 154, 160, 163, 169, 175–177, 186, 191, 196, 226